THE FRENCH TRAGI-COMEDY

Its Origin and Development from 1552 to 1628

DISSERTATION SUBMITTED TO THE BOARD OF UNIVERSITY STUDIES OF THE JOHNS HOPKINS UNIVERSITY IN CONFORMITY WITH THE REQUIREMENTS FOR THE DEGREE OF DOCTOR OF PHILOSOPHY.

BY

HENRY CARRINGTON LANCASTER

GORDIAN PRESS, INC.
NEW YORK
1966

Originally Published 1907
Reprinted by Gordian Press, Inc. 1966

Library of Congress Catalog Card No. 66-29465

Printed in U.S.A. by
EDWARDS BROTHERS, INC.
Ann Arbor, Michigan

TO MY MOTHER.

TABLE OF CONTENTS

NOTE:—The few abbreviations used for the titles of books cited in the following pages are explained by reference to their authors, listed in the Bibliography.

In quoting names, titles, and passages from French authors, I have endeavored as far as possible to reproduce the original orthography, accentuation, etc., rather than to use the system current in contemporary French.

INTRODUCTION.

Toward the middle of the sixteenth century there developed in France a variety of the *drame libre* that represented, in a classical form, the essential qualities of the medieval drama. Under the term *tragi-comédie* it included types as various as the medieval *genres* from which they sprung, united by the common possession of a happy *dénouement*, a classical form and name. After a period of confusion, which lasted throughout the sixteenth century, came the predominance of the *romanesque* tragi-comedy, which grew to be, not only the leading type of the *genre*, but the most popular dramatic kind at Paris, so continuing till succeeded in the public favor by the classical tragedy and comedy. The tragi-comedy continued for some years to be written, but toward 1672, after an existence of one hundred and twenty years, came to an end as an independent *genre*.

It had been as M. Faguet describes it, "tout un genre, et un genre très important et précieux."[1] It had formed an integral part in the evolution of the French drama, filling the stage between the sixteenth century dramatists and Pierre Corneille. For forty years the chief expression of the form of dramatic art that is popular in its appeal, it must be studied for any complete history of the French people or their stage. By such study can be seen both how the scholastic drama of the sixteenth century became popularized, and whence Corneille drew his practical knowledge of the stage. The history of the tragi-comedy shows that the French had for a long period cultivated a type of dramatic composition akin to that which reached such perfection in England and Spain, so that their failure to produce a Shakspere, or Lope, is not assignable, as many have intimated, to the repressing influence of classical rules.

The tragi-comedy, furthermore, deserves study as giving an

[1] *La Tragédie française au XVIe siècle*, 233.

excellent example of the *évolution des genres,* about which the late M. Brunetière wrote so suggestively.[1] In its development may be observed the creation of the *genre* out of other dramatic forms, its early inclusion of a number of rudimentary types, the survival and predominance of the *romanesque* as the fittest of these, the growth of this successful form in the hands of Hardy and his contemporaries with occasional reversions to the older types, its literary culmination in the *Cid,* later decline, loss from the depredations of nearly related forms and final extinction. This evidences a whole cycle of literary evolution, which repays investigation, not only for its own sake, but for that of other *genres* in which the process may be equally true, but less apparent.

It is my purpose to trace this evolution as far as the year 1628, which marks the end of the development of the tragi-comedy and the beginning of the twenty years in which its greatest sucesses lie. It is the year in which Hardy completed the publication of his extant plays, while Rotrou brought out his first tragi-comedy and a comedy that started the French imitation of the Spanish drama. In the following year, moreover, Corneille began his dramatic career and Scudéry composed his first tragi-comedy. Thus 1628 dates, in a way, the end of one generation of tragicomic authors and the beginning of another. As the first period (1552–1628) includes the beginnings of the *genre* in France and the development of its various dramatic qualities, so the second period (1628–1672) covers years of popularity, in which the causes of its subsequent decay may be detected, and years of disintegration, which resulted in the absorption of the *genre* by the tragedy and the comedy.

At some time I hope to treat the second of these periods, but at present I confine myself to the first. The following pages will therefore be devoted to an investigation of the sources of the tragi-comedy, as they are found in France and other parts of Europe, to the development of the *genre* in the former country, and to a study of the tragi-comedies written from 1552 to 1628, in order to show their authorship, structure, sources, treatment of subject, character, and incident.

[1] Especially in *L'Évolution des Genres.*

In this investigation I have relied chiefly on the plays themselves, extant at Paris in the Bibliothèque Nationale and the Bibliothèque de l'Arsenal. I have also used various catalogues of plays, of which the chief are those by La Croix du Maine, du Verdier, Beauchamps, Frères Parfaict, Léris, Allacci, Riccoboni, La Vallière, Soleinne, and Brunet.[1] Of these the last three have been of especial value to me from the extent and comparative reliability of their information. Other catalogue-writers, those named above as well as those of lesser importance mentioned in my bibliography, have been consulted with caution.

My indebtedness to other authors, chiefly for general accounts of the period, or the history of other dramatic *genres*, is indicated in my bibliography. Among the works that have been of greatest assistance to me may be mentioned the enlightening criticisms of M. Brunetière and M. Lanson, the excellent treatises of M. Rigal on Alexandre Hardy and the contemporary theater, and the valuable historical researches of MM. Faguet, Petit de Julleville, Creizenach, Marsan, Ebert, Fournel and Chasles.[2]

Not only does no special treatment of the tragi-comedy exist, but literary historians of the period have assigned it only a few pages at most, usually only a few lines. Certain plays, it is true, have received much attention, as those of Hardy, Mairet, Scudéry, and Rotrou, the *Bradamante* of Garnier, and the *Tyr et Sidon* of Schelandre.[2] But minor authors have been neglected, and no comprehensive account of the whole field has been presented. Criticism, in fact, has been largely reduced to a matter of definition, which in some cases is based on scant acquaintance with extant forms of the *genre*, though in others it is both apt and suggestive. Before beginning an historical investigation of the plays, I must turn to those definitions that are of importance.

The Frères Parfaict[3] hold that the tragi-comedy is "une action singuliere qui se passe entre des personnes d'une naissance distinguée, même entre des Rois et des Princes, dans laquelle il n'y a aucun danger pour la vie des principaux Personnages."[3] They

[1] For titles of works, dates, etc., see *Bibliography*.

[2] For references, cf. the *Bibliography*.

[3] *Histoire du Théatre françois*, III, 455.

naïvely add, that this rule has not been observed in the *Bradamante* of Garnier. Had they investigated further, they would have found that there are few tragi-comedies that do not follow the example of the *Bradamante.* As a matter of fact, it is exceedingly common for the lives of the principal persons to be endangered, so that this definition appears somewhat absurd. It is of interest, however, to note that the Frères Parfaict do not define the *genre* as a mixing of tragic and comic elements.

Guizot comes nearer the truth in a purely negative way when he declares that it is difficult to determine the difference between the tragedy and the tragi-comedy, for "elle ne tient ni à la nature du sujet ni au rang des personnages." [1]

Fournel describes rather than defines the *genre* in his statement that "La tragi-comédie fut comme un asile légal ouvert à ceux que gênaient les lois naissantes, une sorte de compromis politique avec les actes d'indiscipline qu'on ne pouvait empêcher et auxquels on voulait du moins enlever prudemment les apparences de la révolte. . . . Elle fut introduite par le besoin de la variété, et le désir de tirer parti d'un grand nombre de sujets curieux qui se dérobaient aux classifications exclusives." [2]

This view of the freedom that is essential to the tragi-comedy had been expressed at the end of the sixteenth century by Marc de Papillon (1597) in the following quatrain :

> Je n'ensuy en cette œuvre icy
> La façon de l'ardeur antique,
> C'est pourquoi je la nomme aussi
> La Nouvelle tragi-comique. [3]

Ebert is of the same mind as Papillon, when he assigns to the tragi-comedy "*unter andern Freiheiten* auch die Einmischung des Komischen," [4] Larroumet implies the freedom of the *genre* when he writes that it "emprunte ses éléments au roman ; dans le roman l'imagination se donne libre carrière." [5] Brunetière declares that "la liberté, c'est son domaine et aussi son moyen." [6]

[1] *Corneille et son temps*, 135.

[2] *La Littérature indépendante*, 12, 13.

[3] *Nouvelle tragicomique*, preface.

[4] *Franz : Tragödie*, 131.

[5] *Revue des cours et conférences*, 1897, 35.

[6] *Revue des Deux Mondes*, 1901, vi, 143.

The relation between the tragi-comedy and the romance, referred to in the citation just made from Larroumet, is hinted at by Fournel when he speaks of the "côtés romanesques"[1] of the former *genre*. It is more clearly indicated by Rigal, who defines the tragi-comedies of Hardy as "nouvelles dramatisées,"[2] a formula by which he explains several characteristics of this *genre*.

The ordinarily serious nature of the plot has attracted the attention of Desmarests, who mentions "les accidents graves et funestes,"[3] and of d'Aubignac when he describes subjects and characters as "heroïques."[4] They have been followed by Samuel Chappuzeau, who considers "de nobles advantures"[5] a characteristic of the tragi-comedy. Lessing, too, agrees with Desmarests, for he writes: "Tragikomödie hiess die Vorstellung einer *wichtigen* Handlung unter vornehmen Personen, die einen vergnügten Ausgang hat."[6]

Critical observation has frequently noted the high rank of the leading personages in the tragi-comedy. Vauquelin mentions "les plus grands et les Rois."[7] Desmarests declares that "les principaux personnages sont Princes."[3] Both d'Aubignac[4] and Chappuzeau[5] refer to the "personnes illustres," who carry on the action. The Frères Parfaict and Lessing, as quoted above,[8] are evidently of the same opinion. This aristocratic feature of the fully developed *genre* is not to be doubted, but in a number of *non-romanesque* tragi-comedies the aristocrats are omitted. The freedom from rule that characterizes the tragi-comedy allows it to mingle personages of various social classes at any period of its history. There is a tendency, however, even in the sixteenth century toward placing aristocrats in the leading rôles, a usage that becomes the rule in the *romanesque* tragi-comedy of the seventeenth century, which is at that time the only important type of the *genre*. It should be noted, however, that the tragi-comedy does not have princes and princesses disguised as shepherds

[1] *La litt. ind.*, 14.
[2] *Alexandre Hardy*, 502.
[3] *Scipion*, preface, Paris, 1639.
[4] *Pratique du Théatre*, 189.
[5] *Le Théatre françois*, 12.
[6] *Hamburgische Dramaturgie*, 234.
[7] *Art poétique*, III, 166.
[8] Pp. xi and xiii.

and shepherdesses, for, if such persons take part in a play, it is called a pastoral, or *tragi-comédie pastorale*, *genres* that differ from the tragi-comedy in style and incident, tracing their origin to another source.

Little attention has been paid to the non-historic nature of the tragi-comedy, which seems, indeed, to be denied in Faguet's definition of the *genre* as a "drame *historique* à dénouement heureux."[1] Unless this is an attempt at differentiating the tragi-comedy from the comedy by pointing out the tendency of the former to historic imitation in the manner of the romance, the definition is certainly incorrect. The tragi-comedy cannot be called truly historic, as Brunetière has well shown. "Des aventures privées sont la matière propre de la Tragi-comédie," he writes. "Mais des *aventures privées* ce sont des aventures qui ne sont pas en quelque sorte *authentiquées* par l'histoire, du moins au su de tous, et des aventures qui n'ont pas d'existence publique, ni certaine. Ce sont aussi des aventures dont l'enchaînement n'a rien de *nécessaire*. Et ce sont donc encore des aventures que le poète reste maître d'arranger, de combiner, de compliquer, d'enchevêtrer, de développer à son gré."[2] In another place he writes: "Mais le fond de la pensée de Corneille, comme de celle de ses contemporains, comme de celle aussi de Hardy, c'est qu'il n'y a de vrais sujets de tragédie que les sujets historiques, et que par conséquent tous les autres appartiennent à l'espèce de la tragi-comédie. Seulement, comme les frontières de l'histoire sont flottantes, et que Corneille lui-même, dans ses sujets historiques, dans son *Cinna* même, et dans ses *Othon* ou dans ses *Sertorius*, n'a jamais pu prendre sur lui de ne pas les transgresser."[3]

If historic plot is not made the only difference between tragedy and tragi-comedy, this statement may be considered true of the *romanesque* type of the latter *genre*, for its members approach the historic plot only in the four plays that are based on

[1] *La Tragédie française*, 212.
[2] *Revue des Deux Mondes*, 1901, VI, 143.
[3] *Ibidem*, 1890, CI, 702.

mythology. Now the mythological plot was treated by the French classic dramatists along with subjects held to be matters of history, and, as far as the well-established nature of the myth was concerned, it served equally well the classical end. On the other hand, the facts that mythological plots are non-historic and that certain of them lend themselves to romantic treatment made possible their use in four tragi-comedies, *Procris, Ariadne Rauie, Alceste,* and *Les Travaux d'Ulysse.* But the authors of the *non-romanesque* tragi-comedies drew upon supposedly historic sources, when they based their plays on the Bible or lives of saints, while even contemporary history is represented in the tragi-comedy called *L'union Belgique.* The non-historic subject is, therefore, a fixed characteristic of the fully developed tragi-comedy, but not of all its early or subordinate types.

The two characteristics of the tragi-comedy that have given rise to the most varied opinions among critics are the happy *dénouement* and the mixing of tragic and comic elements. The first of these has been rejected as an essential by several writers. Ebert writes: "Obwohl es im Anfang zugleich stets, und auch späterhin meist solche sind, die einen glücklichen *Ausgang* haben: dies war aber keine *wesentliche* Eigenschaft der Tragi-comédie: und so finden sich auch in Frankreich später nicht selten Tragi-komödien mit tragischem Schluss." [1] Rigal is more cautious in his statement: "Ce sont les dénouements heureux, élément nullement indispensable, au début du moins, des tragi-comédies, mais qui s'y rencontre si fréquemment." [2] In support of his position he quotes *Aristoclée* and the *première journée* of *Tyr et Sidon* (1628). Brunetière goes much further, declaring that the tragi-comedy "n'est pas davantage—en dépit du *Cid,* auquel Corneille a donné d'abord le titre de *tragi-comédie,*—une tragédie qui finirait bien, dont le dénouement, au lieu d'être sanglant, serait heureux, et, par exemple, une *Orestie* qui se terminerait par des noces." [3] "Et, s'il était vrai que, comme on le répète encore, le propre de

[1] *Entwicklungs-Geschichte der Franz: Tragödie,* 131.

[2] *Alexandre Hardy,* 432.

[3] *Revue des Deux Mondes,* 1901, VI, 143.

la tragi-comédie fût de se terminer heureusement, Corneille n'en aurait donc pas écrit de plus caractérisée que *Cinna*, la dernière pourtant de ses pièces à qui l'on disputera jamais le nom de tragédie !"[1]

Other critics have, however, taken a very different view. "La Tragi-Comédie nous met deuant les yeux de nobles auantures entre d'Illustres personnes menacées de quelque grande infortune, qui se trouve *suiuie d'un heureux euenement*," declares Chappuzeau.[2] Lessing holds that the tragi-comedy must have "einen vergnügten Ausgang."[3] Fournel emphasizes "la nécessité d'un dénoûment heureux."[4] Before Ebert (1856), indeed, this fact does not appear to have been questioned. It is especially worthy of note that the critics who knew the plays as contemporary products are unanimous in assigning to them a happy dénouement.

> "Quand il y a du meurtre et qu'on voit toutefois
> Qu'*à la fin sont contens les plus grands et les Rois*,
> Quand du graue et du bas le parler on mendie,
> On abuse du nom de Trage-comedie."[5]

Here Vauquelin objects to the use of the term, but at the same time testifies to the fact that it was applied in his day to those plays characterized by a happy ending. Mairet states that, "Le meslange est fait de parties Tragiques et Comiques, en telle façon que les unes et les autres faisant ensemble un bon accord, ont en fin une joyeuse et Comique catastrophe."[6] Georges de Scudéry holds that "à cause de sa fin"[7] the tragi-comedy leans to comedy rather than to tragedy. "La fin est heureuse,"[8] writes Desmarests. Finally the truth of the matter is most clearly stated by d'Aubignac as follows: "Mais ce que nous avons fait sans fondement, est que nous avons osté le nom de Tragédie aux Piéces de Theatre dont la Catastrophe est heureuse, encore que le Sujet et les personnes soient Tragiques, c'est à dire heroïques, pour leur donner celuy de Tragi-Comedies. . . . Or ie ne veux pas absolu-

[1] *Ibidem*, 1890, CI, 702.
[2] *Le Théatre françois*, 12.
[3] *Hamburgische Dramaturgie*, 234.
[4] *La litt. ind.*, 14.
[5] *L'Art poëtique*, III, 165–8.
[6] *La Silvanire*, preface, Paris, 1631.
[7] *Observations sur le Cid*, 8, Paris, 1637.
[8] *Scipion*, preface, Paris, 1639.

ment combattre ce nom, mais je pretens qu'il est inutile, puisque celuy de Tragédie ne signifie pas moins les Poëmes qui finissent par la ioye, quand on y décrit les fortunes des personnes illustres."[1] He then proceeds naïvely to object to the use of the term, as informing the audience of what the conclusion of the play is going to be and consequently destroying the interest that would be excited in the spectator's mind, were he kept in suspense until the end: "Mais des-lors qu'on a dit Tragi-comedies on découvre quelle en sera la Catastrophe." It is scarcely necessary to point out the fact that this is the most valuable kind of evidence, the testimony of an author to the existence of a practice to which he is theoretically opposed. D'Aubignac admits that plays which he would himself call tragedies are called tragi-comedies merely on account of their happy *dénouement.* There can be no doubt, therefore, that in the tragi-comedies with which he was acquainted this form of ending was an established fact.

But it is not difficult to come to this conclusion without the aid of critical authority. An examination of the extant plays reveals with sufficient clearness the state of the case. For the period from 1552 to 1636, when, if ever, the tragi-comedy may be considered an independent kind, there are extant eighty-three *romanesque* tragi-comedies, all of which show a happy *dénouement.* In *Philandre et Marisée*, it is true, the leading characters die, but are depicted as arriving in heaven after a most unfortunate life, so that this play is included in the list. An apparent exception is found in *Les Amours infortunées de Léandre et d'Héron* by le Sieur de la Selve, Avocat de Nîmes. The play was published at Montpellier. The author asks for critical consideration, as he writes in Languedoc, far from Paris and the knowledge of court manners. His use of the term, tragicomedy, does not appear to indicate contemporary usage, but rather his ignorance of it. Certainly the ideas of an obscure provincial on the meaning of the *genre* are of no value when they are opposed to those of the leading dramatists of the time. The play should undoubtedly be classed as an irregular tragedy. Nor does Rigal's citation of the *première*

[1] *Pratique du Théatre*, 189.

journée of the *Tyr et Sidon* (1628) indicate that an unhappy *dénouement* may occur in a tragi-comedy, for the *première journée* is not here a complete play, but must be considered in connection with the *seconde journée*, which brings the story to a happy end. This is true of all such divided plays. Hardy's *Theagene et Cariclée* and Du Ryer's *Argenis et Poliarque*, for example, have no *raison d'être* if their *journées* are considered, as far as the plot is concerned, as separate plays. Moreover, the citation of *Tyr et Sidon* in this connection is especially inapt, as this very *première journée* did actually appear alone in 1608 with its unhappy *dénouement* and was then called a *tragédie*. The term *tragi-comédie* is applied only in 1628 when the play was reworked and followed by the *seconde journée* with a happy *dénouement*. This explanation of the change of *genre* is much more logical than that offered by Rigal, who holds that it was due to the increased popularity of the tragi-comedy, thus hoping to prove the large extent of Hardy's influence. Now, it is quite possible that the tragi-comic vogue may have influenced the addition of this *seconde journée* with the happy *dénouement*, but there is no evidence that it could have induced an author to apply the title, *tragi-comédie*, to a play that ended in sadness—a condition that was opposed to the essence of its meaning. On the other hand, I may cite in support of my view the two plays that appeared in 1646 under the title, *Rodogune*. For the first four acts the plots are substantially the same, but in the fifth there is a differentiation between the two plots. Corneille ends his play unhappily and calls it a tragedy; Gabriel Gilbert brings his to a happy conclusion and styles it a tragi-comedy. The case is evidently an exact parallel to that of *Tyr et Sidon* in its two editions.

Modern ideas concerning the *dénouement* of the tragi-comedy appear to be largely based on two plays by Hardy, of which the classification is in doubt.[1] The first of these, called *Procris ou la Jalousie infortunée*, is styled tragi-comedy on the title-page and at the head of the argument, but tragedy at the top of subsequent pages and in the argument itself, where the author writes "catas-

[1] Cf. Rigal, *Alexandre Hardy*, pp. 401 and 226, note.

trophe qui finit la *Tragedie.*" Hardy seems to have looked on it from the standpoint of the murdered Procris and consequently styled it a tragedy. The term tragi-comedy, twice found and due, perhaps, to the publisher, can, however, be justified from the point of view of Cephale, the hero, and his friend Aurore, whose loves were greatly expedited by the death of the former's wife.

But in *Aristoclée,* the second piece of uncertain classification, there is no doubt as to the unhappiness of the *dénouement,* which induces Lombard to call it a tragedy.[1] Rigal, who classes it among the tragi-comedies, admits that there is difficulty involved, for "si le sujet a une couleur romanesque, du moins est-il emprunté à Plutarque; si les personnages en sont bas, du moins le dénouement en est-il terrible."[2] He states later[3] that it is the only tragi-comedy that preserves the unity of action, a distinctive trait of the tragedy. The personages can scarcely be called "bas," moreover, for one is noble, as Rigal admits in his analysis of the play,[4] and the others seem to enjoy an honorable, if bourgeois rank in their town. The social position of the characters is, in fact, just the same as in Hardy's *Scédase,* to which neither Rigal nor any one else has denied the title of tragedy.

These characteristics show that the play should be classed as a tragedy, whatever title may have been given it, but it is by no means sure that Hardy called it a tragi-comedy. In this connection Rigal writes: "M. Lombard écrit, au sujet d'*Aristoclée,* qu'elle 'n'est marquée ni comme tragédie, ni comme tragi-comédie.' C'est une erreur; elle est au contraire désignée comme tragi-comédie, et sur son titre, et sur son titre courant. Si Hardy parle, dans l'argument, de cette 'tragédie conduite à sa perfection,' c'est que la tragi-comédie est une subdivision de la tragédie et on ne lit jamais que ce dernier mot dans les privilèges." Now, this explanation may be correct, but it is to be observed that Hardy does not use the term, tragedy, in the argument of any play whose *dénouement* is undoubtedly happy. This fact is significant. It is

[1] *Zeitschrift für neu-franz: Sprache und Litteratur,* 1880, 367.

[2] *Alexandre Hardy,* 226.

[3] *Ibidem,* 502.

[4] *Ibidem,* 451.

perfectly possible that he considered *Aristoclée* a tragedy and called it so in his argument. No one would, indeed, doubt this, were it not for the fact that *tragi-comédie* is written as the title and *titre courant*, where, however, its presence may be due to the printer.

The evidence of eighty-three tragi-comedies, of which the *dénouement* is happy, shows clearly that *Aristoclée* and *Léandre et Héron* cannot be considered tragi-comedies and that *Procris* is so called only from the point of view of Cephale and Aurore. A similar regularity in regard to the happy ending is found in the *non-romanesque* tragi-comedies. There is no doubt that such a termination belongs to the tragi-comedies of biblical plot and to those that resemble the *moralité* and farce. It need be remarked only that in those based on saints' lives, the fact that the protagonist occasionally dies at the close of the play does not constitute an unhappy *dénouement*, for the object of such religious compositions is to show the reward of a pious life, a reward that is fully won only with the hero's death, which was, therefore, regarded by the dramatist as a happy event rather than as a disaster.

As quoted above,[1] however, Brunetière objects that if a happy *dénouement* is "le propre" of the tragi-comedy, Corneille's *Cinna* would be an excellent example of this *genre*. He accordingly argues that the tragi-comedy is differentiated from the tragedy by the non-historic nature of the former. Now this is true, but the two *genres* are, before the Cid (1636), kept apart as strongly by the nature of the *dénouement* as by the historic truth of the plot. That this was happy in the tragi-comedy has been sufficiently indicated. An unhappy ending, on the other hand, was essential to the definitions of the tragedy given during the Middle Ages and the XVI century. Vauquelin, as quoted above,[2] called attention to the fact that a tragedy may end happily, but his words were unheeded. Dramatists continued to follow Scaliger's precept that there should be an "exitus infelix",[3] until Corneille, realizing that an unhappy *dénouement* was not essential to the Greek tragedy, made the *genre* chiefly depend on psychological analysis of character and passion with special emphasis on the

[1] Page xiv. [2] Page xvi. [3] *Poetices*, III, 97, p. 367.

human will and the struggles in which it is involved. The nature of the *dénouement*, therefore, became unessential. *Cinna* and *Nicomède* could be considered tragedies as well as *Rodogune* and *Polyeucte.*

This usage is supported by the precept of d'Aubignac, quoted above.[1] As the idea that a tragedy might end happily became established in France, the tragi-comedy began to decline, for one of its principal *raisons d'être* had lain in the fact that it satisfied a popular craving to see the story finish in happiness, by which means it had succeeded in supplanting the tragedy in spite of the latter's artistic superiority. Now that the tragedy had acquired this important prerogative of the tragi-comedy, the latter lost its popular hold, began to decline while Corneille was writing, and ceased to exist not long after d'Aubignac had attacked it (1657). From this point of view, therefore, there is no incompatibility between the classification of *Cinna* as a tragedy and the fact that the happy *dénouement* is an essential characteristic of the tragi-comedy.

Another point that has evoked critical discussion concerns the mixing of tragic and comic elements that appears to have given rise to the name tragi-comedy. Desmarests holds that such mixing is not essential, for the tragi-comedy is "une pièce dont les principaux personnages sont Princes, etc., encore qu'il n'y ait *rien de comique qui y soit mêlé.*"[2] "Il n'y a rien qui ressente la Comédie," writes d'Aubignac. "Tout y est grave et merveilleux, rien de populaire ny de bouffon."[3] According to Robiou, tragi-comedies "n'ont rien de comique, ou du moins, si le comique s'y rencontre, c'est à l'insu de l'auteur et bien malgré lui."[4] Brunetière denies that it is "une composition dramatique où le tragique et le comique, s'aidant l'un l'autre, et se faisant valoir par leur contraste même alterneraient pour le divertissement du spectateur."[5]

Vauquelin, on the other hand, notes that here "auecques le

[1] Page xvii. [2] *Scipion*, preface, Paris, 1639.

[3] *Pratique du Théatre*, 189.

[4] *Essai sur l'histoire de la littérature*, 401.

[5] *Revue des Deux Mondes*, 1901, VI, 143.

Tragic le Comic se raporte" and that "du graue et du bas le parler on mendie."[1] Mairet's opinion has been already quoted.[2] Scudéry calls the *genre* "un composé de la Tragedie et de la Comedie,"[3] and declares that "ce beau et divertissant poeme, sans pancher trop vers la severité de la tragédie, ny vers le stile railleur de la comédie, prend les beautez les plus delicates de l'une et de l'autre: et sans estre ny l'une ny l'autre on peut dire qu'il est toutes les deux ensemble et quelque chose de plus."[4] Ebert mentions the "Einmischung des Komischen."[5] Fournel calls attention to "la fusion des deux genres opposés en un seul ouvrage."[6] Rigal more specifically points out "le mélange dans la même pièce de personnages de conditions sociales différentes; c'est l'intervention de personnages *médiocres* dans une action pathétique, ou de personnages *illustres* dans une action médiocre."[7]

Now, if a reader confines himself to a limited number of tragi-comedies, he may reach any of these conclusions as to the mixture in style and characters. This fact is well brought out by Fontenelle, who writes: "Dans ce temps là la Tragi-Comédie étoit assez à la mode, genre mêlé où l'on mettoit un assez mauvais tragique, avec du comique, qui ne valoit gueres mieux. Souvent cependant, on donnoit ce non à de certaines Pièces toutes sérieuses, à cause que le dénouement en étoit heureux."[8] It seems, indeed, that the existence of the familiar and comic in speech and character was not essential, but was frequently admitted. There is apparently no evolution in the matter, as these elements are exceedingly apparent at various periods in such plays as *Lucelle* in 1576, *L'Ephésienne* in 1614, *L'Innocence Descouverte* in 1609 and 1628, *Les Folies de Cardenio* in 1625, and *L'Ospital des Fous* in 1635.

But there is a broader sense in which the name tragi-comedy is well chosen, in spite of the fact that familiar and humorous

[1] *Art poétique*, III, 164 and 167.
[2] See page xvi.
[3] *Observations sur le Cid*, 8, Paris, 1637.
[4] *Andromire*, preface, Paris, 1641.
[5] *Franz: Tragödie*, 131.
[6] *La Litt. ind.*, 14.
[7] *Alexandre Hardy*, p. 431.
[8] *Vie de P. Corneille*, in *Oeuvres de Fontenelle*, IV, 207.

elements frequently do not enter into it. Cloetta[1] and Lanson[2] have shown what constituted the medieval and XVI century idea of the difference between tragedy and comedy. The same view was held in the XVII century while the tragi-comedy was developing. During all this time, that difference was based on four characteristics, which were, perhaps, external, but served well enough to guide the pre-Cornelian dramatist. These were: the historic or non-historic subject, the high or low rank of the personages, the terrible or happy *dénouement*, the noble or familiar style. Now it has been shown that in respect to these qualities, the fully developed tragi-comedy occupied middle ground between the older *genres*. It is non-historic, but imitates history by a plot that savors of the romance rather than of the comedy of manners. The leading personages are of noble birth, but bourgeois and plebeians are allowed. The *dénouement* is never tragic, but frequently threatens to become so, in a manner foreign to the comedy. The style is serious in the main, seldom rising to tragic heights, yet sinking with no great frequency to comic familiarity and humor. From this point of view, it is evident that there is a mixing of tragic and comic elements which justifies the name, tragi-comedy.

While it approaches both classical *genres* in its form, where the use of Alexandrines, division into five acts, and subdivision into scenes is the rule, the tragi-comedy is differentiated from them by its looseness of structure, which presents the story *ab ovo*, with no regard for the unities of action, time, and place, and makes the tragi-comedy essentially a variety of the *drame libre*. Although the action in the tragi-comedy may spring from the will of the persons, it is more often produced, unlike that of the classical tragedy, by purely external causes. As psychological problems are seldom put, study of character and emotion is replaced by multiplicity of incident, cleverness of intrigue, and variety of personages and verse-forms. Mixing of opposing styles is freely employed, so that concrete are found with abstract statements,

[1] *Beiträge zur Litteraturgeschichte des Mittelalters*, I, 14–54.
[2] *Revue d' Histoire littéraire de la France*, XI, 541–85.

humorous with grave dialogues, lyrical with narrative verse-forms. Startling stage-effects are obtained by duels, murders, *enlèvements*, and other romantic means, which classicists avoid or keep behind the scenes. Dramatic effort is directed towards arousing the curiosity, rather than the passions of the audience. In the more fully developed type of the *genre*, love is the main-spring of the action, marriage is the chief end, all that is *romanesque* the means.

In defining the tragi-comedy, a distinction must be made between the early conception of the *genre* and that which was subsequently had of it. During the sixteenth century, the name could be applied to any play of medieval origin which possessed a happy *dénouement* and a form that was at least partially classic. This usage continued sporadically throughout the period of the *genre's* existence in the seventeenth century. But the more highly developed type of the *genre*, conveniently termed the *romanesque* tragi-comedy, which was extensively cultivated at Paris during the seventeenth century and became the only important variety of the tragi-comedy, possessed characteristics that may be summed up as follows:

1. The structure is that of the *drame libre*, by which the story is dramatized from its beginnings without regard for any dramatic unity except that of interest.

2. The events treated are serious, secular, non-historic, and *romanesque*.

3. The *dénouement* is happy.

4. The leading personages are aristocratic, but bourgeois and plebeians may be introduced in subordinate rôles. The shepherd of the pastoral is excluded.

5. The addition of comic passages, though frequent, is not an essential characteristic.

6. The form is classic in the predominant use of Alexandrines, the division into five acts, and the subdivision into scenes.

CHAPTER I.

THE SOURCES OF THE FRENCH TRAGI-COMEDY.

While the classic tragedy of France is derived directly from that of Greece and Rome, the *drame libre*, of which the tragi-comedy forms a part, is the secularized and modernized representative of the medieval drama, from which it inherited its stage, its traditions, and its audience. Its existence shows that there is in France a continuous dramatic development from the middle ages to modern times, a fact that has been somewhat obscured by the preponderance of the classic tragedy during the seventeenth century. At the same time, the French *drame libre* has followed the example of the *genre* in other countries by uniting with its medieval elements certain subsidiary features of the ancient classic drama.

It is the purpose of the present chapter to demonstrate the truth of these statements as far as they concern the tragi-comedy, which has been shown[1] to be that form of the *drame libre* which, when fully developed, displays a *romanesque* and non-historic theme, a happy *dénouement*, predominantly classic form, and aristocratic personages in the leading rôles. The method of procedure will be to indicate the indebtedness of the tragi-comedy (1) to the French medieval plays in their various *genres*, (2) to the Greek and Roman stage, (3) to the Renaissance drama of Western Europe that has combined under the title, tragi-comedy, the characteristics of medieval and classic plays.

I. The Relation of the French Tragi-Comedy to the Medieval Drama.

Although the medieval prototypes of the tragi-comedy have neither taken on a classical form and name, nor abandoned a

[1] Page xxiv.

religious and supernatural spirit that is foreign to later dramas, they exhibit the essential characteristics of the younger *genre* in an unmistakable fashion. Freedom of construction, romantic elements, happy termination, aristocratic leading personages, and frequent comic additions characterize certain medieval dramas as strongly as they characterize the tragi-comedy. Some of these qualities belong to all non-comic medieval plays, while others are exemplified only by certain varieties. For the full understanding of the influence exerted by the characteristics of the medieval drama on those of the tragi-comedy, it is necessary to take up these characteristics in detail.

1. That the construction of the medieval play is the same as that of the tragi-comedy is evidenced by the following contrast of the former *genre* with the French classic tragedy: "Le théâtre classique noue une action restreinte, . . . le théâtre des mystères déroule une action étendue. Dans l'un, les scènes s'appellent et pour ainsi dire s'engendrent l'une l'autre. Dans le théâtre du moyen âge, elles se succèdent. Le lien n'est pas dans le style; il est dans l'événement lui-même, et quelquefois il n'est nulle part."[1]

The unity of action, in a classical sense, is absent. The story is acted from its beginnings or as nearly so as possible. Thus, the medieval *mystère* of *Sainte Geneviève*[2] opens with the saint's birth, and recounts her various disconnected miracles. In *Griselidis*[3] the wooing of the heroine is presented, although this forms no necessary part of a drama designed to describe her patience under the afflictions imposed by her husband. In *L'Abbeesse grosse*[4] the heroine's church-going is first acted, although it has nothing to do with the rest of the play. Examples of such lack of unity in dramatic construction may be multiplied indefinitely.

In a similar manner the unity of action is violated by the tragi-comedy. Details that Racine would put in the mouth of a messenger or *confidante* are acted on the tragi-comic stage along

[1] Petit de Julleville, *Les Mystères*, I, 244.
[2] Bibliothèque Sainte Geneviève, Y, f-10, 183-217.
[3] Bibliothèque nationale MS. fr. 2203.
[4] *Miracles de Nostre Dame*, I, 57-100.

with circumstances of large dramatic interest. The scenes, also, are not developed one out of another, but occur at random, with little logical sequence.[1] Subordinate plots may be added, or the interest may be divided between two principal plots, which, developed simultaneously, are connected only at the end.[2]

Violation of one of the classic unities is readily associated with infringement of the others in both medieval plays and tragi-comedies. In neither *genre* is there any attempt at reducing the time of the action to the prescribed twenty-four hours. On the contrary, the greatest liberty is allowed in this respect. Seven years elapse during the progress of the *Miracle de Theodore;*[3] thirty in *La nonne qui laissa son abbaie,*[4] not to mention the tremendous periods of time involved in the cyclic plays that run from the Creation of the world to the Resurrection of Christ.[5]

In the tragi-comedy, also, considerable periods of time elapse, although they do not ordinarily extend beyond the limits of a natural life. In *La Force du Sang* of Hardy, a child, begot in the first act, is old enough to converse fluently in the third act. In *Philandre et Marisee* (1619), the hero weds the heroine at the beginning of the play, and encounters his son, grown to manhood, at the end of it. Other plays are of briefer duration, but none are confined to the limits of a single day.

A similar freedom is allowed with regard to the unity of place. On the medieval stage "la mère du pape est arrivée en Italie, venant du Sinaï, se traînant vers la Galice;"[6] or the scene of a single play may be laid in Scotland, Hungary, and Italy; as, in *La Fille du Roi de Hongrie.*[7] Similarly, the tragi-comedy follows Ulysses in his wanderings[8] or brings back the Count of Gleichen

[1] Cf. *Lisandre et Caliste* by Du Ryer, *La Sœur valeureuse* by Maréchal, or *Le Prince deguisé* by Scudéry.

[2] Cf. *L'Orizelle* by Chabrol or *Ligdamon et Lidias* by Scudéry. This phenomenon is very common in the *tragi-comédie pastorale.*

[3] *Miracles de Nostre Dame,* III, 67–133.

[4] *Ibidem,* I, 309–351.

[5] Cf. *La Création de l'Homme, la Nativité, la Vie, la Passion, la Résurrection de J.-C.* Petit de Julleville, *Les Mystères,* II, 411.

[6] Petit de Julleville, *Les Mystères,* II, 264.

[7] *Miracles de Nostre Dame,* V, 1–88.

[8] *Les Travaux d'Ulysse* (1631) by Durval.

from Palestine to Germany by way of Rome.[1] At times the limits of the space are smaller, but they are never reduced to those of the classic stage.

This freedom in regard to the latitude of space in which the action could be located was, indeed, one reason for the popularity of the tragi-comedy at the beginning of the sixteenth century. M. Rigal[2] has indicated the importance of the medieval *mise en scène* in delaying the development of the French classic stage and in hindering its popularity during the sixteenth century. Now, M. Lanson has shown that M. Rigal has gone too far in denying popular representation to the tragedies of Jodelle, Garnier, Montchrestien, and their followers,[3] yet it is certainly true that the presence of the elaborate apparatus of the medieval stage in the *mise en scène* of the *Confrères de la Passion* kept alive the medieval drama at the end of the sixteenth century and went far to popularize its successor, the tragi-comedy, at the beginning of the seventeenth century. For by the presentation of various places on the stage at one time, the *mansions* and the complicated medieval decorations associated with them could be utilized by the tragi-comedy in a manner impossible to the classical tragedy. Hence the tragi-comedy obtained favor with the theatrical managers and received large popularity with audiences that demanded striking stage effects rather than the discussion of a psychological problem.

The broad view taken of the dramatic unities by the authors of the *miracles* and *mystères* induced a prolixity of treatment that extended the presentation of the subject beyond the limits of a single performance, giving rise to the division into *journées*, which procedure forms a familiar characteristic of the medieval stage. One finds, for example, *La Passion de Jesu-Crist* in twenty *journées*,[4] *Sainte Barbe*[5] in five, and in *La Destruction de Troie*[6] in three *journées*. Many other plays, showing a varying number of

[1] *Elmire ou l'Heureuse Bigamie* by Hardy.

[2] In *Théâtre français avant la période classique.*

[3] Cf. *Études sur les origines de la tragédie classique en France. Revue d'histoire littéraire de la France*, x, 177–231 and 413–36.

[4] MS. Bib. Nat. fr. 12536.

[5] *Ibidem*, 976.

[6] *Ibidem*, 1415.

such time divisions as those indicated, can be mentioned, together with those whose performance is limited to a single *journée.* Now, despite the fact that the tragi-comedy has largely adopted the form of the classical tragedy, this medieval phenomenon persists in five cases : *Les chastes et loyales amours de Theagene et Cariclée,* by Hardy, contains eight *journées ;* while *Les Heureuses Infortunes* (1618) by La Brousse, *Tyr et Sidon* (1628) by Schelandre, *La Genereuse Allemande* (1630) by Mareschal, and *Argenis et Poliarque* by Du Ryer, contain time divisions into two such parts. The tragi-comedy thus betrays its medieval origin even in its form, that part of it which had undergone classical influence to the greatest extent.

It should be noted here that these phenomena of dramatic construction apply to the non-comic medieval drama, to the *miracles* and *mystères* rather than to the more condensed *moralité* and farce. The tragi-comedy is, indeed, in its mature form the outgrowth of this religious drama rather than of its contemporary *genres* that tended towards the comedy, although both the *moralité* and farce are represented by early tragi-comedies.

2. The second important characteristic of the fully developed tragi-comedy is the non-comic, secular, non-historic, and *romanesque* nature of the subjects treated.[1] In this respect it finds prototypes in certain medieval plays as surely as it finds them in the matter of its dramatic structure.

It is true that, in the sixteenth and early seventeenth centuries, the name *tragi-comédie* is applied to a number of plays that are derived from the comic side of the medieval drama. The farce is represented by *La Nouvelle tragicomique* (1597) of Papillon and by three undated plays published at Rouen toward 1620: the *Rebellion des grenouilles contre Jupiter, La Subtilité de Fanfreluche et Gaudichon* and the *Enfans de Turlupin.* The *moralité* appears in *L'Homme iustifié par Foy* (1554), *La Gaule* (about 1561), *Garnier Stoffacher* (1584), *Le Desesperé* (1595), *Caresmė prenant* (1595), *L'union Belgique* (1604), *Zo'anthropie* (1614), besides causing the introduction of allegorical characters into several other tragi-comedies. These, however, are exceptional cases in the

[1] See above, p. xxiv.

seventeenth century, while in the sixteenth their occurrence is an evidence of the fact that the term, *tragi-comédie*, could at that time be applied to any representative of the medieval drama that had a happy *dénouement* and at least a partially classical form. The mature *romanesque* type of tragi-comedy, and its early religious representative that derives its plot from the Bible, grow directly out of the medieval mystery and miracle play, especially from the *Miracles de Nostre Dame* and the *Mistére du Viel Testament.*

These medieval forms have no connection with the comedy of manners. Presenting a plot of which the interest lies in the events narrated rather than in the problems discussed, or the customs portrayed, they are to be chiefly distinguished from the tragi-comedy by their prevailingly religious spirit, which is largely lacking in the younger *genre.* This secularization is a matter of historical development that may be readily explained.

The earliest dramatic monuments of the middle ages, *Adam* and the *Résurrection* fragment are essentially religious, but with the *Theophile* and the *Saint Nicolas* secular interests are apparent. The tendency to introduce these interests into the plays is especially observable in the fourteenth century *Miracles de Nostre Dame,* which are at times dramatized romances, with *Nostre Dame* introduced to accomplish the *dénouement.* Good examples of such dramas are *Amis et Amille,*[1] *Ostes roy d'Espaingne,*[2] and *La Fille du Roi de Hongrie.*[3] The interest is here in the events, to which the rôle of *Nostre Dame* is subordinated. So far, indeed, is the expression of this feeling carried, that plays are developed from which the religious element is entirely lacking, as is the case with *Griselidis.*[4]

In the fifteenth century this secular spirit is less apparent. The *Mistére du Viel Testament* shows the reappearance of Biblical plots, a number of which are again met with in early tragi-comedies. Jacob's theft of the paternal blessing, his flight, marriage, and return, the finding of Moses by Pharaoh's daughter, the sufferings

[1] *Miracles de Nostre Dame,* IV, 1–67.
[2] *Ibidem,* V, 315–88. [3] *Ibidem,* V, 1–88. [4] Cf. page 2 above.

of Job, the romantic adventures of Tobit[1] are repeated in the tragi-comedies of *Jacob* (1604), *Jokebed* (1597), *Job* (1572), and *Thobie* (1579). The story of Abraham, described at length in the *Mistére du Viel Testament*,[2] reappears in a lost tragi-comedy concerning "deux grieves tentations desquelles le patriarche Abraham a été exercé."[3] In the same century, prototypes of the *romanesque* form of tragi-comedy can be found in *Le Roi Avenir*,[4] *Judith* and *Esther* from the *Mistére du Viel Testament*,[5] and in *La Destruction de Troie*.[6] These are continued in the early sixteenth century by *Saint Louis*[7] and in several of the *Douze Mystères de Nostre Dame de Liesse*;[8] by the lost *Roy de Castille et la royne sur la mer*, *Histoire romaine intitulée du Roy de Gascogne*, and *Le jugement du Roy d'Aragon*, played at Béthune, 1506, 1509, and 1526, respectively;[9] by *Huon de Bordeaux* (1557) and a drama in which *un roi Mabriant* figured, two pieces known to have been played at Paris by the *Confrérie de la Passion*.[10]

By a parliamentary act of November 17, 1548,[11] moreover, *mystères sacrés* were prohibited and only *mystères prophanes* allowed, so that dramatic authors were forced to seek secular subjects, or to disguise their religious plays under a classical form. This partly accounts for the two features of the tragi-comedy that chiefly distinguish it from the medieval drama, its secular character and its classical form. The fact that secular *miracles* and *mystères* are occasionally found, while religious tragi-comedies are common in the sixteenth and still persist in the seventeenth century, evidences the result of a literary evolution.

In the middle ages the *miracles* and *mystères* possessed religious and secular elements, of which the former predominated. The

[1] *Mistére du Viel Testament*, II, 139–246; III, 238–245; V, 1–51, 52–129.

[2] II, 28–79.

[3] See below, page 57.

[4] Petit de Julleville, *Les Mystères*, II, 474.

[5] V, 271–354; VI, 1–179.

[6] Petit de Julleville, *Les Mystères* II, 569.

[7] *Ibidem*, 583.

[8] *Ibidem*, 608.

[9] Petit de Julleville, *Répertoire*, 358, 360, 376.

[10] J. A. Dulaure, *Histoire physique, civile et morale de Paris* (Paris, 1821), III, 125 and 127 in the edition of Laynadier.

[11] *Ibidem*, 124.

Renaissance so promoted the secular dramatic spirit that in the latter half of the sixteenth century both religious and secular plays occurred side by side, descended from the medieval plays, but now bearing the name *tragi-comédie*. In the seventeenth century the evolution is completed with the triumph of the secular form, which was then used by all but a few conservatives.

Another case of development in the character of the subject treated in tragi-comedies is observed in the growth of the idea that an historic plot was to be avoided. Before the Renaissance, historical subjects, like the *Baptême de Clovis*[1] or the *Siège d'Orléans*,[2] were treated side by side with the marvellous legend of *Robert le Dyable*.[3] These were probably regarded as equally historic by their authors, whose choice of subject was unaffected by such considerations, as the exactness with which they dramatized their sources depended rather on the poverty of their imagination than on a developed historical sense. In the early tragi-comedies, subjects believed by their authors to be historical were confined to those derived from the Old Testament narrative, alongside of which occur *romanesque* dramas based on Ariosto and Boccaccio. When the *genre* was fully developed in the seventeenth century, the non-historical had so replaced the historical subject, that treatment of the latter became practically confined to the classical tragedy.[4]

These statements, however, apply only to the conscious choice of a non-historical theme. It is only with the development of a general sense of the difference between the historical and the non-historical that such choice became possible. As a matter of fact, however, the non-historical theme was freely treated in the middle ages and in the seventeenth century, so that the tragi-comedy finds prototypes in this as well as in other respects among the *miracles* and *mystères*.

Not only are such medieval subjects non-historical, but they possess frequently the *romanesque* qualities of the tragi-comedy.

[1] *Miracles de Nostre Dame*, VII, 193–277.

[2] Petit de Julleville, *Les Mystères*, II, 576.

[3] *Miracles de Nostre Dame*, VI, 1–77.

[4] An exception occurs in *L'union Belgique* (1604.)

Similar themes are acceptable to authors of medieval plays and of tragi-comedies, as is shown by a comparison of the plots of the *Miracle de Nostre Dame de la Marquise de la Gaudine*[1] and of *La Polyxene Tragicomœdie* (1597) by Jean Behourt. In the former, the uncle of the marquise seeks in vain to seduce her during her husband's absence. Desiring revenge for his repulse, he puts a dwarf in her bed while she sleeps, pretends to find him there, murders him, and accuses the marquise of adultery. The husband on his return condemns her to be burned alive. Fortunately a knight whom she has formerly befriended arrives at this juncture, proclaims her innocence, and challenges whosoever may deny it. The uncle accepts the challenge, is conquered, and admits the falsity of the accusation. The marquis and marquise are reunited, while the knight is rewarded with half the former's lands. The rôle of *Nostre Dame* is subordinate, as she descends from heaven only to comfort the marquise and assure the knight of her innocence. The same plot is found in *La Polyxene,* where the knight is made the lover of the lady he rescues, to whom he is united in marriage after her husband's opportune death in battle. The subsidiary religious element introduced by the presence of *Nostre Dame* is wanting in *La Polyxene.*

The *romanesque* expression of love that is characteristic of the tragi-comedy is also found in the *miracle* and *mystère.* The love of a man and a maiden is recounted in *La nonne qui laissa son abbaie,*[2] in *Tobie,*[3] and in the fifth of the *Mystères de Nostre Dame de Liesse,*[3] but, as a rule, the heroine of these medieval *genres* is a married woman, while in the tragi-comedy the removal of obstacles to marriage forms the *dénouement* of the piece. This change is probably brought about by the freer position of unmarried women after the middle ages. In both cases, however, love is an important element of many plays, whether it be before or after the marriage of the heroine.

The favorite medieval theme of a wife unjustly slandered by an unsuccessful and revengeful lover has already been noted in the

[1] *Miracles de Nostre Dame,* I, 121–170.

[2] See page 3 above.

[3] See page 7 above.

case of the *Marquise de la Gaudine.* It occurs again in *Berthe,*[1] *L'Empereris de Romme,*[2] *Oste roi d'Espaingne,*[3] *La Fille du Roi d'Hongrie,*[3] and in number seven of the *Mystères de Nostre Dame de Liesse.*[4] With these may be compared numerous tragi-comedies in which the virtue of the heroine has been calumniated; as, for example, *Genevre* (1609), *Madonte* (1631), and *La Virginie* (1633).

The woman's innocence is proved by resort to single combat in *Oste Roi d'Espaingne,*[3] as it was in the *Marquise de la Gaudine,* and as it is again in the tragi-comedies, *Genevre* and *Madonte.* Duels for this and other reasons are, indeed, exceedingly frequent in tragi-comedies and may also be found in the medieval drama. An especially *romanesque* effect is produced when a woman puts on armor to fight, disguised as a man. *La Fille d'un roy*[5] illustrates this use for the medieval drama, as do *La Sœur valeureuse* (1634), *Omphalle* (1630) *and L'infidelle Confidente* (1631) for the tragi-comedy. Such combats and the deaths that often accompany them are portrayed, moreover, on the stage. In neither tragi-comedy nor medieval drama is there any of the classic shrinking from the melodramatic that places behind the scenes all violent displays of physical force.

The exposure and subsequent recognition of children, disguises, *enlèvements,* assignations and other adventures furnish elements of the *romanesque* to *miracle, mystère* and tragi-comedy. *Amis et Amille*[3] is comparable with Scudéry's *Ligdamon et Lidias* in its portrayal of adventures due to a marvellous resemblance, with Hardy's *Gesippe* in the setting forth of a friendship unto death. The medieval hermit of *Le Roi Avenir,*[6] *Saint Guillaume du desert,*[7] and other plays reappears in such tragi-comedies as *Madonte* (1631) and *L'Orizelle* (1632). The medieval notion of humor derived from the antics of a deranged person appears

[1] *Miracles de Nostre Dame,* v, 153–251. [2] *Ibidem,* iv, 237–313.
[3] See above, page 6. [4] *Ibidem.*
[5] *Miracles de Nostre Dame,* vii, 1–117.
[6] Petit de Julleville, *Les Mystères,* ii, 474.
[7] *Miracles de Nostre Dame,* ii, 153.

notably in *Robert le Dyable*[1] and *Un Parroissian esconmenié.*[2] It is preserved in *Les Folies de Cardenio* (1625) and *L'Ospital des Fous* (1635).

Although the supernatural elements connected with almost every *miracle* or *mystère* largely disappeared with the secularization of the medieval play, they left traces in the tragi-comedy that are by no means rare. The miracle of the fiery furnace, the magic properties of Tobit's fish, the prophecies of the magician in *La Nouvelle tragicomique,* the appearance of the *diablon* in *Le Desesperé* occur in plays to which the term, *tragi-comédie,* is applied in its sixteenth century sense, but similar examples of the use of the supernatural can be cited from seventeenth century plays. *La Clotilde* (1613) and *Richecourt* (1628) are belated *miracles,* as was the *Tragi-comédie de Saint-Étienne* (1605). In *Philandre et Marisee* (1619) the heroine returns from heaven to accompany her husband thither. In *L'Inconstance punie* (1630), the fickle protagonist is punished by a bolt from the skies. A magician appears in *Omphalle* (1631), in *Les Passions esgarees* (1632) and in a number of *tragi-comédies pastorales.*

These examples are sufficient to prove the persistence of medieval dramatic qualities in the tragi-comedy as far as the subject of the plays is concerned. It has been shown that the *romanesque* characteristics of the *miracle* and *mystère* form an integral part of the tragi-comedy, for not only did similar topics appeal to the authors of each *genre,* but similar means were employed in the development of the themes. The chief distinction to be made regarding the subject matter of the *genres* is that the tragi-comedy is largely secular, while the medieval drama is religious. It has been shown,[3] however, that this character of the tragi-comedy is the result of the spirit of its age, expressed by popular approval of the secular, and legal prohibition of the religious drama, but that the change has not been sufficiently complete to prevent survivals of supernatural elements even in the tragi-comedy of the seventeenth century.

3. The happy *dénouement* that constitutes a third feature of the

[1] *Ibidem,* II, 1–77. [2] *Ibidem,* III, 1–65. [3] Page 6 *seq.*

tragi-comedy occurs very frequently in the *miracles* and *mystères*. It is characteristic of a religious drama that virtue is rewarded therein and vice punished. Even plays in which the holy protagonist is martyred cannot be considered tragic on account of the heavenly consolation held out to the suffering saint. More immediate, however, is the hero's reward in the fourteenth century *Miracles de Nostre Dame,* where Our Lady plays the rôle of *deus ex machinâ,* producing the astonishing results that are brought about in a tragi-comedy by a combination of circumstances often little less miraculous than those depicted in its medieval prototype.

In the fifteenth century, the plays of the *Mistère du Viel Testament* show the punishment of vice and reward of virtue that characterize Old Testament narratives. The happy *dénouement* is also found in plays that deal with Christ's Resurrection, but not with those that have to do with the Passion, if they be taken individually. It is less common in the *Cycle des Saints,* though the termination cannot be considered unhappy in such plays as *Saint Clément*[1] or *Sainte Barbe,*[2] where the souls of the martyrs are carried to heaven by angels. Even the element of the tragic that is present in a martyrdom is lacking in *Sainte Geneviève,*[3] *L'Institution de l'Ordre des Frères Prescheurs,*[4] *Marie Madeleine,*[5] *Saint Nicolas,*[6] and *Saint Remy.*[7] This happy termination is further characteristic of *Le Siège d'Orléans,*[8] but is lacking in *La destruction de Troie.*[9]

While both endings are found in the sixteenth century, the happy *dénouement* predominates, characterizing especially the *Douze Mystères de Nostre Dame de Liesse.*[10]

It is evident, then, that while both forms of *dénouement* existed in the *mystères* and *miracles,* the happy termination is there predominant. This fact is in keeping with the theory of the development of the *drame libre* out of the medieval drama, for it contains plays of tragic ending like *Philanire femme d'Hippolyte* (1577) by the side of the tragi-comedy with its happy *dénouement*; but

[1] Petit de Julleville, *Les Mystères,* II, 493.
[2] *Ibidem,* 486. [3] *Ibidem,* 515. [4] *Ibidem,* 522.
[5] *Ibidem,* 533. [6] *Ibidem,* 541. [7] *Ibidem,* 555.
[8] *Ibidem,* 576. [9] *Ibidem,* 569. [10] *Ibidem,* 608.

just as in the middle ages, the play of happy termination predominated, so in the sixteenth and seventeenth centuries the tragi-comedy with its happy ending is the leading form of the *drame libre*.

4. The rank of the personages in the *miracle* and *mystère* is much the same as in the tragi-comedy. Kings and princes, popes and prelates, biblical leaders and members of the heavenly hierarchy play principal rôles in the medieval drama, serving as prototypes to the aristocratic protagonists of the tragi-comedy. In both kinds, however, bourgeois and plebeians may be added, if the author so desires.

In *L'Empereur Julien*[1] figure the emperor, *Nostre Dame* and angels, the seneschal, two cavaliers, three clerks, three bourgeois and attendants. In *Griselidis*[2] the marquis is allied to a shepherdess, daughter of an humble peasant. *L'Incarnation et la Nativité de J.-C.*[3] includes among its *dramatis personæ Dieu le pere*, *Octavien empereur de Romme*, leaders of the Jews, shepherds and women of Bethlehem. Besides heavenly personages, the emperor, and prelates, *Saint Crespin et Saint Crespinien*[4] contains *le messagier*, *le geollier*, *Rogier le bon homme*, *Pavie bonne fame*, *le ladre*, *l'aveugle*, *le fol*, his *vallet*, etc. In *Saint Christophe*[5] (1527) the three ranks are represented by King Darius, two *bourgeoys* and Purdoyn, *varlet du tavernier*.

Among tragi-comedies that show the same mingling of men of various ranks may be mentioned *Lucelle* (1576), Hardy's *Felismene*, *Les Heureuses Infortunes* (1618), *Lisandre et Caliste* (1632), in which a physician, a banker, servants, shepherds, fishermen and a butcher are introduced along with leading characters of princely rank. Many other examples can be cited to show that in this respect the tragi-comedy shows a freedom of treatment unknown to the classical stage and derived from the usage of the medieval drama.

5. Another attribute of the tragi-comedy is the addition of

[1] *Miracles de Nostre Dame*, II, 171–226.

[2] See above, page 2.

[3] Petit de Julleville, *Les Mystères*, II, 430.

[4] *Ibidem*, 498.

[5] *Ibidem*, 491.

comic elements as a frequent, if not an essential characteristic. Similarly "le comique, dans le mystère, était en somme épisodique plutôt que nécessaire; un accident, non un élément intégrant du poème; une broderie très prodiguée sur un fond sérieux." [1] Usually spoken by some special character as the *fou*, or the *diable* when he is not tragic, this element was of exceedingly common occurrence, as the reading of almost any *miracle* or *mystère* will show.[2]

These statements are equally true of the tragi-comedy, though there are probably more plays in this *genre* that are entirely free from comic elements than there are in its medieval predecessors. Among tragi-comedies in which this feature is particularly evident may be mentioned *Lucelle* (1576), *Bradamante* (1582), *Ariadne Rauie* (about 1606), *L'Ephesienne* (1614) *Les Folies de Cardenio* (1625), *Tyr et Sidon* (1628), *L'Innocence Descouverte* (1628), *Lisandre et Caliste* (1632), and *L'Ospital des Fous* (1635). In these, as in the *mystères*, the comic element is introduced to add interest to the play, but is not essential to its existence. It is usually found in the mouths of subordinate personages.

The many resemblances indicated between the tragi-comedy and the medieval plays show clearly that it derived from them its essential dramatic qualities as well as the stage on which it was acted. There was no break here in the historical development of the French theater, for the tragi-comedy was the chief of the modernized seventeenth century forms of the medieval drama. But all medieval dramatic forms were not represented in it to an equal extent. The farce, as already mentioned,[3] was imitated by only four so-called tragi-comedies besides portions of such plays as *Lucelle* and *L'Innocence descouverte*. As, moreover, it had already inspired the comic elements in many of the *mystères*, the greater part of its influence on the tragi-comedy was probably exerted through that medium.

The *moralité* has been shown[4] to give rise to several tragi-comedies of the sixteenth century. From it, furthermore, the

[1] Petit de Julleville, *Les Mystères*, I, 278.
[2] *Ibidem*, 266-278. [3] See above, page 5. [4] *Ibidem*.

younger *genre* introduced allegorical characters into such plays as *Polyxene* (1597) and *Pasithée* (1624). Of greater importance, however, was the influence of the *moralité* in deepening the study of the moral ideas that prompted the actions of the various personages. The *moralité* has been called the commentary on the text of the *mystère* and as such it has influenced the tragi-comedy, which shows an advance beyond the *mystère*, from a psychological point of view, although it is still greatly inferior in this regard to the classical tragedy.

The tragi-comedy, however, is concerned more largely with incidents than with their cause. When it teaches, it does so by example rather than precept. In this respect it closely resembles the *miracle* and *mystère* and shows its lack of essential connection with the *moralité*. The *miracle* and *mystère*, moreover, are the only medieval forms that show fully the construction of the tragi-comedy, its serious *fond* and joyous *dénouement*, its aristocratic protagonist, its addition of the comic, and especially its choice of the *romanesque* in subject and detail. There is no doubt that the tragi-comedy originated in them rather than in any other medieval form.

It is worthy of note that the tragi-comedy in its secular and *romanesque* subject seems nearer to the fourteenth century *Miracles de Nostre Dame* than to the *Mystères* of the fifteenth century. It is probable, however, that many representatives of the *miracle* were known during the fifteenth century, although they have not been preserved, for they reappear in the sixteenth century *Miracles de Nostre Dame de Liesse*. The fifteenth century *mystère* shows, furthermore, sufficient resemblance to the tragi-comedy to be regarded as its prototype, even had the *miracle* failed to survive, for when either *genre* is secularized and given classical form, the differences between it and the tragi-comedy are such as can be readily explained by the modernity of the younger *genre*. So it is that medieval *mystères* with biblical plot reappear as tragi-comedies, and that belated *miracles* occur in the seventeenth century under the title, *tragi-comédie*. By this time, however, the great majority of tragi-comedies had undergone influences that had changed the appearance, if not the essential qualities of the *genre*. It is these influences that must now be discussed.

II. The Relation of the French Tragi-Comedy to the Drama of Greece and Rome.

1. While the special influence of the drama of Greece and Rome on the tragi-comedy is concerned largely with the form and name adopted by the latter *genre,* there is a general influence of more far-reaching effect that has been exerted by the ancient stage in company with other Greek and Latin literary kinds. This influence is not concerned in the creation of the tragi-comic *genre,* but is important in deepening and secularizing its character, in doing away with much medieval crudity and confusion, and in individualizing the author and the personages he treats. These phenomena are noticeable in Renaissance literature as a whole and are due to the ancient stage only as it forms a part of the *corpus* of classic literature.

From the individualization of the author results the fact that, while medieval plays were largely anonymous, the authors of all but thirteen tragi-comedies are known to us by name.[1] The personal spirit is shown, also, in the large number of dedications and introductory writings attached to tragi-comedies. This reacts upon the personages of the play, whose characters are more varied, and show the results of more careful thought than do those of the medieval drama. There is visible here and elsewhere a toning down of the medieval exaggerations that indicates a tendency toward realism, causing the disappearance of the miraculous from most tragi-comedies.

The style has developed from the naïve character of the *mystère* to a degree of subjectivity that becomes *préciosité* with Scudéry and other authors. Classical allusions abound, frequently occurring in the speech of most unsuitable persons. The employment of such terms as *Fleuve stygieux,*[2] *Parques fatales,*[3] *Champs Heliseens,*[4]

[1] These are: *Jacob ou Antidolatrie, Purification du temple de Jérusalem, Henry et Kunégonde, Ignace de Loyola, Lambertiade, La Gaule, Rebellion des grenouilles, Fanfreluche et Gaudichon, Enfans de Turlupin, Saint Étienne, Alexandre et Annette, Richecourt,* and *Agimee.*

[2] *La Gaule,* I. [3] *Ombre de Garnier Stoffacher,* II. [4] *Thobie,* II.

however, while showing classical influence, is not altogether a departure from medieval usage, for there also classical pedantry at times ran riot.[1]

The tragi-comedy frequently employs classical names for its personages, as, Mercure,[2] Bellone,[3] Hospes,[4] Hamarthie,[5] and many others. *Richecourt* (1628) is partly written in Latin, while a quotation in that language closes *Philandre et Marisee* (1619). These are only a few instances of the enormous influence exerted on the tragi-comedy by classical literature, as a whole. It is evident that changes thus brought about characterize other *genres* as well as the tragi-comedy. For a more special influence on this new dramatic kind, brought about by the classical drama only, one must look elsewhere.

2. The influence of Seneca can be detected in a number of tragi-comedies. The violent expressions of emotion, invocations of heavenly powers, elaborate circumlocutions, mythological allusions, overworked metaphors, and labored monologues that characterize this author's plays are found in such tragi-comedies as *La Gaule*, *Bradamante*,[6] *L'Ombre de Garnier Stoffacher*, *Theagene et Cariclée*, *Genevre*, *Les Heureuses Infortunes* and *L'Innocence Descouverte*. The plot of the latter play may be partly drawn from Seneca's *Phaedra* or Euripides's *Hippolytus*, though the happy *dénouement* and addition of extensive comic passages show that the imitation amounts to little more than the repetition of the theme of a woman's incestuous passion and her desire for vengeance on the stepson whom she had failed to seduce.

A number of tragi-comedies draw their plots from Greek and Latin authors,[7] but only one of them traces its source to a classical play. This is Hardy's *Alceste*, which, the author states, is derived

[1] Cf. Petit de Julleville, *Les Mystères*, II, 261 *seq.*

[2] *La Gaule.* [3] *Garnier Stoffacher.* [4] *La Nouvelle tragicomique.* [5] *Zoanthropie.*

[6] For special influence here, cf. H. M. Schmidt-Wartenberg, *Seneca's Influence on Robert Garnier*, Darmstadt, 1888.

[7] Two on *Theagene et Cariclée; Arsacome*, *Procris*, *Alceste*, *Ariadne Rauie*, *L'Ephesienne*, *Heureuses Infortunes*, *Gesippe*, *Phraarte*, *Aretaphile*, *Clitophon*, *Les Travaux d'Ulysse.* All but the last are by Hardy or by contemporary authors. *Aristoclée* and *Léandre et Héron*, improperly called tragi-comedies, also have classical subjects.

from the *Alcestis* of Euripides. He does not understand Euripides's dramatic principles, however, using him as he used Cervantes, merely for the story set forth in his play. A comparison of the two dramas is of interest, as it shows the difference in the constructions of a classical tragedy and a tragi-comedy.

Euripides's drama consists of a few important scenes closely connected in interest and played by a small number of persons. The ideas of death and guest-friendship that run throughout the play give unity of action to the plot, which is also one in place and time. The beauty of the play is largely derived from the study of character and the portrayal of the heroine's noble sacrifice. The thread of the narrative, after the preliminary debate between Apollo and Death, is taken up just before the demise of Alcestis, after she has consented to die for her lord.

Hardy, on the other hand, begins his narrative with the gods, when Juno sends a messenger to bid Hercules go in search of Cerberus. In Act II Admète laments his approaching end, while listening to protestations of affection from his father and mother. Then the message of the oracle is brought that allows one of them to die for him. They refuse and Alcestis offers to sacrifice herself. In Act III Hercules arrives and is told the situation by Admète, whom he promises to aid by descending to the *Royaume des morts*. This he actually does in the following act, much to the disgust of the infernal powers. Finally he returns to earth with Alceste, whom he reunites to Admète.

Hardy is far from Euripides, whom he follows but little. He has combined with the Alcestis narrative the account of one of Hercules's labors, including his rescue of Theseus. The violation of the unities is conspicuous. While Euripides selects artistically the scenes of philosophical importance, Hardy puts the story on the stage from beginning to end, hoping to sustain the interest by the succession of surprising events. It is evident from this example that, even where the same plot is dramatized, the tragi-comedy in its essential elements, as a *genre*, is entirely independent of classical influence.

3. There is, however, an obvious influence of the classical drama on the tragi-comedy in the matter of the form in which the

latter *genre* is written. Like the French classical tragedy, the tragi-comedy is mainly composed in Alexandrine verse, the French equivalent of the iambic hexameter. In five early plays, it is true, the Alexandrine is altogether lacking; for *Lucelle* (1576) and *Iokebed* (1597) are written in prose; *L'homme iustifié par Foy* (1552) and *Les Enfants dans la Fournaise* (1561) chiefly in verses of ten syllables, *Caresme Prenant* (1595) in verses of eight syllables. It must be noted, however, that these plays are all in the sixteenth century, before the tragi-comedy is fully developed. In the following century, the Alexandrine is the verse-form commonly employed in dialogue and monologue portions of the great majority of tragi-comedies.

The tragi-comedy, however, shows much greater liberty than the French classical tragedy with respect to its verse forms. While the Alexandrine is the prevailing form employed, verses of eight or six syllables occur in lyric passages, letters, love dialogues and soliloquies. Echo-rimes are found in a number of instances and sonnets are sometimes inserted. The subject of the use of verse-forms in the tragi-comedy will be treated below.[1] For the present it is sufficient to note that, while the classic influence predominates in determining the use of the Alexandrine, shorter verses are employed with considerable freedom.

The division into five acts is employed in the tragi-comedy after the Horatian precept and the Senecan example. The exceptions that occur are found chiefly in sixteenth century plays. There is no such division, for example, in *Trois Enfants dans la Fournaise* (1561) or in *La Nouvelle tragicomique* (1597). *La Gaule* (about 1561) is divided into four acts; *L'Ombre de Garnier Stoffacher* (1584) into three. The subdivision into scenes is slightly less common; it is absent not only from the plays that show no act-division, but also from *La Gaule, L'Ombre de Garnier Stoffacher, La Polyxene* (1597), *L'Ephesienne* (1614) and *L'Éthiopique* (1609). Concerning such divisions the author of *L'homme iustifié par Foy* writes: "Touchant la disposition et ordre que i'ay tenu en la Tragique Comedie ie l'ay disposée par Actes et Scenes, non tant

[1] Pages 81, 99, and 146.

pour l'imitation de Poetes comiques, que pour la division des propos et des dialogues." Be this as it may, the classical influence is evident where the division is made. The authors of the fully developed tragi-comedy carried it as far as did those of the French classic tragedy, though they did not show the same exactitude in changing the scene with every variation in the number of persons on the stage.[1]

Another example of the classical influence is found in the chorus, which, however, never occupied an important place in the tragi-comedy and soon disappeared from it altogether. Where the chorus occurs, it shows a wide variety of function. In a number of tragi-comedies it plays the purely external rôle of commenter on the action, without taking any part in it.[2] In others it remains external in reality, but bears something of the spirit of the play by assuming a name appropriate to it. Thus, one finds *Chœur de Babyloniens* in *Les Enfants dans la Fournaise* (1561); *Chœur des soldats, des anges,* and *des vaincus* in *Richecourt* (1628). In *L'Ombre de Garnier Stoffacher* (1584) there are three choruses, who debate with one another and with the characters, but who represent lyric elements throughout. Here the chorus plays the double rôle of personage and commenter. This is true also of the chorus in *Tobie* (1579). The evolution from the lyric to the dialogue-rôle is shown at a further developed stage in *Agimee* (1629), where the *Chœur des Luteciens* and the *Chœur des Bergers* dance and play with the actors, so that they are scarcely more lyric than the latter. The last step before its disappearance is taken when the chorus becomes a band of men like the Roman mob in *Julius Cæsar.* This is its function in Hardy's *Theagene et Cariclée* and *Phraarte.* In general, however, Hardy has abandoned the chorus in his tragi-comedies, thereby setting an example that was followed by his successors, except by the monk that wrote *Richecourt* and by the author of *Agimee,* which is practically a *tragi-comédie pastorale.*

[1] Cf., for example, *Madonte,* I, 2 and 3; *Ligdamon et Lidias,* I, 1, and V, 1. *Argenis et Poliarque,* II, 1 and IV, 2.

[2] Cf. *La Gaule, Polyxene, Jacob, Geneve, L'Ephesienne, Philandre et Marisee.*

In its length, the tragi-comedy also shows the effect of classical influence; for, while it is rarely as short as a Greek or Latin tragedy, it is briefer than the usual *miracle*, or *mystère*. The idea had now become established, futhermore, that the play must be acted at a single performance, a custom that had not always been adhered to during the middle ages. The few tragi-comedies that violate this rule have been noted above.[1]

In these matters of form, however, as in its style and secular spirit, the tragi-comedy has received from the stage of the Greeks and of the Romans only what came in fuller measure to the French classical tragedy. None of these characteristics serves to mark it as a *genre* different from contemporary dramatic kinds. In this respect, indeed, the only service rendered to the tragi-comedy by the classical drama is the formation of its *genre* name, first used, however in an entirely different sense from that in which it was applied in France.

4. The term, tragi-comedy, first occurs in the Prologue to the *Amphitruo* of Plautus, where Mercury calls the play a *tragicomœdia*[2] because gods and kings are introduced into the comedy along with slaves. The passage runs as follows:

> Quid? contraxistis frontem quia tragœdiam
> dixi futuram hanc? deu'sum commutauero.
> eandem hanc, si uoltis, faciam <iam> ex tragœdia
> comœdia ut sit omnibus isdem uorsibus
> utrum sit an non uoltis? sed ego stultior,
> quasi nesciam uos velle, qui diuos siem.
> teneo quid animi uostri super hac re siet:
> faciam ut commixta sit, <sit> tragico[co]mœdia;
> nam me perpetuo facere ut sit comœdia,
> reges quo ueniant et di, non par arbitror
> quid igitur? quoniam hic seruos quoque partis habet,
> faciam sit, proinde ut dixi, tragico[co]mœdia.[3]

---

[1] Page 5.

[2] The versification shows that this is the proper form, rather than *tragicocomœdia*, which appears in the MS. and has been repeated in a number of plays of an academic type such as the *Hypocrisis* of Gnaphaeus (1544), the *Gedeon* of Libertus ab Hauthem (1575), etc.

[3] *Amphitruo, prologus*, 52–63. *T. Macci Plauti Comœdiœ*, edited by W. M. Lindsay, Oxford, 1903, 2 vols.

This passage has been noted in connection with the French tragi-comedy by Scaliger,[1] and after him by d'Aubignac,[2] Voltaire,[3] Lessing,[4] and others. The second of these, after mentioning Plautus, declares that the name is "une raillerie qu'il fait dans son Prologue, en ioignant les noms de ces deux Poëmes comme il en avoit mêlé les Personnages." Plautus's intent is certainly humorous, but he is at the same time serious in his objection to applying the term, *comœdia*, to a play in which gods appear. A *tragicomœdia* is, therefore, a *comœdia* into which are introduced personages ordinarily confined to the *tragœdia.* Such a use of the word is approved by Lactantius Placidus, who writes in his *Commentarius in Statii Thebaida,* "Tiryntha Deus. Iuppiter mutatus in Amphitryonem concubuisse cum Alcmena Electryonis filia dicitur in urbe Tirynthia. unde natus est Hercules, unde et Tirynthius dicitur. de qua Plautus tragicomœdiam dixit."[5] In other words, the mingling of men of different rank gives rise to the tragi-comedy.

Now, this basis of nomenclature does not apply to the French tragi-comedy, for, although this *genre* frequently permits similar mixing, it has at times only such personages as would be admitted into a Greek tragedy.[6] Furthermore, if the mingling of rank were the only essential to constitute a tragi-comedy, the *Amphitruo* would be called a *tragi-comédie* in France; yet Rotrou, whose numerous tragi-comedies show that he well understood the nature of the *genre,* called his *Deux Sosies,* which is a reworking of the *Amphitruo,* not a *tragi-comédie,* but a *comédie.* In so many other respects, also, does the *Amphitruo* fail to meet the requirements of the French *genre,* that the name *tragi-comédie* seems to be practically the only evidence of connection between them.

No historical objection can be raised against the derivation of the term from Plautus's use of it; for the *Amphitruo,* never entirely lost during the middle ages, was studied under Pope Paul II

[1] *Poetices,* 34.
[2] *Pratique du Théâtre,* 194.
[3] *Remarques sur le Cid,* I, 4, verse 75, in *Oeuvres Complètes* (*Paris,* 1784, 69 vols.) *L,* 112.
[4] *Hamburgische Dramaturgie,* 234.
[5] Ricardus Jahnke, *P. Papinius Statius,* III, 200, Leipzig, 1898, 3 vols.
[6] Cf. *Bradamante* (1582), *Aretaphile* (1618) or *L'Indienne Amoureuse* (1635).

(1464–71), was played at Rome, and subsequently (1487 and 1491) at Ferrara, and was published at Venice in 1472, 1482, 1495 and 1499.[1] It was sufficiently well known in France and Spain to be translated by Meschinot in 1509 and Villalobos in 1515; it was acted, moreover, at several German towns during the first half of the sixteenth century.[2] With the spread of the play came the knowledge of the term *tragicomœdia*, which seems to have been looked upon by the sixteenth century playwright as a classic label for any dramatic production that bore a resemblance, however slight, to both tragedy and comedy. Thus applied to various kinds of plays in France and other European countries, it did not attain a fixed meaning till the beginning of the following century. The influence of the tragi-comedies that sprang up after this fashion in other countries, on the development of the *genre* in France, must now be discussed.

III. The Relation of the French Tragi-Comedy to that of Other European Countries.

The French tragi-comedy has been shown to derive its leading characteristics from the medieval drama, just as it takes its form and name from the classical Latin stage. These elements were united in French plays toward the middle of the sixteenth century after they had given rise to tragi-comedies in other lands. The question whether these older tragi-comedies did not exert an influence on the development of the *genre* in France may, therefore, be aptly put. For the discussion of the reply to this question, I have prepared a list of all tragi-comedies that I have been able to find, written before 1582, the date of the publication of Garnier's *Bradamante*. This play, although the tenth French work called tragi-comedy, has been chosen because it gives a conspicuous early example of the form that the *genre* ultimately took, and because, with its appearance, the tragi-comedy won for itself so definite an

[1] Cf. C. von Reinhardstöttner, *Plautus, Spätere Bearbeitungen*, 21, 50, 51, 162; and Brunet, *Manuel*, IV, 705–8.

[2] Cf. Reinhardstöttner, *ibidem*, 138, 174, 35 *seq.*

existence that it is idle to look for forces that acted later in the creation of the *genre*. The tragi-comedies are arranged according to the dates of their first editions;[1] with the titles, names of authors, places of publication, and dates of reprints as late as 1582. This list of tragi-comedies forms Appendix A.

As the three earliest tragi-comedies hold a position chronologically detached from other plays of this *genre* and fall into no group that might be investigated as a whole, they will be first discussed in the order in which they were published.[2] The subsequent plays will then be treated[3] in four groups, according to the language in which they were composed. The order of treatment will be as nearly chronological as possible, beginning with the Spanish and Portuguese plays, and following them with those written in Italian, in Latin, and in the Teutonic languages.

A. The Earliest Tragi-Comedies.

1. *Fernandus Servatus* (1494), the first tragi-comedy, was written in Latin prose by Carlo Verardi and done into hexameters by his nephew, Marcellino. The historical subject, the attempted assassination of Ferdinand, King of Spain, by a lunatic, has been altered for dramatic and religious purposes. Tisiphone, sent to earth by Pluto, induces Ruffus to attempt the King's murder. After he has succeeded only in wounding him, the Queen prays for the King's recovery and is comforted by Saint James. The King then enters miraculously healed and the chorus commends the example set by the royal pair.

This slight production is chiefly interesting as showing the continuation of medieval ideas of dramatic composition despite the introduction of certain classical names and traditions. The story is acted from the first inception of the plot. The unity of place is lacking, for the scene is laid in the infernal regions as well as at the court of Ferdinand and Isabella. The strong religious spirit that pervades the piece culminates in the appearance of Saint

[1] Unless their existence at an earlier date is well established.

[2] Pages 24–27. [3] Pages 27–34.

James, and in the King's miraculous recovery. The classical names, Pluto and the Furies, are mere epithets attached to medieval personages, in whose assembly Creizenach[1] sees the influence of the plots laid by devils in the medieval drama. In these respects it shows resemblances to early French tragi-comedies, to which it bears further resemblance in its serious subject, aristocratic personages, and happy *dénouement.* The chief distinction, indeed, to be made between it and such a play as *Les Enfants dans la Fournaise* (1561) lies in the fact that its subject is drawn from contemporary rather than from biblical history. This variation indicates that the author was an innovator, as is shown by his composing this play and the *Historia baetica* in prose. The spirit in which he writes is evident from his prologue to the latter play, where he states his opposition to the writers of classical comedy:

Apporto non Plauti, aut Næuii comœdias,
Quas esse fictas scitis omnes fabulas,
At nouam nobis veramque fero historiam,
Per quam licebit nosse, ut summi principes
Ferdinandus & coniunx, domuerunt Bæticam
. . . .
Præsertim cum ulta hic tyrannorum scelera
Non sitis audituri, aut fastus regios,
Intolerandam vel bonis superbiam,
Quæ sæpe describi solent tragœdiis.
Neque audientur lenonum hic periuria,
Seruorum technæ, aut meretricum blanditiæ,
Auara non usquam lena hic inducitur,
Milesue gloriosus, aut sycophanta impudens,
Edaxue parasitus, vel matrona impudens,
Paterue durus, aut amator cupidus,
Et reliqua, quæ in Graiis nostrisque comicis.
Spectata præbent voluptatem plurimam.
Verum pudica, honestaque hic sunt omnia.
. . . .
Requirat autem nullus hic comœdiæ
Leges ut obseruentur, aut tragœdiæ,
Agenda nempe est historia, non fabula.[2]

It was in this reformer's spirit that Verardi rehabilitated the

[1] *Geschichte,* II, 9.
[2] *Expugnatio Regni Granatæ. Caroli Verardi Cæsenatis in Historiam Bæticam. Prologus. Hispaniæ Illustratæ,* II, 862 (Frankfort, 1603, 4 vols.).

title, *tragi-comœdia,* and applied it to the Renaissance treatment of a medieval play. As his selection of a plot from contemporary history was not followed in France, he altered nothing in the medieval essentials inherited by the tragi-comedy, simply showing that it was possible to treat them under a more classical form. In this way he introduced the grafting of classical elements on the medieval stem, and though he did not carry far this procedure, not even dividing his play into acts and scenes, he thus rendered an important service to the formation of the *genre.* That his play was known outside of Italy and could consequently influence the mingling of classic and medieval elements in other countries is evidenced by its reprint at Strasburg in 1513.

2. Kitzscher's *Profectione* (1501), the second play to be called a tragi-comedy, was probably influenced by the works of Verardi, as it concerned a contemporary event of some importance and was written by a German who had studied in Italy. Like the *Historia baetica,* too, it is composed in Latin prose without divisions into acts or scenes, and its author declares in his prologue that it is a true history, neither tragedy nor comedy. The play deals with the departure of the Duke of Pomerania on a pilgrimage and the lamentations of the duchess till she receives good tidings from the messenger, who narrates at length the incidents of the duke's journey. The classic unities of place and of action, if action there be, are here preserved, though the unity of time is violated. Although allied by aristocratic personages, serious subject, and happy *dénouement* with the French tragi-comedy, it is opposed to the latter in the source of its subject, which is derived from contemporary history. The play is too academic in character to have met with great popularity. Its chief service seems to have lain in introducing the term *tragicocomedia* to the German writers of Latin.

3. The *Celestina* was first called a tragi-comedy in 1502. Its plot is too well known to be analyzed here. The play is a comedy of manners with a tragic ending and by no means a tragi-comedy in the French sense. The following explanation has been made of the use of the term *tragicomedia:*

"Otros han litigado sobre el nombre, diciendo que no se habia de llamar comedia, pues acaba en tristeza, sino que se llamase tragedia. El primer autor quiso dar denominacion del principio, que fué placer, é llamóla comedia: yo viendo estas discordias entre estos estremos, partí agora por medio la porfía, é llaméla *tragicomedia.*" [1]

As the unhappy ending, which suggests the first part of this compound term, does not occur in the French tragi-comedy, the *Celestina* does not seem to have aided in the creation of the *genre* as known in France. On account of its great length, it was probably not considered a dramatic work at all, but a prose romance of daily life. The only service this work rendered the tragi-comedy was that of spreading its name through the various countries of Europe in which the enormous popularity of the *Celestina* caused it to be repeatedly translated or reprinted.

It is in this spreading of the name of the new *genre*, indeed, that lies the importance of these early tragi-comedies. They did not affect the matter of the medieval drama, nor did they show the classical form of the fully developed French tragi-comedy. What they brought about was the use of the *genre* name and the beginning of tendencies that resulted in the application of a classical form to the French tragi-comedy.

B. Non-French Tragi-Comedies from 1513 to 1582.

A glance at the list of tragi-comedies given in Appendix A shows that:

1. Eleven were written in Spanish and Portuguese between 1513 and 1542. The earliest nine of these were the work of Gil Vicente, one of the first European dramatists to modernize the medieval drama. Most of his *tragicomedias* are in the nature of *Festspiele*, courtly productions of an allegorical and mythological nature, that show a robuster tone in the introduction of well-drawn personages from the lower walks of life. They are mostly slight compositions, a kind of interlude without divisions into acts and scenes.

Two of them, however, *Dom Duardos* and *Amadís de Gaula*, bear striking resemblance to the French tragi-comedy in their

[1] In the author's prologue, *Biblioteca de Autores españoles*, III, 12.

romanesque subjects, derived from chivalric romances, their construction, termination, personages, and comic elements. They differ from the French species, indeed, only on the formal side, for the divisions into acts and scenes is not made, and the verse form is much more lyric than that of the French *genre.* These two plays, written, with the exception of stage directions, entirely in Spanish, seem to be the forerunners of the later *comedia.* We have no evidence that they exerted any influence in France, as there is no indication of a knowledge of Vicente's work in that country. In a consideration of the French tragi-comedy, however, his drama is of interest, as it exemplifies the fact that similar medieval and classical influences at work in France and Portugal produced plays of much the same kind.

The two tragi-comedies by Spaniards are of less interest. The *Tragicomedia alegórica del Paraíso y del infierno* is an allegorical play of medieval spirit imitated from an *auto* by Gil Vicente; the *Lysandro y Roselia* is a prose continuation of the *Celestina.* Neither of these works appears to have exerted any influence on the French tragi-comedy, nor do they offer examples of parallel development, as was the case with the work of Gil Vicente and as will be found true of the Italian tragi-comedy, to which attention must now be paid.

2. The first Italian *tragicommedia,* the *Cecaria,* is a pastoral drama on the recovery of three men, struck blind by love. The name *dialogo,* applied to the early editions of it, might well have been retained. It is by no means a tragi-comedy in the French sense of this term, yet this is the only Italian tragi-comedy composed before 1582 that was translated into French as a *tragicomédie.* It so appeared in 1594 as *Les Aveugles.*

La Potenza d'Amore relates an unsuccessful lover's attempt at suicide. The leading personages appear to be bourgeois. Minor rôles are played by Pedante, Zani, and Collubrino, a magician. The play is a comedy of manners rather than a tragi-comedy in the French sense.

The greater number of early Italian tragi-comedies are based on classical narratives. *Apollo e Leucotoe, Il Ratto d'Helena,* and *Il Giudizio di Paride* speak for themselves. *La Cangenia* may be added to these, as in it the author treats the conflict between the Carthaginians and the Romans. Now, had these plays influenced the French *genre*, it is impossible that the classical subject would not have been employed there as well. In reality, however, the first French tragi-comedies that show plots derived from classical authors were written by Hardy fifty years later.[1]

The only Italian tragi-comedy, in fact that is similar to the French form of the *genre* is the *Quintilia* (1567), a play which is *romanesque* in its love intrigue and in the discovery by a father of a long lost son; aristocratic in its personages, who belong to the court of Sicily, where the spectator is introduced by the ghost of the king; serious in the main, but comic in such subordinate characters as Trulla, the court buffoon, and Gallofria with his Bergamasco dialect. The play comes, however, rather late to influence the French tragi-comedy in its origin, for not only had the *genre* name appeared in France four times before the *Quintilia* was published, but one of the plays to which the name was applied belongs to the *romanesque* type of tragi-comedy, typified by the Italian play, and it was acted as early as 1564. There is, moreover, no evidence that the *Quintilia* was known in France during the formative period of the tragi-comedy. One sees here another example of parallel and independent development already noted in the two dramas of Gil Vicente.[2]

While the Italian tragi-comedy had no influence on the French play of the same *genre* name, an Italian comedy, the *Amor costante* (1540) by Alessandro Piccolomini is the source of *Lucelle tragi-comédie de Louis Le Jars* (1576). The latter play is however, an exceptional variety of tragi-comedy,[3] nearly approaching the *comédie bourgeoise*, and has small influence on other members of the *genre*. It shows the qualities that would have belonged to the tragi-comedy, had that form of the drama originated in Italian plays of the Renaissance rather than in the products of the medieval stage.

[1] *Procris* and *Alceste*, for example.

[2] See above, page 27.

[3] See below, page 62.

Italian influence is exerted on the *Bradamante* (1582) and the lost *Genièvre* (1564), tragi-comedies that derive their plots from the *Orlando Furioso.* As Garnier is known to have drawn his play directly from Ariosto, and as the author of *Genièvre* seems to have done the same thing, there is no influence of the Italian drama on these plays, which followed their epic source, as the medieval *mystère* followed the Bible or a *roman d'aventure.* One sees here the same phenomenon that he observes in regard to the Spanish influence on the French drama. Just as the *novelas* of Cervantes furnished plots to Hardy in the first years of the seventeenth century, while the influence of the Spanish drama did not begin before the appearance of Rotrou's *Bague d'Oubli* (1628),[1] so the *Orlando Furioso* furnished plots for French tragi-comedies of 1564 and 1582, when the Italian tragi-comedy was unknown in France.

Italian dramatic influence was of another sort, being exerted on the comedy and the pastoral. The strolling Italian comedians, who played farces and other pieces of a light order, apparently did not indulge in the more serious tragi-comedy. The pastoral and its allied form, the *tragi-comédie pastorale,* came later in the wake of the *Aminta* (1580) and the *Pastor fido* (1590). These forms were too late to influence the formation of the French tragi-comedy, which seems, on the other hand, to have been one of the formative forces in the *tragi-comédie pastorale.* This latter *genre* however, is but a variety of the pastoral and consequently lies outside the scope of this dissertation.[2]

The early Italian tragi-comedy, like that of Gil Vicente, offers a parallel to the French, while exerting no influence upon it. All three kinds are medieval products, modernized by a classical influence that is particularly noticeable in Italy. Somewhat different is the influence of the Latin tragi-comedy, which, as next in chronological order, must now be considered.

3. One of the chief sixteenth century forms of the French tragi-comedy is that which clothes in a largely classical form a

[1] Cf. Martinenche, *La Comedia espagnole,* 167.
[2] Cf. Marsan, *La Pastorale Dramatique,* 402–18.

plot derived from the biblical narrative. In the tragi-comedies of which the subject is known, are told the stories of the sacrifice of Isaac, the three children in the fiery furnace, Tobit, Jacob, Jokebed, and Job. As these accounts had furnished plots to medieval French dramatists, the sixteenth century writers of tragi-comedies may have reworked them in classical form without other influence. As, however, the Latin Renaissance drama, especially of countries to the east of France, exhibits the same or similar biblical plots with classical form and frequently with tragi-comic title, it seems probable that the Latin Renaissance drama exerted an influence on this form of the French tragi-comedy in teaching its authors the application of a classical form to a medieval drama.

The school of Latin dramas, just referred to, began with the *Acolastus* of Gnaphaeus in 1529 and spread through much of Western Europe. The plays are called indiscriminately *comedia, tragedia, historia, tragicocomedia, drama comicotragicum,* etc. *Comedia* is the most usual term employed; *tragedia* is ordinarily applied to a play that ends unhappily; the other terms are used with little discrimination, except that they are commonly characterized by a happy *dénouement.* The plays are medieval in their violation of the unities, religious spirit, and comic elements, while in their form, title, and style they show the effects of classical imitation. Written chiefly in the Rhine valley, Bavaria, and Belgium, they were published largely at Bâle, Augsburg, Cologne, and Antwerp, whence they inspired productions in France, England, and Portugal. In the first of these countries they were followed by a number of plays called tragedies, tragi-comedies, and, rarely, comedies. A number of examples can be cited to indicate the similarity of subject between the Latin and French plays and their indiscriminate use of *genre* name.

The sacrifice of Isaac was dramatized by Ziegler in 1543 without name of *genre*[1] and by Philicinus in 1546 as a *Dialogus.*[1] Beza in 1551 wrote of his *Abraham sacrifiant:* "Pour venir à l'argument que je traite, il tient de la tragédie et de la comédie,

[1] Goedeke, *Grundrisz,* II, 137.

et pour cela ay séparé le prologue et divisé le tout en pauses à la façon des actes des comédies, sans toutefois m'y assujettir. . . . Et parce qu'il tient plus de l'un que de l'autre j'ay mieux ainsi l'appeler tragédie." [1] In 1588 a tragi-comedy was given at Montbéliard "en laquelle figure l'histoire des deux griêves tentations desquelles le patriarche Abraham a été exercé." [2]

Again, Schoepper called his *Monomachia Davidis et Goliae* a *tragicocomœdia,*[3] Desmazures styled *David combattant,* which treats the same subject, a *tragédie saincte.*[4] Judith is the heroine of a *drama comicotragicum* by Betulius [5] and of a *tragédie sacrée* by Pierre Heyns.[6] The latter author tells the story of Moses' rescue from amid the bulrushes in a *tragi-comédie,* an event which forms part of the *Exodus, comœdia tragica* by Laurimanus.[7] Susanna, heroine of a number of Latin plays, will be noted [7] as furnishing the title to Betulius's *Comœdia Tragica* and to Godran's *Susannae Helchiae filiae tragica comœdia.*[7] The latter is particularly important, as it was written by a Frenchman and published at Dijon. Furthermore, *Tobie,* the tragicomedy composed by Mlle des Roches and Jacques Ouyn, treats the same subject as *Tobias, Comœdia sacra* by Laurimanus.[8] The *Tragicomœdia ex Daniele prophetâ* [7] has the same source as the *Tragi-comedie. L'Argument pris du troisieme chapitre de Daniel.*[9]

These and other examples that can be cited show the indiscriminate method of *genre* classification and the similarity of subjects treated in Latin and French. The plays are important as giving early examples of the fusion of medieval dramatic material with classical dramatic form, a phenomenon that is characteristic of the French tragi-comedy. Violation of the unities, biblical plot, happy *dénouement,* comic elements, mingling

[1] Lanson, *Revue d'hist. litt.*, XI, 579.
[2] See below, page 57. [3] See Appendix A.
[4] La Vallière, *Bibliothèque du Théâtre françois,* I, 181.
[5] See Appendix A.
[6] *Le Miroir des Vefves, Tragédie sacrée d'Holoferne et Iudith,* Amsterdam, 1596.
[7] See Appendix A.
[8] Goedeke, *Grundrisz,* 139. [9] See below, page 49.

of persons of various ranks, classical division into acts and scenes, and classical *genre* name are found in both cases. The biblical drama is, indeed, practically the same, whether written in Latin or French, except that the latter has a greater popularity by reason of its use of the vernacular. In this respect, therefore, the biblical Latin drama differs from the Italian, Spanish, and Portuguese tragi-comedy, with the exception of *Celestina*, for, while the latter shows no influence on the French *genre*, the former has aided in the creation of one branch of it and has given to the whole the name it derived from the works of Verardi, Kitzscher, and, possibly, Rojas.

This statement cannot, however, be applied to all the Latin dramas of the period, for the Latin biblical tragi-comedies of Portugal and the Latin tragi-comedies of non-biblical plot show no influence upon the French *genre*. Of the four plays belonging to the latter class that will be mentioned below,[1] the *Voluptatis ac virtutis pugna* seems an echo of the medieval morality on the war of the virtues and vices, the *Hypocrisis* and *Inclyta Aeneis* are classical, in plot, while the *Ecclesia Militans* is a priestly treatise on the history of the Catholic church. The Portuguese Latin drama seems too remote to have influenced the French stage, with which, furthermore, most of its biblical plays are contemporary. The subjects treated by the Portuguese, *Josephus*, *Prodigus*, *Sedecias*, *Golias*, are the same as those already found further north. In Portugal, however, despite the early spontaneous productions of Gil Vicente, the *tragicomedia* assumes an especially classical meaning, furnishing the chief name to the drama which the Jesuits opposed to the more natural work of Vicente and his followers. Here, perhaps, as in the neighboring University of Salamanca, the term was practically the equivalent of *tragedia*.[2] At any rate, there is no evidence of its influence in France.

4. The tragi-comedy written in Teutonic languages appeared

[1] Pages 87, 92, 93.

[2] Vidal y Diaz, *Memoria historica de la Universidad de Salamanca*, 69 (Salamanca, 1869): "Cada año se representara una *comedia* de Plauto o Terencio o *tragicomedia* . . . . las dichas *comedias o tragedias*." Cf. Creizenach, *Geschichte*, II, 79.

too late to influence the formation of the *genre* in France. This is particularly true of the Danish play, *Susanna* of 1579.[1] Of German plays of the period treated (1513–82), I have found the term only in Valentin Boltz's *Tragicomœdia Sant Pauls bekerung* (1546)[1] and in Hederich's *David und . . . Absolon* (1567).[1] It does not appear to have been in general use till much later, for, even in 1592 it has to be translated by Hoius when he writes, *Tragicocomœdia Actapostolica, Das ist: Die Historiē der heiligen Aposteln Geschicht.*[2] This term, *historie*, is applied to the German versions of Sixtus Betulius's *Susanna* and *Judith.*[3] It is, indeed, only by the *Susanna* and other Latin reworkings of German plays that any influence came to the French tragi-comedy from plays written in the German language.[4]

Not only do the English tragi-comedies come too late to influence the French, but two of the three examples mentioned below[5] are essentially opposed to the French conception of the *genre.*[6] *Appius and Virginia* is a tragedy, *The Glasse of Gouernement* a belated morality that inclines toward the bourgeois comedy. *Damon and Pithias*, on the other hand, resembles closely the French *genre*, in which Chappuzeau wrote (1656) a *Damon et Pythias ou les parfaits amis.* There is no further evidence, however, of a knowledge of the English play in France and, as the French play on the same subject appeared a century after the formation of the *genre*, it must be concluded that there is here, as in the case of Italian and Portuguese plays, merely another interesting example of independent developments, in which like causes have produced like effects.

To sum up briefly the matter of the relations between the French tragi-comedy and that of other European nations, the following statements are made:

[1] See Appendix A.

[2] See Geodeke, *Grundrisz*, II, 385.

[3] *Ibidem*, 345.

[4] It must be remembered, however, that, as in the case of the *Judith*, the Latin is often the original version.

[5] See Appendix A.

[6] Sir Philip Sidney considers the *genre* as "mingling Kings and Clownes," in which the authors "match Horn-pypes and Funeralls." *Apologie for Poetrie*, 65, *Arber's Reprints*, II, London, 1868.

1. The only foreign dramatic influence since classical times that has affected the formation of the French tragi-comedy is that of the Latin biblical drama of Germany, Switzerland and the Netherlands. This influence is directly exerted only on French plays with biblical plots, and is not to be compared in importance with the influence of the medieval or classical drama, as it serves only to unite the elements already existing in them and to transmit these united elements to a part of the French tragi-comedy.

2. The tragi-comedies of the Spanish Peninsula, Italy, and England differ decidedly from those of France in most cases. *Dom Duardos, Amadís de Gaula, Quintilia* and *Damon and Pithias*, however, offer close resemblances to the *romanesque* type of French tragi-comedy, but there is no evidence that they influenced its formation.

3. The name, *tragi-comœdia*, taken from the prologue of Plautus's *Amphitruo* and first applied to a play by Verardi, spread to France and other European countries through these two works, Kitzscher's *Profectione*, and Rojas's *Celestina*. The Latin drama of Germany, Switzerland, and the Netherlands aided the introduction of the name into France.

In the latter country the title *tragi-comédie* was applied to a number of literary dramatic kinds, of which the origin went back to the medieval, the form to the classical drama. They represented the morality, farce, biblical mystery, and *romanesque* mystery. These varieties existed side by side until, under Alexandre Hardy, the *romanesque* tragi-comedy became the definitive form assumed by the *genre*. It will be the object of the next chapter to trace the history of the tragi-comedy during this period of hesitation, which lasted throughout the latter half of the sixteenth century.

CHAPTER II.

THE FRENCH TRAGI-COMEDY OF THE XVI CENTURY.

An examination of plays written in France during the latter half of the sixteenth century makes it clear, that the term *tragi-comédie* could at that time be applied to almost any survival of the medieval stage which showed a happy *dénouement* and a form that was at least partially classic. It indicated the *moralité* of social or political tendency, the *mystère*, represented by plays of biblical or *romanesque* plot, and occasionally even the farce.[1] Not until the time of Alexandre Hardy (1593–1631) did any one of these forms become sufficiently predominant to be considered the typical tragi-comedy. With him, indeed, the *romanesque* play attained so large usage that other seventeenth century forms of the *genre* may be regarded as mere reversions to obsolete types, created by authors unable to keep abreast of the times. But during the half-century before Hardy, the tragi-comedy passed through its formative period, when the various medieval *genres* represented by it were acquiring a more artistic form and content, and the public was becoming accustomed to the use of the new name. Limited to this period of development, the present chapter deals with plays written between 1552 and 1600, the date of the first French tragi-comedy and the approximate date of Hardy's first extant play.[2]

The list of plays in Appendix B, I (page 108 below) gives the French tragi-comedies in the order of their appearance during the

[1] Examples of the *miracle*, called tragi-comedy, occur at the beginning of the seventeenth century.

[2] Rigal in *Alexandre Hardy*, 77, shows that *Theagene et Cariclée*, Hardy's first extant play, was written after 1593 and before 1601. As the year 1600 falls between these dates, it forms a convenient, if necessarily inexact limit to the formative period of the tragi-comedy. It may be added that none of the plays treated in this chapter evidence influence from Hardy's work.

sixteenth century. The titles, forms, and authorships of the plays are stated, with the places and dates of their representation and the names of the persons to whom they are dedicated. I have also indicated, in foot-notes, references to them that are found in catalogues of plays and, where such exist, more recent critical opinions concerning them. With the exception of La Vallière's *Bibliothèque* and the works of Brunet and Soleinne, these catalogues are so exceedingly unreliable that they have been consulted with the greatest caution.

These plays may be conveniently classified according to their resemblance to (1) the *moralité*, (2) the *mystère* of biblical plot, (3) the *mystère* of *romanesque* plot, (4) the farce, (5) the pastoral and foreign play. The first three groups contain the great majority of the tragi-comedies written during the sixteenth century; the fourth is of small importance; while the fifth, largely composed of translations, has nothing to do with the history of the *genre*. I shall discuss the five classes in the order given.

I. The Moralité as Tragi-Comedy.

The *Tragique Comedie Françoise de l'homme iustifié par Foy* is a theological *moralité*, in which Henry de Barran, a Huguenot pastor of Béarn, preaches the Calvinistic dogma of Justification by Faith. In spirit it is like such other Protestant *moralités* as *L'Affligé*, *Aucun*, *L'Homme fragile*, and *La Maladie de Chrestienté*.[1] After expressing contempt for those who seek to please an audience by farcical representations, the author explains in his prologue the didactic principles of his own composition. "Ie n'ay fait autre chose que prendre les sentences de la sainte Escriture, sur lesquelles ceste doctrine [Justification by Faith] est fondée, et les mettre par tel ordre en vers françois, sachant que ceste maniere de composer n'est pas indigne de l'Escriture sainte, attendu que quelque partie d'icelle y a esté composée. Bien est vray, que ie n'ay eu si grand soucy de la proprieté et perfection de ceste Rithme (ce que assez monstre le bas stile de mon escriture) que de la verité de la doc-

[1] Petit de Julleville, *Répertoire*, 32, 37, 67, 79.

trine laquelle est Crestienne et non poetique, comme aussi ie ne suis point Poete." As might be expected from this declaration, the production is more appropriate to the pulpit than to the stage.

The personages, *La Loy*, *L'esprit de Crainte*, *Satan*, *Peché*, *La Mort*, *Concupiscence*, *L'Homme*, *Rabby*, *Paul*, *Foy*, and *Grace*, are all abstractions or types. Paul represents the Protestant, Rabby the Catholic preacher, but slightly disguised by their biblical costuming. In the first act *L'esprit de Crainte*, sent by *La Loy*, seeks to win *L'Homme* against *Concupiscence*, *Peché*, and *La Mort*, children of Satan. *L'Homme* decides to cast in his lot with the latter, despite the warnings of Rabby and Paul, who here work together, though they use different methods according to their respective adherence to *La Loy* and *Foy*. The nature of the struggle is shown in the following lines:

"Paul parle à l'Homme :
Enten, amy, Dieu a soucy
De toy, et t'aime grandement :
Cesse donc toy pareillement
D'estre enuers luy mal-gracieux.
Satan : O L'heretique ingenieux !
Qu' à cent diables soit le meschant :
De cestuy faut craindre le chant,
Tant doux et tant melodieux.
Concupiscence : Ie luy rendray si odieux,
Que luy feray abandonner.
(À l'Homme) Si tu te veux plaisir donner
N'enten à ce fallacieux.
L'Homme à Paul : Laissons ce Dieu là-haut és cieux." [1]

The last line is repeated in reply to remarks from the two preachers. The act ends with the victory of *Concupiscence*.

Paul and Rabby return, however, in the second act and persuade *L'Homme* to accompany them. After they have seen him frightened by *La Loy* and *L'esprit de Crainte* and beaten into confession by *Peché* and *La Mort*, they vie with each other in their efforts to show him the proper method of salvation. The contest results in the victory of Rabby, who leads *L'Homme* before *La Loy*. The consequences of this action are seen in the third act, when *L'Homme*

[1] I, 7.

is overwhelmed by the difficulties of obeying *La Loy* till Rabby covers her face, to the satisfaction of *L'Homme* and Satan. The former, under the tutelage of Rabby, now becomes a finished Pharisee.

"I'y vueil porter franges bien amples,
Auec philacteres fort grans." [1]

He secretly receives *Concupiscence*, while Paul soliloquizes on the evil effects of hypocritical preaching.

In the fourth act, Paul and Rabby renew their dispute, which is ended by the former's unveiling *La Loy* and thus forcing *L'Homme* to confess his sins. Attacked by *Peché* and *La Mort*, *L'Homme* is now abandoned by Rabby, and rescued by Paul from a meditated suicide. The act closes with a revelation of *Foy* and *Grace*. Though the play might well end here, it is continued by a fifth act in which Paul, *Grace*, and *La Loy* hold a theological debate, after which *L'Homme* is assured of his ultimate salvation. A needless conclusion is added to point the moral.

In the course of this play, five actions, resulting from the efforts of Satan, *La Loy*, *Foy*, and their adherents to obtain possession of *L'Homme*, are successively presented. The first act recounts the preliminary victory of Satan over *La Loy* and *Foy*; the first four scenes of the second set forth the victory of *La Loy* and *Foy* over Satan. Concerned in neither of these contests to a large extent, *Foy* is next defeated in the person of Paul, by *La Loy*, represented by Rabby. Then comes the ultimate defeat of *La Loy* by Satan through the hypocrisy of Rabby and the final victory of *Foy*, which frees *L'Homme* from the infernal powers. There is, therefore, no unity of action in the classical sense. The two other unities also appear to be violated, though there are no definite statements as to the place and time of the action. The play is held together, on the other hand, by a unity of interest in the final salvation of *L'Homme*.

The fact that the subject is here taken from the New Testament is kept constantly before the reader, not only by translations of biblical passages, but by marginal references to the chapters and

[1] III, 5.

verses in which they are to be found. The thoroughly didactic treatment, which finds expression in prosaic monologues or lengthy debates, is lightened by no appeal to the spectator's imagination. The personages are the purest abstractions, representing the powers of good and evil, busy with the fate of *L'Homme.* The latter, a colorless personality who changes beliefs and desires at every fresh encounter, may please the theologian, but makes no appeal to an audience. It is difficult, indeed, to find anything here in the presentation that is apt to interest the spectator in the fate of the protagonist or the method by which his salvation is accomplished.

That the writer is not entirely devoid of dramatic talent, however, is shown by his keeping the various details of the plot constantly before the spectator. Thus, Paul is introduced into the first act and is assigned a monologue in the fourth scene of the third, although he has little to do with the contest between *La Loy* and the agents of Satan, which contest forms the principal *motif* of these acts. Had he been first presented in the fourth act, his rôle would have been that of a *deus ex machinâ,* instead of forming an integral part of the play.

The *Tragicomédie, La Gaule,* is a *moralité* of another sort, appealing to the spectator's love of country rather than to his hope of salvation. Political subjects had already been treated in *moralités,* notably in *Le Nouveau Monde, La paix de Peronne,* and *Le concile de Basle,*[1] of which the last-named introduced *France* into its plot, just as the play here under discussion concerns *La Gaule.* The three estates, which take part in the latter play, are found in other *moralités*; as, *L'Eglise Noblesse et Povreté, Le Ministre de l'Eglise Noblesse le Laboureur e Commun,* and *Tout le Monde,*[2] besides the *Tragedie sur la defaite et occision de la Piaffe et de la Picquorée.*[3] *La Gaule* may be further compared with the fragmentary *moralité sur la France,*[4] which resembles it in form as well as in subject, for it is written in Alexandrines and divided into acts.

[1] Petit de Julleville, *Répertoire,* 87, 89, 46. [2] *Ibidem,* 55, 84, 99.

[3] Paris, 1579. Cf. La Vallière, I, 158.

[4] Bibliothèque Nationale, MSS. fr., 25468.

Although *La Gaule* was recommended by Paulin Paris to "ceux qui recherchent les origines du théâtre moderne,"[1] it has been neglected in critical studies of the period to which it belongs. As the first tragi-comedy written in Alexandrines and alternating masculine and feminine rimes, it furnishes an interesting example of the presentation of medieval matter in classical attire. The supposed rescue of *La Gaule* from her many woes by the prowess of Charles IX constitutes the subject, declared in the author's prologue to be historically true.

"Si l'histoire qui est et vraye et profictable
Doit estre aussy plustost receue que la fable,
Mesme lors que l'histoire avec joye finit,
Et que la fable est triste et n'aporte profit
(O Roy sur tous heureux), je croy que ceste histoire,
Laquelle est veritable et finit par ta gloire,
Devrait a tes espritz donner plus de plaisir,
Que fable qu'on eust sceu entre toutes choisir."

The plot, which had been summarized both in the prologue and in the prose argument, is acted by *La Gaule, L'Europe, Le Chœur, Le Temps forgeron, L'estat de noblesse, celuy de l'eglise, Le plebée, Premier, second, troisiesme soldat,* and *Le jeune Roy fils de la Gaule.* The play opens with a long lament by *La Gaule,* beginning with an invocation worthy of Seneca:

"Dieux marins et terrains, puissances des haultz cieux
Manes, toy gouverneur du fleuve Stigieux.
Et du lac Averna! et qui des ombres vaines . . ."

L'Europe, hearing her sobs and noting that "elle n'a plus ny teint ny la couleur vermeille, Qui rendoit sa beauté a l'Aurore pareille," comes to her aid with chosen maxims concerning self-control and silent patience. The chorus ends the act with three strophes on comfort in affliction and the importance of turning to "Dieu qui est pardessus tout."

In the second act *L'Europe* and *La Gaule,* on the former's suggestion, start out to ask aid of *Le Temps,* whom they opportunely encounter. A natural conversation ensues:

[1] *Les* MSS. fr., VI, 418.

"Le Temps, forgeron :
Mesme salut vous soit, mes dames, Dieu vous gard.
Ou allez vous ainsi seuletes a l'escart?
L'Europe : Nous le vous dirons bien ; nous cherchons le repaire
Du Temps, s'il vous plaisoit nous l'enseigner, mon pere.
Le Temps : Dictes moy, qui vous meut de le chercher ainsi
Et vous saurez de moy ce que cherchez aussi."

La Gaule now asks his aid, which is promised, subject to Jupiter's will. Into this act *Le Temps* introduces a pleasing variety by singing a sonnet as he forges the destiny of *La Gaule*. But in spite of his good intentions, he is forced to admit

"Que mon art ne pourroit amendre ton martire,
Je quite tout, a dieu. Celuy travaille en vain
Qui cuide pervertir son destin inhumain."

La Gaule would now despair, but *L'Europe* persuades her to call on the resources of the three estates. With a comment on Time, the chorus closes the act, which is followed by *pause et musique*.

The third act serves to increase the miseries of the heroine, for her estates, after assuring her of their allegiance, excuse themselves on learning that she expects them to aid her. Her distress is increased by the sight of three soldiers, engaged in slaying all persons whom they meet, one of whom cries,

"Je veux Je veux soldats ceste espée baignee
Au pur sang des humains sans aucun espargner."

The chorus repeats the strophes sung at the end of the second act with the addition of six lines at the beginning. One of the repeated strophes runs as follows :

On sait comme le Temps courant
Toujours en empirant
Remplit de sang les champs humides
Il abat bien les pyramides
Et faict a la pleine egaler
Les tours qui perçoient l'air.

In the fourth act, all the gloom of the preceding acts has disappeared. *La Gaule* rejoices over a message delivered to her by Mercury, which shows her how to escape from all her woes :

"Il te fault seulemeut chercher en ta maison
De ton mal douloureux s'entirer guérison
Elle gist en ton filz que Jupiter tant ayme
Qu'il luy a sur le chef posé le diademe."

La Gaule, accompanied by *L'Europe*, now meets the king, who promises to cherish and protect her. She replies with praise of him and his mother, a sentiment that shows the sycophantic spirit of the author in putting the queen mother above the country.

> "Tu as bien une mere plus excellente
> Que je ne suis (O Roy) car son port est divin
> Son renom hurte au ciel, elle est sage et prudente
> Ainsi vivra son los éternel et sans fin."

Praise is also accorded to the other princes "qui te sont plus prochains," to *Monseigneur le Connestable*, and to *Monseigneur le Chancelier*. The play ends in general rejoicing, *L'Europe* crying:

> "Qu'on rompe tout soucy, qu'on le face enfuyr
> Et qu'on crie par tout Vive Charles sans cesse,"

and *La Gaule:*

> "Qu'on chante ïo trois fois, qu'on le chante a grand presse
> Que l'on claque des mains en signe d'alegresse
> Qu'on n'oublie le los de Charles mon enfant
> Et qu'encor on le nomme en tous lieux triumphant."

From these passages it is possible to approximate the date of the play. Allusions to King Charles show that it was written after the accession of that monarch, December 5, 1560. Paulin Paris declared that it dates "des premières années du règne de Charles IX,"[1] evidently basing his conclusion on references to the king's youth. As, however, Charles was only twenty-four years old when he died (1574), he might have been called *le jeune roy* any year of his reign, while a courtier might at any time overlook the troubles brought by his reign in order to refer to him as the savior of his country. On the other hand, a definite lower date can be assigned to the play through the mention of the *conestable* just cited. The description of him as "Nestor mesme et sa barbe chenue" fits exactly Anne, duc de Montmorency, sixty-eight years old and *conestable* when Charles IX came to the throne. As he was killed in battle on November 10, 1567, and as no successor to his office was appointed during the reign of Charles,

[1] *Les* MSS. fr., VI, 417.

the time of his death is the latest possible date that can be assigned to the play.

The structure of this tragi-comedy is exceedingly loose. The preliminary discourses between *La Gaule* and *L'Europe,* the unsuccessful visit to *Le Temps,* and the equally unavailing summons of the estates have so little connection with one another that the omission of any one of them would not affect the rest. All of the classical unities are obviously violated. The solution of the problem given in the fourth act is dramatically illogical, as one cannot understand why *La Gaule* did not turn to this wonderful son in the first instance. As the play stands, the *dénouement* is too readily attained after all the woes depicted. The anti-climax could be pardoned only by Charles IX. The key-note of the play lies, indeed, in this praise of monarchical rule by an author who esteems Catherine de Medici more highly than France and presents her son as the savior of his land, when nobility, clergy, and people had failed to help it. Once, it is true, the author's sympathy is extended to the people, when *L'Europe* predicts that "Toujours le laboureur an travail ne se tue,"[1] but his feeling is ordinarily for the country as a whole in the fixed order of class distinctions.

The personages actively concerned in the play are few in number. They are mainly abstractions that show no great variety in expression. *L'Europe* is a consistent adviser and friend. *La Gaule* appropriately, if unintentionally, personifies the fundamental egoism still characteristic of countries in their political relations. The weakness of her character is shown by the fact that all her actions are based on the advice of *L'Europe* or Mercury. The other personages play subordinate rôles, appearing never more than once on the stage. In alluding to the Supreme Being the author forgets his classical mention of Jupiter and Mercury. By the substitution in the rôles of emotion for didacticism, the play shows a marked advance over *L'homme iustifiê par Foy.* That it was intended for representation is shown by the direction for "pause et musique" at the end of the second act.

L'Ombre de Garnier Stoffacher, Suisse, by Josephe Du Chesne, physician to François de France, brother of Henri III, is a

[1] I.

moralité of the same type as *La Gaule* that shows still weaker dramatic qualities than those exhibited in the latter play. It celebrates the perpetual alliance between Geneva, Zurich, and Berne by recounting the manner in which the timely arrival of Stoffacher's shade averted a civil war. The personages are *Bellone*, *Le Chœur des soldats*, *L'Ombre de Garnier*, *Le Chœur des Cantons*, *Discorde*, *La Paix*, *Le Chœur des trois villes*, *Le Messager*. *Bellone* begins the play by a four-page monologue expressing her fury on account of peace and her desire for war among the Swiss allies. Her terms, though crude, are not lacking in vigor.

> "Qu'ores la solde soit le fruict de vos moissons,
> Vos coutres soyent changez en estocs, et en lances
> Vos esguillons pointus, que pour toutes semences
> Vous iettiez à ce coup sur vos sillons voustez
> Des sacagez meurtris les corps ensanglantez."

The chorus of soldiers ends the act, which has scarcely begun, expressing in eleven strophes their hope for peace and dread of war.

The second act is, in construction, the counterpart of the first, with the substitution of *L'Ombre de Garnier* for *Bellone* and the Chorus of Cantons for the Chorus of Soldiers. Garnier cries:

> "Ie romps, i'ouure, à present de ma prison la porte,
> Bien que du noir tombeau iamais aucun ne sorte,
> De mes cris, de mes vœuz, de mes larmes l'effort
> Eut esmeu à pitié l'impitoyable mort
> Contre sa dure loy m'ayant donné licence
> De visiter encor le lieu de ma naissance."

He invokes peace, reminding the Swiss of the noble deeds of their heroes. Particularly interesting is his simple account of Tell's notable deed, when the tyrant

> "mit sur la teste du fils
> De Telh pour butte las! une pomme iadis,
> Que l'abatre contrainct d'une flesche legere,
> Fut à peine de mort le miserable pere;
> La face lui pallist, et de crainte et de peur,
> Il ne pouuoit guigner ayant l'œil plein de pleur,
> L'arc trembloit en sa main, ainsi mal asseuree,
> N'esperoit guider droit sa sagette aceree:
> Mais à la fin forcé hardiment la lascha,
> Et sans nuire à son fils de son chef l'arracha."

After a five-page exhortation, Garnier returns to the *Champs Elisiens*, leaving the *Chœur des Cantons* to banish *Bellone* and welcome *La Paix*. *Bellone* and *Discorde* wrathfully retire to *l'enfer*, a departure that should end the play. The author, however, sees fit to add another act, in which *La Paix* laments her misfortunes, is interrogated by three friendly choruses, and finally rejoices on hearing that *Bellone* has been put to flight by Garnier. This information is brought by a messenger, who begins his speech happily enough:

> "Quel Echo auiourd'hui r'enforcera ma voix?
> Calme donc tous tes flots, ô beau lac Geneuois,
> Car ayant abordé si pres de ton riuage
> Ie te veux faire part de mon heureux message."

The vows of the chorus at the end of the play are naïvely expressed as follows:

> "Que tout le bestail porte-laine,
> Qui paist en ceste heureuse plaine,
> Plustost s'accorde auec les loups,
> Plustost sans Ours soyent nos montagnes,
> Et sans fonteines nos campagnes
> Que la paix s'esloigne de nous."

No play can be much less dramatic than this. The actors speak almost entirely in choruses or lengthy monologues. There is no intrigue, no action, not even a debate, for the chorus decides at once in favor of Garnier's advice and against that of *Bellone*. Expressions of feeling are crudely attempted when *Bellone* shrieks her fury and Garnier expatiates on the nobility of patriotism. The weak character of *La Paix* recalls that of *La Gaule*. Classical influence is evident in the language, the introduction of the *Ombre* and the *Messager*, and the large use of monologue and chorus.

The two remaining tragi-comedies of this class show a return in character to *L'Homme iustifié par Foy*. *Le Desesperé* preaches the reward of virtue and the punishment of vice by the example of two brothers. The personages are *Le Prologue, le Pere, Charles, Thomas, la Sagesse, la Vertu, la Voupté, l'Abus, l'Ange, le Laquay, le Serviteur, la Mort, le Diablon, Lucifer, l'Epilogue.* Charles avoids *Abus* and *Volupté* to follow *Vertu* and *Sagesse,* while Thomas pursues the opposite course, resulting in brigandage and suicide, which delivers his soul to *Lucifer* and *Diablon.* From grief over this catastrophe, the father also meditates suicide, but is prevented from taking his life by an angel, who bids him rather arrange the marriage of his remaining son. Virtue is thus rewarded amid general rejoicing.

Morality is also taught in *Caresme prenant,* as acted by *Le Prologue, la Concupiscence, le Mespris de religion, le Remords de conscience, la Temperance, le Monde, le Voluptueux, la Continence, Caresme-Prenant, le Dimanche gras, le Lundy gras, le Mardy gras, le Mercredy gras, le Jeudy gras, Cerès, Bacchus, la Gloutonie, Cupidon, Venus, le Mignon de Caresme-Prenant, Morphée, Caresme, Tivan, Jaumet, Arlequin, Guillot, le Mercredy des cendres, Penitence, l'Epilogue.* The following analysis of this play is given by Petit de Julleville:[1] "Cest l'histoire de Carême-prenant (c'est-à-dire Carnaval) battu par Carême. Le Voluptueux s'abandonne à tous les vices, puis il se convertit à la voix de Religion. La fin est édifiante; les détails ne le sont pas tous, quoique le Prologue annonce une pièce 'plus grave que grasse.' La pièce, en vers de huit syllabes, est, à la mode nouvelle, divisée en cinq actes; entre le quatrième et le cinquième, quatre personnages, qui ne sont pas mêlés au reste de l'action, Tivan Savoyard, Jaumet Provençal, Guillot Français, et Arlequin Italien, forment un intermède où se trouvent les allusions promises par le titre 'touchant quelques abus de ce temps.'"

It is evident that neither *Le Desesperé* nor *Caresme prenant* is similar to the tragi-comedy of the seventeenth century. The first tends to become a *drame bourgeois,* where the interest is centered in the affairs of a simple family and the moral lesson derived therefrom. The second has elements of the farce that show resemblance to the fourth class of sixteenth century tragi-comedies.[2] Written by Claude Bonnet, an obscure "docteur en droit civil et canon" of Dauphiné, and published at Aix-en-

[1] *Répertoire,* 43 *seq.*

[2] See below, page 69.

Provence, these tragi-comedies probably exerted little influence on the *genre* now becoming known at Paris.

In general, it may be said that the *moralité* tends to develop into the comedy rather than into the tragi-comedy, and consequently affects the latter *genre* not as a whole, but only in isolated plays. Of these the political *moralités, La Gaule* and *L'Ombre de Garnier Stoffacher*, show the closest resemblance to other tragi-comedies, but even in their case the term is used with the broad sixteenth century sense, which made possible its application to any medieval play of happy *dénouement* that shows in its form some effect of classical imitation.

II. The Mystère of Biblical Plot as Tragi-Comedy.

The Old Testament subjects that furnished material for medieval plays and Latin dramas of the Renaissance were repeated in a number of French plays, written during the latter half of the sixteenth century. Six of these were called tragi-comedies and nearly all the rest tragedies. There seems to be no definite system of nomenclature in them, except that the tragi-comedies end happily, while the tragedies usually contain personages who meet with loss of life or fortune. Exceptions are found before the term, *tragi-comédie*, has come into general use; as, in the case of Beza's *Abraham sacrifiant, Tragedie Francoise* (1550) and Des Mazures's *David Triomphant* and *David Fugitif* (1566). Reprints of Beza's work continue the term *tragédie,* but a play on the same subject is called a tragi-comedy in 1588.[1] The rare application to biblical plays of the term *comédie* is probably due to the fact that light pieces, based on Italian models, were usually so called. Its use at Antwerp in 1589 to designate a play concerning the *Patriarche Abraham et sa servante Agar* seems to show the influence of the numerous Latin plays on biblical subjects, written in the Netherlands and called *comœdiæ.*

The first of the six biblical plays that are to be discussed here is *Tragicomédie. L'Argument pris du troisieme chapitre de Daniel:*

[1] See below, page 57.

avec le cantique des trois enfans, chanté en la fornaise, dedicated to the Queen of Navarre, in the service of whose husband the author professes to be. Lanson,[1] mentioning this with other plays that speak of an audience or theater in their prologue, shows that this evidence is not sufficient to prove the representation of the piece, as such remarks constitute an ordinary, introductory formula. He has not noticed that in this case, however, there is the additional, if not conclusive, evidence of a *Sonnet du S. D. S.* to the author, in which *S. D. S.* seems to have a definite performance in mind, as he writes: "Quand je *voy* sur son dos ta Tragi-comedie Relever," and "On les [the three children] *voit* renaistre en ce *Theatre.*"

The subject of the play is an old one on the French stage, as at the end of *Adam,* the first medieval play extant, Nebuchadnezzar told of the three children: "Chi jo fis mettre en foc ardant."[2] Strangely enough, no play on this subject has been preserved in the *Mistére du Viel Testament.* An *Histoire Tragedienne tirée de la Fureur et Tyrannie de Nabuchodonosor* is mentioned by La Vallière[3] as published at Rouen, without date, but probably at the beginning of the seventeenth century. The subject is the same as that of the play here under discussion, except that after the furnace incident the King goes mad, the ending thus coinciding with the term, *tragedienne,* according to the standards of the time.

The personages of the tragi-comedy are *Nabuchodonosor, Roy de Babylone; Son lieutenant; Asphene, gouverneur de ses Eunuques; troupe de Babyloniens, scavoir, Demie bande et Demie bande; Gendarmes et Satellites premiers et secondes; Les Conseillers; Le herault; La suyte du Roy; Sydrach; Misach; Abdenago.* The prologue, written in Alexandrines, after enjoining silence on the audience, promises to be instructive in presenting a subject that is familiar to all. The play is begun with a tirade by the King:

"Quand ma grandeur s'abbaisse à contempler
Ce qui fut faict pour la terre peupler,
Tous animaux quels qu'ils soyent, ayant vie,

[1] *Revue d'hist. litt.*, x, 415.

[2] *Das Adamsspiel,* 930–43, *Romanische Bibliothek,* vi, Halle, 1891.

[3] i, 463.

> I'ay (à bon droict) de m'estonner enuie
> Du grand honneur deu a ma grauité
> De chascun peuple à perpetuité."

Faguet declares that this speech, "révèle bien le voisinage de la tragédie classique de 1560," and adds, "Il n'y a pour parler si longtemps sur ce ton que les Charles-Quint de 1830 ou les Nabuchodonosor de 1560."[1] The same kind of introductory verbiage may, however, be found in the medieval drama, *De Nabugodonosor et Holofernès.*[2]

Asphene now echoes his master's self-praise by calling him a god. The King tells him of the image that has been made and orders him to set it up. The crudity of the piece is shown in this scene, for the King shows no hesitation in assuming a divine rôle, while Asphene is made to receive information which he must already have known. Now follows a *Cantique d'une petite bande de Babyloniens* on the greatness and folly of their lord:

> "Apres tout flechit et ploye
> Sous nostre Roy d'auiourd'huy,
> Il n'ha nul pareil a luy,
> L'ennemi luy est en proye
> Les astres roulans és cieux,
> Tous pour en heurer son mieux
> Luy vien[nen]t auec fortune;
> Ie croy qu'en enfer profond
> Ses forces effrayer vont
> Le Roy frere de Neptune."

The King reappears, to boast again and to learn that the people are coming to worship the image. He threatens to punish with the fiery furnace all that will refuse to do so, while Asphene advises him to prepare for his appearance at the *théâtre.* The Babylonian bands end this division of the play by a song on the evil influence of flatterers.

The three children, next introduced, discuss "ceste ordure d'image." Some variety is infused into the piece by the rôle of Sidrach, who hesitates to disobey the order of the King. As he is speedily convinced by Abdenago, however, that the divine

[1] *Tragédie fr.*, 103.

[2] *Mistére du Viel Testament*, v, 231.

command alone must be followed, all three unite in refusing to worship the image. After the music has sounded, all the people bow down except the three children, whose disobedience is reported by *Satellites*, to the King. Brought before the King, they are offered pardon, if they will now consent to worship, but when they refuse they are ordered to the furnace seven times heated. The Babylonian bands express their sympathy in a chorus.

Nabuchodonosor, roused to vigorous, if unkingly language by the obstinacy of the children, cries to his attendants:

"O malheureux!
Ne me dépescherez-vous d'eux,
Les laisserez vous sermonner
Encor' long temps, et estonner
Ce poure peuple, grosses bestes,
Ie vous rompray à tous les testes,
Si plus longuement vous songez.
Satellites: Nous sommes prestz.
Le Roy: Qu'ils soient plongez
En la fornaise, au beau milieu,
Et puis on verra si leur Dieu
Tant puissant, les retirera
De là dedans.
Abdenago: Il le fera
S'il luy plaist: car vrayement il peult
Tost nous en retirer, s'il veult.
Satellites: S'il peult, s'il veult, qu'il vous en tire."

To the King's amazement the excutioners are burnt, while the children sing a *canticque* in the midst of the flames. They follow this with a metrical translation of the Apocryphal *Song of the Three Children.* The King now bids them leave the flames, expresses sorrow for his past conduct, and promises to protect them in the future. The children rejoice, while the *Babyloniens* point the moral in a final chorus. An epilogue in Alexandrines ends the play.

Although no division into acts is indicated in this tragi-comedy, the five parts of it are clearly marked out after the Senecan model by the insertion into the midst of the action of songs sung by the *Babyloniens* and the three children. The fact that the unity of action is preserved in the play seems due to the nature of the subject, rather than to the skill of the author, for the biblical narrative is followed with slavish exactitude. This unity would appear more clearly, if the first scene had been omitted. The unity of place is violated, as the action is located before the palace, in the fields, and around the fiery furnace. The unity of time seems also unobserved, as, more than one day was probably required for the erection of the image and the incidents that follow in the drama.

Some attempt at character-drawing is shown in the speeches of the important persons. *Nabuchodonosor* is the first of a long line of blustering, tragi-comic kings, whose overbearing manner is accompanied by a feeble intellectual endowment. The leader of the eunuchs is an humble sycophant. The happy attempt to discriminate the characters of the three children is visible only at first. They subsequently become merely three names, attached to a single character, thus losing in dramatic interest what they gain in fidelity to their biblical prototypes.

The spirit of the play, as well as its crude style and uneven versification, shows it to be essentially medieval, despite the fact that the choruses and the Prologue and Epilogue are in classical Alexandrines. It is of importance as the first French tragi-comedy in which the events are of dramatic significance, as well as the moral lesson taught by it. This play thus begins a tendency that results in the typical tragi-comedy which neglects psychological study and moral teaching for the interest aroused by the dramatic event.

The story of Job's sufferings and restoration to health and wealth furnished the plot of many plays written during the fifteenth and sixteenth centuries. It is found in the *Mistère du Viel Testament* (36536–37848) and in the *Pacience de Iob* of which eight *rédactions* can be indicated between 1478 and 1600. A *Jeu de la Pacience de Job* was given at Metz in 1513, and a *Moralitas Patientie Job* at Draguignan in 1534. A Latin play on the same subject was published at Marburg in 1543, and at Bâle in 1547, while another was represented at Prague in 1550.[1] It was, there-

[1] *Mistère du Viel Testament*, v, pages iii-x. Petit de Julleville, *Répertoire*, 391, mentions a *Vie de Job*, played at Rouen, 1556.

fore, no unfamiliar theme that was acted in the *Histoire* or *Tragicomedie de Iob* at Poitiers, July 27, 28, and 29, 1572, "en magnifiques habits et theatres, toutesfois mal representée."

Now, parts of this play have been preserved in the *Oeuvres de Scevole de Sainte Marthe* under the title, *Pour le Prologue de la Tragicomedie de Iob* and *Cantiques de Iob.* These fragments, which are all that is left of the play, show a decided advance in stylistic excellence over contemporary tragi-comedies. After summoning the muses and praising the use of verse, the author professes adherence to the tenets of the medieval stage:

"Les vers, qui sont le fruit des estudes de ceux
Que le vulgaire lourd estime paresseux,
Ny eux mesmes iamais sous la mort ne perissent,
Ny ne souffrent perir ceux-là qui les cherissent.
. . . .
Or les Poëtes vieux, et ceux dont la pensee
De payennes erreurs est encore insensee,
Ont rendu iusqu'ici les Theatres tous pleins
Des miseres de Troye et des malheurs Thebains:
Mais nous qui du vray Dieu connoissons mieux la gloire
Auons voulu changer les fables à l'histoire,
A fin de contenter le Chrestien auditeur
D'un poëme Chrestien, et non pas d'un menteur:
Vous proposant ici, auec vostre silence,
D'un des enfans de Dieu la loüable constance."

The plot outlined in the prologue adheres closely to the biblical account, exaggerating somewhat, however, Job's unhappiness by placing him on a dung-heap "pleine de fascheuse odeur, et groüillant de vermine." The prologue is followed by a *discours sur le mesme sujet,* which appears to have found no part in the play. Later in the volume, however, the author adds the *Cantique de Iob,* which includes the following pleasing strophes with their happily chosen simile:

"Quand sus la campagne humide,
Par l'orage courroucé
Le nocher palle et timide
Voit son nauire froissé,
Quelle attente luy demeure
Sinon que bien tost il meure?
Toutesfois souuent un aiz

Le porte sur le riuage :
Et là sauué du naufrage
Il rend les vœux qu'il a faits.
   Ainsi quand l'aspre tourmente
Du malheur qui s'irritoit,
Ceste maison florissante
De fond en comble abbatoit,
Qu'est-ce qu'on pouuoit attendre
D'un si euident esclandre
Qu'une ruine à iamais?
Et toutesfois ce bon pere,
Du fond de telle misere
Se voit tiré desormais."

The poetic feeling shown in these lines makes the reader regret that this tragi-comedy has survived in only fragmentary form.

As the *Tobie* (1579) of Mlle des Roches may best be discussed in connection with Ouyn's *Thobie* (1597)[1], the next play to be considered is *Iokebed,* written by Pierre Heyns, a schoolmaster of Antwerp. This play is bound with two others by the same author under the title,

La { Iokebed / Susanne / Iudith } miroirs des { Meres / Mesnageres / Vefves }

As the heroine of the second of these plays is not the Apocryphal Susannah, but a Dutch *bourgeoise,* the title *comédie* is appropriately employed here. *Iudith,* involving the slaying of Holophernes, is called a *tragédie* ; while *Iokebed* is a *Tragi-Comedie de Moyse.*

The plot of the latter play includes the accounts of the midwives, who saved the new-born Hebrews in Egypt, of the birth of Moses, and of his finding by Pharaoh's daughter, events that I find dramatized in no earlier French plays except the *Mistére du Viel Testament,*[2] which shows no closer connection with Heyns's work than that which is necessitated by the fact that the two compositions have a common source. Unlike the author of this portion of the *Viel Testament,* Heyns crowds into his play a number of allegorical personages, who hold lengthy scholastic arguments crowded with platitudes. The play thus resembles the

[1] See below, page 57.

[2] Lines 22067–22829.

medieval *moralité* as well as the *mystère.* By its division into acts it shows classical influence; by its use of prose, an approach to contemporary comic productions. Its didactic nature is obvious from the following list of *dramatis personæ: Audience* and *Operation,* who speak in dialogue the prologue and conclusion; *Disposition-Divine; Gent-Israëlite; Affliction, sa servante; Sagesse-humaine, concubine de Pharaon; Cruauté, sa chambriere; Iokebed, mere de Moyse; Marie, sa fille; Foy; Esperance; Sciphra* and *Puha, sages-femmes; Thermuth, princesse: Compassion, fille d'honneur; deux ou trois muëttes; Abda* and *Bersa, nourrices Egyptiennes.* All of these rôles, it may be noted, are suited to the sex of Heyns's female pupils.

The play opens with a heavy dialogue between *Audience* and *Operation* as to whether hearing or action is more efficacious in matters of salvation and election. This tragi-comedy, they state, purposes to teach God's providence, the subject of a disquisition by *Disposition-Divine* in the first scene. This virtue, finding *Gent-Israëlite* in tears, demonstrates her lack of resignation by a theological catechism. Meanwhile *Sagesse-Humaine* and *Cruauté* determine to destroy the Hebrews. In the second act *Gent-Israëlite,* when lamenting again, is advised by Iokebed to rejoice with her in time of trouble. *Affliction* now weeps with *Gent-Israëlite,* till *Foy* comforts them by means of a dream, predicting the Exodus. Iokebed adds that she has been assured of salvation, to be won for her people by the child in her womb.

The allegorical figures continue to discourse in the next act, when *Sagesse-Humaine* plans the massacre of the innocents. *Disposition-Divine* gives *Cruauté* power to accomplish this, but sends *Compassion* to win over the midwives. After considerable argumentation, the latter agree to save the children, despite their scruples over the prevarication involved. In the fourth act *Cruauté* takes from *Compassion* a dead infant, which the latter had intended to substitute for Moses. Iokebed laments this misfortune, till she is comforted by *Disposition-Divine* with the suggestion to hide the infant in the bulrushes. A crude attempt at displaying Iokebed's emotion on parting with Moses may be distinguished amid the pedantic utterances of the actors. The rest of the play is taken up with the finding of Moses by Thermuth, an event that inspires the only part of the play in any degree dramatic. The discovery of the infant is the occasion of the following dialogue :

" *Thermuth:* O quelle douce harmonie y rend aussi le gasoüillement et ramage d'un million d'oiselets organisans, qui font resonner melodieusement leurs voix musicales, parmi ces arbres branchus ! Vrayment, je ne vei oncques saison plus plaisante, ne place plus commode pour se refraichir.

" *Compassion:* Ie n'y ay esté qu'une seule fois, Madame, mais elle m'a tant pleu, que j'ay estimé vostre excellence y devoir aussi trouver du plaisir comme elle fait maintenant, dont je suis bien joyeuse. Mais voyez, Madame, que peut estre cela, que je voy-là descendre sur la riviere ?

" *Thermuth:* Il semble que ce soit un coffret, il n'est guere loing de la rive, on y pourroit bien avenir de ceste branche coupée, prenez-la et essayez à l'attirer à nous, e me l'apportez, que je voye ce qu'il y a dedans, mais gardez vous du faux Crocodile.

" *Compassion:* Ie le feray, Madame : Ie l'ay. Le voicy, Madame.

" *Thermuth:* Qu'est ceci ? un coffre vivant ? il y a de la vie dedans, ce me semble. Helas, c'est un enfant pleurant ! O quelle mere desconfortée peut avoir perdu ce povret trouvé. Ha ce sera un des enfans Hebrieux.

" *Compassion:* Il pourroit bien estre, Madame." [1]

The intensely pedantic nature of this tragi-comedy is evident from the preceding analysis. Unity is absent from the plot, for the first two acts are concerned with the woes of *Gent-Israëlite,* the third with kindly actions of the midwives, the fourth and fifth with the birth and rescue of Moses. The scene is laid in the house of Iokebed, on the banks of the Nile, and elsewhere. The time involved is probably several months. The inconsistency of the allegorical characters is obvious in the case of *Sagesse-Humaine* and *Gent-Israëlite,* of whom the former is both an allegorical figure and Pharaoh's concubine, while the latter represents the Hebrews as a whole and also one of Iokebed's neighbors. *Affliction* is a useless echo of *Gent-Israëlite,* as *Esperance* is of *Foy,* and *Cruauté* of *Sagesse-Humaine.* No distinction is made between the two midwives. *Disposition-Divine* is a heartless pedant, whose ideas of sympathy are contracted to the limits of a catechism. The rôle of Iokebed does not appeal to the reader, for her lack of personality is not compensated by the

[1] v, 2.

didactic sentiments that she voices. The only part of the play, indeed, that is fairly true to life is that concerned with the finding of Moses, from which a citation has just been made.

The *Tragi-comédie en laquelle figure l'histoire des deux griëves tentations desquelles le patriarche Abraham a été exercé* has been mentioned above.[1] The subject of the sacrifice of Isaac, probably indicated by this title, had been treated in several plays of the sixteenth century, notably in that of Théodore Beza, published at Geneva five times[2] before 1588, the year in which the play under discussion was represented at Montbéliard. As this town is not very far from Geneva, it is probable that the latter play was influenced by Beza's work, if it was not a direct imitation of it. As the tragi-comedy is lost, however, no definite conclusions can be reached regarding it.

The Apocryphal story of Tobit is found in the *Mistére du Viel Testament*,[3] after which it is first dramatized in the *Acte de la Tragi-comedie de Tobie* of Mlle des Roches. From statements made in the prologue of the latter play it seems that the author outlined a dramatization of the whole story, but versified only the one act and fragmentary passages, all of which have been incorporated by Iacques Ouyn into his own play, published in 1606, but written as early as 1597, the date of the privilege.[4] Ouyn does not hesitate to acknowledge what he has borrowed from Mlle des Roches, "laquelle dicte Acte iay apropriee en son rang quatriesme, qui m'a a la verité beaucoup ou plus cousté à entrer, que si ie ne l'eusse iamais veuë."[5] In the final form of the play the story is dramatized in full, with the following personages as interlocutors: *Thobie, le pere; Anne, sa femme; Thobie, leur fils; Raphael, Ange dit Azarie; Raguel; Anne, sa femme; Sarra; Le voisin; La servante; le chœur; Gabel; voisins.*

[1] Page 32.

[2] In 1550, –53, –61, –65, and –76. Cf. *Mistére du Viel Testament*, II, page xlix *seq.*

[3] Lines 38585–39688.

[4] A play on this subject called the *Ystoire de Tobie* was played at Amiens in 1581. Cf. *Mistére du Viel Testament*, V, page xviii.

[5] *Thobie, Argument.*

Thobie *le pere*, having decided to dwell at home after the death of Sennacherib, has sent his son to invite friends to dinner. The young man returns from his errand with the news that "un corps mort sur la terre gisait." His father wishes to bury the body, but remembers that he has a relative visiting him, whom he ought not to leave. The arrival of this relative occasions a natural and prosaic conversation :

> "Soyez bien revenu mon Compere Thobie
> Vrayment ie ne pensois iamais vous voir en vie,
> Dieu sçait combien de fois ie vous ay regretté,
> Et combien vostre fils chez moy ay souhaitté.
> *Thobie le pere:* Ne parlons de cela, quittons la facherie
> Mon fils, donne à laver, etc."

They proceed to dinner, in the midst of which the host excuses himself to bury the dead body, much to the dissatisfaction of his guest and his wife. The former says :

> "Inviter ses amis, pour ainsi les quitter,
> A proprement parler, c'est, c'est les despiter,"

while Anne declares :

> "Mais c'est un vitupere
> D'aller iournellement dans chasque Cymetiere
> Enfouir tant de corps, cela ne m'agrée point."

Her husband now returns blinded, and explains how he became so. Anne does not lose the opportunity of pointing out her foresight :

> "Ne disois-ie pas bien, voyez, comme il endure.
> Tu scauras maintenant si ton Dieu aura cure
> De ton affliction."

Though rebuked by her son, she laments the loss of income, sure to follow her husband's affliction.

In the second act Anne describes to her son the family of their relative, Raguel, the beauty of his daughter, Sarra, and the fate of her seven unfortunate husbands, "tous estranglez et en terre estendus" by Asmodeus. She then distresses her husband by telling him of Sarra's misfortunes. This act forms a digression that violates the unity of the play and serves merely to inform the audience of the state of affairs in the house of Raguel.

Thobie *le pere* now sends his son *en Ragez* to collect money owed him by Gabel. Azarie, the disguised angel, accompanies him as guide. On the way, young Thobie is bitten by "un animal ou bien quelque poisson," certain parts of which Azarie advises him to preserve. This brings the reader to the fourth act, written by Mlle des Roches in a style superior to that of Ouyn. After explaining the magic properties of the fish's parts, Azarie bids Thobie ask for shelter at the house of Raguel hard by and seek to win the hand of his daughter. Thobie hesitates for fear of sharing the fate of Sarra's seven husbands, observing naïvely:

"Les hommes ont souvent des femmes deux ou trois
Mais la vie iamais ils ne l'ont qu'une fois."

But Azarie explains how he can escape by a proper use of the fish's parts. A *Chœur des Femmes* indicates the way to the house, where the two are well received and Thobie explains the object of his journey. When alone with Azarie, he admits that he has fallen in love with Sarra, who is presented in the next scene conversing with *la servante.* The latter accuses her of having murdered her husbands, whereupon Sarra replies:

"On vous prend seulement pour faire le menage
Et non pour babiller et causer à chascun."

Shortly after, she soliloquizes concerning her love for Thobie, whom she fears to marry, lest he suffer the fate of the other victims of Asmodeus. When she has been convinced, however, that Thobie will escape, the marriage is quickly arranged.

Ouyn resumes the dramatization in the fifth act with a conversation between Azarie and Gabel, the debtor of Thobie *le pere.* As the latter consents to pay his debt, Thobie prepares to return home with the money. The scene in which Thobie and his wife take leave of the latter's parents is from the pen of Mlle des Roches, as is also a lamentation from Thobie *le pere* and Anne over the absence of their son. Their grief is turned into joy by the arrival of the young people, who bring the fish-gall by which the father's eyesight is restored. The identity of Azarie is now disclosed and the play ends with a thanksgiving from young Thobie.

This tragi-comedy may with equal propriety be called a *drame bourgeois*, if one considers the rank of the personages represented in it and the sentiments they express. The character of Anne, a typical housewife swayed by small practical considerations, is very well drawn. Thobie *le pere* is too austere, his son too timid and sanctimonious to obtain sympathetic appreciation. The delineation of Sarra's character does credit to Mlle des Roches, especially when she expresses the conflicting emotions induced by her love of Thobie and her fear that he may suffer the fate of her former husbands:

"Dois-ie brusler touiours sans descouvrir ma flamme?
Dois-ie faire mourir celui qui tient mon âme?
Faut-il donc tant souffrir et ne le dire pas?
Faut-il mener aussi mon ami au trespas?
Ah! mon Dieu! meurs plutost, Sarra, que d'estre cause
De la mort de celui où ta vie est enclose." [1]

Faguet [2] has pointed out that this tragi-comedy shows dramatic unity only in the part written by Mlle des Roches, who concerns herself chiefly with the love of Thobie and Sarra. Her single act, however, forms a small part of the play published by Ouyn. The latter author has dramatized freely the whole Apocryphal story in accordance with the principles of the *drame libre.* Two distinct plots, one concerned with the welfare of Thobie *le pere,* his blindness and recovery, the other with the affairs of young Thobie and Sarra, are crudely connected in order to fill five acts. The unities of place and time are obviously violated, as the action takes place in different countries during the space of several months, at the least. There is, however, a unity of interest in the affairs of young Thobie, while the lesson of divine providence is taught throughout.

This is the last fifteenth-century tragi-comedy of biblical plot. While its religious and *bourgeois* spirit distinguishes it from tragi-comedies of the following century, it anticipates them in the important place assigned a love-affair, an element lacking in

[1] IV, 6. The entire scene is a happy addition to the Apocryphal account.
[2] For reference see Appendix B, I.

preceding biblical members of the *genre*. In this respect it resembles the tragi-comedies of *romanesque* plot that are now to be discussed.

III. The Mystère of Romanesque Plot as Tragi-Comedy.

Especial importance is attached to this group of secular and *romanesque* plays, which furnished to the *genre* its best known sixteenth century examples and formed the type that became, in the hands of Hardy, the tragi-comedy *par-excellence*. First among them chronologically is the lost play on Ariosto's story of Ginevra,[1] performed at Fontainebleau in 1564. The fullest account of the presentation tells of a "*tragi-comedie* que la Royne, mere du Roy fit iouer en son festin, la plus belle, et aussi bien et artistement representée que l'on pourroit imaginer, et de laquelle le duc d'Aniou, à present roy, voulut estre, et auec luy, Marguerite de France sa sœur à present royne de Navarre, et plusieurs princes et princesses, comme le prince de Condé, Henry de Lorraine duc de Guise, la duchesse de Nevers, la duchesse d'Uzés, le duc de Rets auiourd'huy mareschal de France, Villequier et quelques autres seigneurs de la cour. Et après la *comedie* qui fut admirée d'un chacun . . ."[2]

The other writers cited by Madeleine in his admirable study of the play make certain the subject of the piece, but do not give the name. It has been called *Genièvre* on account of this subject. The evidence that it was considered a tragi-comedy comes from Castelnau, who, however, also calls it a *comedie*. As the other authors refer to it by the latter appellation, it seems probable that it was known as a comedy, but the character of its subject classes it among tragi-comedies, a conclusion supported by the usage of Claude Billard, who published in 1610 a *Genevre tragecomedie*. The loss of the play is unfortunate, as it would furnish an early

[1] *Orlando Furioso*, IV, 56–72, V, VI, 2–16.

[2] Castelnau, *Mémoires*, in *Mémoires relatifs à l'Histoire de France* (Michaud et Poujoulat, Paris, 1857), X, 499.

example of a modern *romanesque* play, the appearance of which in France is due to no foreign dramatic influence. The subject treated is thoroughly in keeping with those employed in tragi-comedies of the seventeenth century.

The *Lucelle* of Louis Le Jars displays *romanesque* qualities that make appropriate its classification here. In many respects it is rather a *comédie bourgeoise,* not in keeping with the later traditions of the tragi-comedy. As the work has been fully analyzed by Faguet, Toldo, and Schlensog,[1] I shall give only a brief outline of the plot.

The personages are *le Baron de Sainct-amour, le sieur de Bel-acueil, Bonaduenture, le sieur Carpony, Lucelle sa fille, Marguerite, Philippin l'alteré, Ascagne, le Capitaine Baustruld, le sire Claude.* The baron seeks to win the hand of Lucelle, daughter of Carpony, a banker of Lyon. He obtains the father's consent, but has no success with Lucelle, who loves Ascagne, her father's clerk. As the latter realizes his humble position too fully to speak his love, Lucelle makes known her passion, finds it reciprocated, and accomplishes a secret marriage. Carpony, finding the lovers together, is so deeply offended that he sends for poison, which he forces them to drink. When they have become unconscious, Baustruld arrives with the surprising information that Ascagne is the disguised *Chastelain de Posnanie,* son of the *Prince Palatin de Vualachie en Pologne.* Carponi falls into great distress over the murder he has committed, but Claude *apoticaire* suddenly enters with the pleasing intelligence that the poison was only a sleeping draught. The lovers, restored to consciousness, arrange a marriage amid general rejoicing. Even the baron seems to be satisfied, as he discovers that he is some relation of the new-found prince.

To this *romanesque* plot are added numerous farcical discourses from the valet, Philippin, and lengthy generalizations from the baron. The unity of action is violated by these digressions, by the large part of the first three acts devoted to the baron's courtship, and by the *dénouement,* which, instead of developing from the preceding action, is accomplished by the arrival of a *deus ex machinâ.*

[1] For references see Appendix B, I.

The violation of the unities of time and place are shown by Schlensog.[1]

The fact that the play is thoroughly *bourgeois* in spirit is not disguised by the lofty rank assigned the hero at the end of it. Ascagne's conversation and bearing place him in the middle class of society along with Carpony and Lucelle. The baron, whose rôle is subordinate, is the only aristocrat in the work. This fact, taken in connection with the large comic element introduced into it by the valet, the author's use of prose, and the derivation of the plot from an Italian comedy,[2] makes of the play a *comédie bourgeoise* rather than a tragi-comedy. A play of somewhat similar type is Ouyn's *Thobie*,[3] which lacks, however, the farcical elements of *Lucelle.*

The decided difference that exists between *Lucelle* and other plays of this *romanesque* group seems due to its Italian dramatic origin. Had other sixteenth century tragi-comedies been derived from Italian plays, the term would soon have become the equivalent of comedy. As it was, *Lucelle* stood largely alone, finding no follower in the *genre* before *L'Innocence Descouverte* (1609), where, however, though the comic element was equally large, the principal personages were aristocrats.[4]

Undoubtedly the best known tragi-comedy of the sixteenth century is the *Bradamante* of Robert Garnier, long considered the first example of the *genre* in France. It is the most thoroughly *romanesque* tragi-comedy before Hardy's *Theagene et Cariclée.* As it has been exhaustively analyzed by Ebert, Faguet, and others,[5] I shall give merely a brief account of the plot. The personages are Charlemagne, Nymes (*duc de Bauieres*), Aymon, Beatrix, Renaud, La Roque, Bradamante, Leon, Roger, Hippalque, La Montagne, Marphise, Basile (*duc d'Athenes*), *Ambassadeurs de Bulgarie* and Melisse. The plot, derived from cantos 44, 45, 46

[1] *Lucelle*, 13–14.

[2] *L'Amor costante* by Alessandro Piccolomini (1540).

[3] See above, page 57 *seq.*

[4] For an excellent criticism of the composition of *Lucelle* and the characters of its personages, cf. Faguet as cited in Appendix B, II.

[5] Cf. Appendix B, I.

of the *Orlandc Furioso,* concerns the marriage of Roger and Bradamante. The latter's parents insist on her marrying Leon, son of the Emperor of Constantinople, although she is in love with Roger. Charlemagne, however, has decreed that she shall marry him only who can conquer her in a duel. Leon, who has saved Roger's life, but does not know his name, now appears with this warrior, who has promised to fight Leon's battles for him. Roger, disguised under Leon's armor, is thus forced to fight against his beloved Bradamante, knowing that if he is victorious, she will be married to Leon. Despite his anguish at this state of things, he fights so skillfully against Bradamante that he is declared victorious and she is awarded to Leon. The lovers are both in despair, but their friends, by reminding Charlemagne that he has promised Bradamante to Roger, persuade him to let the matter be decided by a duel between that knight and Leon. To this the latter agrees, trusting that his friend Roger, whose identity he does not know, will fight for him against the Roger with whom he is unacquainted. Now, however, he finds Roger lamenting in the woods the loss of Bradamante, discovers who he is, and generously yields her to him. Meantime the consent of Bradamante's parents to her marriage with Roger is obtained through the timely arrival of ambassadors from Bulgaria, come to offer Roger the crown of their country. The marriage is arranged amid general satisfaction, while Leon is solaced by the promise of Charlemagne's daughter—a double *dénouement* that recurs frequently in the tragi-comedy of the seventeenth century.

The *romanesque* elements of this non-historic plot, based on love, developed by a duel between two lovers, and concluded by the offer of a throne to the hero; the lofty rank of the personages, who include Charlemagne and the son of the Emperor of Constantinople; the serious subject and happy *dénouement*; the comic elements that appear, especially in the character of Aymon; the violation of the unities; the use of Alexandrines, division into acts and scenes, and absence of the chorus:—these qualities make this the tragi-comedy of the sixteenth century that most nearly approaches the type established for the *genre* by Hardy and his contemporaries. It differs, however, from subsequent tragi-comedies by the evidences of classic influence in the structure of the piece, for though it violates the unity of action by the arrival of the ambassadors, an event unconnected with the rest of the play, yet there is an obvious attempt at selecting for dramatization only those parts of Ariosto's tale that closely concern the love intrigue. Earlier incidents, such as Roger's display of prowess in Bulgaria, his capture by the Greeks and rescue by Leon are recited, not acted. The duel between Roger and Bradamante takes place behind the scenes, according to classical rule and contrary to the usage of later tragi-comedies. Classical again is the subordinate rôle of Hippalque, a typical *confidante.* Such elements were, indeed, to be expected from the pen of Garnier, whose other plays were essentially classical. It is surprising that, despite the influence of his tragedies, he created the tragi-comedy that in many respects most closely resembles the type established in the seventeenth century.[1]

The resemblance in plot existing between *La Polyxene* and the medieval *Miracle de la marquise de la Gaudine* has been indicated above.[2] As the former play has been neglected by critics of the French stage, it demands a somewhat detailed analysis. The author states that the plot is taken from "le docte Boisteau au premier livre des histoires Tragiques[3] histoire 6." The latter writer translated it from the *novella* of Bandello called *Amore di don Giovanni di Mendozza e della duchessa di Savoia.*[4] Though thus based directly on a collection of tales, the story goes back to the *Marquise de la Gaudine*, the plot of which is derived, according to Petit de Julleville,[5] from "une ancienne chanson de geste qui nous est parvenue dans une rédaction française italienisée, que M. Guessard a publiée sous le titre de Macaire."[6]

[1] I do not discuss this play at greater length, as it has been admirably criticized by Ebert and Faguet. For references see Appendix B, I.

[2] Page 9.

[3] Cf. Pierre Bouestuau, *Histoires tragiques*, Paris, 1559.

[4] *Novelle di Matteo Bandello, novella* 44, Florence, 1832.

[5] *Les Mystères*, II, 253.

[6] Cf. *Macaire Chanson de Geste*, in *Anciens Poëtes de la France*, IX, François Guessard, Paris, 1859–70. 10 vols.

The personages of the drama are: *Irenophile, Gentilhomme, l'amateur de paix; Irene, Princesse, paix; Megalprepie, Damoiselle, la magnifique; Dromon, le Courrier; Opade, Gentilhomme de la suite; Polyxene, Duchesse, ayant plusieurs hostes; Evandre, Duc de Savoye, homme genereux; Le fol amour; Philomache, Page, aymant a se battre; Philippe, Page, aymant les chevaux; Eubolie, Damoiselle, donnant bon conseil; Eulalie, Damoiselle, la bien disante; Le Saint amour; Mysogyne, Marquis, haineux des femmes; Mandosse, Chevalier; Pancalier, Conte; Appian, Medecin; Dicandre, Premier juge, homme iuste; Semnandre, second juge, homme severe; Les cinq chœurs, dont le second seul est de filles.* The play begins with a four-page prayer for peace, spoken by Irenophile. Megalprepie and Irene converse on the same topic till a courier announces to the latter the victory of her brother, Mandosse, over the enemy. Irene resolves to go to Rome to return thanks. The chorus ends the act by invoking peace in the following dull lines:

"Lors cesseront les assassins
Les bruslemens et les ruines
Les violemens et larcins
Les outrages et les rapines.
Tost reprendra Justice en main
Sa iuste balance et espee
Alors sera du genre humain
Tout extortion extirpee."

On her pilgrimage Irene visits Polyxene, to whom she so eloquently describes her brother's prowess, that this duchess falls in love with him, although she has never seen him. At first she struggles against this love, while the chorus praises chastity, but in the third act she is forced by *Le fol amour* to leave home with Irene, under pretence of paying her vows to Saint Jacques, but resolved in reality to abandon herself to Mandosse. The chorus now deplores unchastity. The two women are cordially received by Mandosse, but Polyxene, fearing that he does not love her, determines to continue on her way. This resolution forces him to declare his love and beg her to return quickly, which she promises to do. But, meanwhile, *Le Saint amour* stirs up Polyxene's husband to follow her, although he does not doubt her chastity. The announcement of his approach awakens her dormant virtue, so that she resolves to give up Mandosse and return home with the duke. Not long after this, *Le fol amour* takes revenge for this action by inciting Pancalier, a despairing lover of Polyxene, to put his nephew under her bed, while the duke is away from home, to pretend to find him there, to kill the nephew and accuse Polyxene of adultery. The latter is sentenced to be burnt unless some champion can be found to defend her innocence. Her friends send for Mandosse while the chorus ends the fourth act by commenting on Fortune's sudden changes.

Disguised by his armor, Mandosse now comes to the rescue, conquers Pancalier and forces him to confess his guilt and the innocence of Polyxene. The latter sends for her unknown protector, only to find that he has disappeared. Shortly afterward she learns of her husband's death in battle, an event that moves her to cry,

> "O gouverneur du monde, ô Monarque eternel
> Pourquoy tiens mon ame en cest enclos charnel ?"

But she recovers from her grief as soon as Mandosse, hearing of the duke's death, returns to prove his identity as her champion. She falls into his arms exclaiming :

> "Pauure ame des tourmens tant de fois agitee,
> Et lasse des assaux de fortune irritee,
> Prens maintenant courage en te voyant au port,
> En voyant pres de toy ton aide et ton support :
> . . . .
> Mais un poinct seulement me chagrine et soucie,
> De pouuoir satisfaire à ceste grand'bonté.
> Mandosse : I'estimeray, Madame, estre en tout surmonté
> Par vous en courtoisie, en grace en gentillesse,
> Si vous vous baissez tant enuers ma petitesse
> De me prendre à Espoux.
> Polyxene : Vrayment, mon bon Seigneur,
> Ie reçoy plus icy de faueur et d'honneur
> Que ie n'en pourrois rendre, et bien froide et petite
> Est ceste recompense."

The structure of this piece is decidedly faulty, for the main plot is dramatized almost exclusively in the fourth and fifth acts, while the first three, following Bandello's narrative, are full of extraneous matter that serves merely to give the play sufficient length. The action takes place in both Spain and Italy during several months, at least. The story is told *ab ovo,* beginning with the causes of Irene's journey, which was itself the cause of the love-affair between Polyxene and Mandosse. The preliminary discourses are delivered at great length, while the important parts of the plot are too quickly narrated, characteristics worthy of the didactic author, a schoolmaster of Rouen, known by his *Petit-Behourt,* an abridgment of Despautères's *Rudiment.* His pedantry is further shown by his use of such names as, Irenophile and Megalprepie. Classical influence is seen in the *courrier* and *confidantes,* as well as in the use of the five choruses and the recitation of certain events that should have been acted. On the other hand, the abstract personages show the influence of the *moralité.* This play is in one respect more dramatic than *Bradamante,* inasmuch as the duel is here acted on the stage, whereas in Garnier's play the contest between Roger and Bradamante is described to the audience by a third person.

The tragi-comedy has an unnecessarily large number of personages, of whom many are altogether useless and few possess individuality. Irene, a colorless personality, appears in the first two acts to be the heroine of the piece, but is insignificant in the rest of it. The characterization of Polyxene is inconsistent, for she is first represented as a woman of easy virtue, but later held up as a model of irreproachable chastity. One is not moved by the portrayal of slandered innocence when one knows that the innocence has been preserved through forced separation from the desired lover. Mandosse is a knightly character of few words and mighty deeds, an agreeable contrast to the prolix abstractions, who concern themselves with peace and different kinds of love. Despite the addition of these personages from the *moralité,* the play is, however, essentially *romanesque,* as the plot is based on love, the heroine becomes enamored of a hero whom she has never seen, she is saved from the stake by a duel, and she recognizes her disguised rescuer by means of a ring she has given him before the contest. Such elements make this play, like others of its class, the prototype of the tragi-comedies written by Alexandre Hardy.

Before leaving the subject of tragi-comedies that have a *romanesque* plot, mention should be made of two sixteenth-century plays that have the characteristics of such tragi-comedies, though classified as belonging in other *genres*. The first of them is the *Comedie des Amours de Theseus et de Dianira* (5 acts, prose) by Gerard de Vivre of Ghent, published at Paris, 1577, and republished in *Trois Comedies françoises de Gerard de Vivre, Gantois* at Rotterdam and Antwerp, 1589, and again at Antwerp, 1602.[1] Theseus and Dianira elope to Egypt, where they are captured by Tyrrhene, who falls in love with Dianira, believing her to be the sister of Theseus. Informed by a letter from her father that this is not the case, Tyrrhene is about to put the lovers to death, when Anchises, supposed father of Theseus, shows that the young man is the son of Tyrrhene. This discovery appeases the ruler's wrath, so that the piece ends in the marriage of the lovers.

Equally romantic in plot is *La Sophronie Tragédie* (5 acts, verse) by Aymard de Veins, published at Rouen, 1599, and at Troyes, 1619.[2] Aladin, king of Jerusalem, seeks to save his city from capture by getting possession of an image of the Virgin, which suddenly disappears. When he condemns all the Christians in his power to be put to death for the theft, Sophronie accuses herself of having stolen the image, in order to save her co-religionists. Olinde, her lover, endeavors to save her by implicating himself. Aladin orders both to be killed, but frees them at the last moment on the intercession of Clorinde, the famous female warrior. The lovers are then happily united.

Despite changes of names and incidents, the plot of the first of these plays is evidently derived from the romance of Heliodorus on which Hardy based his *Theagene et Cariclée;*[3] that of the second comes from Tasso's *Gerusalemme Liberata* (II, strophes

[1] La Vallière, I, 214–5; Brunet, V, 1356–7; *Mistère du Viel Testament*, I, p. xc.

[2] La Vallière, I, 325–6; Brunet, V, 114.

[3] See below, page 120. Stiefel is evidently mistaken in deriving this play from *Cleitophon and Leucippe* of Achilleus Tatius, for its plot is much nearer that of *Theagenes and Charidea.* Cf. A. L. Stiefel, *Nachahmung italienischer Dramen*, 258.

1–53). These romantic plots of love unto death, rescue at the last moment, oriental surroundings, aristocratic personages, and happy *dénouement,* make the plays true tragi-comedies. The fact that they were called *comedie* and *tragédie* shows that the term *tragi-comédie* was not fully established even at the end of the sixteenth century.

IV. The Farce as Tragi-Comedy.

The farcical elements that have been shown to play an important part in *Lucelle* and *Caresme prenant*[1] constitute practically the whole of *La Nouvelle tragicomique,* a late example of the medieval farce. The piece is so constructed that the reader cannot be certain whether it was written as a play or a *nouvelle.* Sainte-Beuve analyzed it as a *drame satirique.*[2] The greater part of it is dialogued after the manner of medieval plays, in which the change of scene, though unmarked, is sufficiently indicated by the context. Towards the end, however, events are related by different personages of the play, not in dramatic monologues, but in synopses that tell of what occurs between the dialogues, interior speeches corresponding to the prologue and epilogue. The system is the same as that employed in *Pericles Prince of Tyre,* where Gower relates the undramatized events of the story. However subject to objection such a system may be, it does not prevent the piece in which it is used from being looked upon as a dramatic production.

The personages of the play are: *Ambrelin, laquais; Dominicq le seigneur; Vouly; Griffon advocat; Arcquigue; Bergers; Magis le sçavant; Candelin le portier de la ville; Hospes, maistre hostelier; Chicanoux; Gonophage, femme de l'advocat; Furcifer le brigand.* Dominicq, apprized of the loss of "deux mille escus" and the death of the servant in charge of them, seeks aid from Griffon, whom he persuades to consult Magis. Griffon is at first unwilling to do so, calling the sooth-sayer:

[1] See above, pages 62 and 47.

[2] *Tableau,* 235.

> "une grosse teste,
> Un homme mal formé qui n'est rien qu'une beste."

Yielding at last, Griffon seeks out Magis, whose dwelling is shown to him by shepherds. When Griffon tells of the lost treasure, the sage replies:

> "Vous changez de discours et n'ay changé de teste;
> Suis-je pas mal formé? Suis-je pas une beste?
> Griffon, vous l'avez dict.
> Griffon: Magis, pardonnez-moy."

But Magis is resolved on vengeance and, after telling Griffon where to look for the thief, assures him that he will remember the insult when he finds the man.

Soon the lawyer reaches Paris, secures guards, and proceeds to hunt for the robber in a house of ill-repute, kept by Hospes. After considerable parleying, they proceed to the room where *Furcifer le brigand* is lodged, break open the door, and find him in company with no other than the wife of Griffon. The dialogue stops temporarily while Hospes relates the scene, beginning:

> "Si jamais on a veu une ame perturbée
> Il falloit voir Griffon, sans combat combatu,
> Voyant sa femme, etc."

He is so greatly surprised that he makes no effort to arrest Furcifer, merely asking him to explain his presence in such company. Furcifer assures him that he objects to no woman whom he can buy. Then Candelin, taking up Hospes's recitation, tells how Furcifer quietly left the house and sent the guard to arrest Griffon on the ground that he "luy retenoit sa femme et beaucoup de son bien." The lawyer submits to the arrest for fear of scandal. A brief dialogue follows between him and Dominicq, who deplores the loss of his money, reminding Griffon that he has failed to recover it because of his scepticism regarding magic. Hospes continues the story by telling how Griffon was let out of prison after apologizing to his wife's family, who then allowed him to be reunited to her, celebrating the reconciliation by "un beau festin," which brings the play to a happy termination.

This badly dramatized tragi-comedy contains two nearly distinct actions, of which one is concerned with an attempt to recover stolen property, the other with the betrayal of an advocate by his wife. A weak attempt to unite the two is made by introducing the rôle of Magis into the play, Griffon's light opinion of him and its subsequent punishment. Unnecessary personages are introduced into the piece; as, Vouly, an adviser, Arcquigue, who merely comments on the play without mingling in the action, the shepherds, whose introduction into the action may be due to the rising popularity of the pastoral. The piece is thoroughly *bourgeois* in its subject and in the rank and conversation of its personages. The dialogue is full of vulgar humor. Dominicq's grief over the loss of his gold and his servants is largely burlesqued. The scene at the inn is full of jests at the expense of Griffon, the butt of the play.

The spirit of the piece is, indeed, that of the farce rather than the tragi-comedy. The fact that the author calls it a *nouvelle tragi-comique* rather than a tragi-comedy seems to indicate his realization that it did not fulfill the conception of the *genre* already developed in the public mind. At the time when it was written, however, it could be called a tragi-comedy, as it continued the traditions of certain medieval plays, ended happily, and showed by the use of Alexandrines the effect of classical influence upon its form. A few examples of similar farcical tragi-comedies will be noted in the discussion of seventeenth century plays.[1]

V. The Pastoral and Foreign Play as Tragi-Comedy.

This group, of no importance in the history of the *genre*, is limited to three plays, to which the term, *tragi-comédie*, has been loosely applied. In 1527 two translations of the *Celestina* appeared at Paris and a third at Lyons. Reprints were made at the former city in 1529 and 1542. The name, *tragi-comédie*, appears in the titles of none of these. In 1578, however, was published *La Celestine . . . tragi-comédie jadis espagnole*,[2] indicat-

[1] See below, page 94.

[2] See Appendix B, I.

ing the increased popularity of the tragi-comedy, although the term is here a translation and is not used in the French sense, for the *Celestina* is not a tragi-comedy according to French ideas, but, if it be considered a dramatic production, it is a comedy of manners with tragic *dénouement.* Its influence is not exerted on the tragi-comedy, but on the comedy through the *Contents* of Odet de Tournebu.[1]

Les Aveugles, as a translation of the *Cecaria,* retains the title, *tragi-comédie,* though it is in reality a pastoral. To the latter *genre* belongs also *Tragi-comedie pastorale ou Mylas,* an adaptation of the *Aminta,* with the new *genre*-name taken from the *Pastor fido.* This is the first occurrence of this term in France, where it is used a number of times in the sixteenth century to indicate a variety of pastoral that has been influenced by the tragi-comedy.

Another example of the pastoral is found in *Amour Vaincu, tragecomedie,* in which *Amour* seeks to bring all the gods under his sway, but falls in love himself with a nymph who laughs at him. After conquering a number of divinities, he is captured when asleep and deprived of his weapons, so that the play ends in the usual pastoral fashion with the return of all the lovers to their former mistresses.

These plays have no connection with other tragi-comedies of the sixteenth or seventeenth centuries. The application of the term, tragi-comedy, to them is due either to a translation of it from the foreign original, or to a confusion that existed at this time between the tragi-comedy and the pastoral, owing to Guarini's denomination of the *Pastor fido* as a *tragicommedia pastorale.*

The preceding investigation of tragi-comedies written during the sixteenth century shows that the name was at that time applied to a number of dramatic kinds, derived from the medieval stage. Distinctions among the classes of tragi-comedies, thus formed, must not be rigorously made, as certain plays can be put into more than one class. Thus, *Iokebed* resembles the *moralité* and the biblical *mystère; Polyxene,* the *moralité* and *mystère* of *romanesque*

[1] Paris, 1584.

plot; *Thobie* is both biblical and *romanesque*. Since the tragi-comedy in the sixteenth century might include any play of happy *dénouement*, which was derived from the medieval drama and showed in its form evidence of classical influence, there is no reason for calling the lost *Genièvre*, *Lucelle*, or *Bradamante* the first tragi-comedy.[1] According to the conception of the *genre* in vogue at that time, *L'Homme iustifié par Foy* or *Les Enfants dans la Fournaise* were not only considered tragi-comedies, but belonged to divisions of the *genre* that left a larger number of examples than did the *romanesque* type, which later became the only form of tragi-comedy. To deny this fact is to attempt to foist upon the tragi-comedy of the sixteenth century the meaning attached to it at a subsequent period.

But, although tragi-comedies of the sixteenth century vary more widely than they subsequently did, they have in common many characteristics which influenced the later composition of the *genre*. Their failure to observe the unities has been discussed after the analysis of each play. Many of the scenes of this *genre* do not grow logically out of those that precede, but follow one another largely by chance. Plays like *L'Homme iustifié par Foy*, *La Gaule*, *Iokebed*, *Thobie*, *Caresme prenant* include more than one important action. The *dénouement* is accomplished by a *deus ex machinâ* in *La Gaule*, *Lucelle* and *Bradamante*.

The time of the action is not always clearly indicated, but appears to vary from a period of more than a year in *Iob*, *Lucelle*, *Le Desesperé* and *Polyxene* to one of a few days in *Bradamante* and *Les Enfants dans la Fournaise*.

Though the scene is laid ordinarily within a limited locality, as, in a city; it may represent places at some distance from one another. In *La Nouvelle tragicomique* the action takes place within Paris and outside of it, while in *Polyxene* and *Thobie* it is found in more than one country. Instead of the classical unities, however, these tragi-comedies display a unity of interest in a

[1] Madeleine, *Revue de la Renaissance*, IV (1903), 30, and Tilly, *French Renaissance*, II, 99, claim this title for *Genièvre;* Schlensog, *Lucelle*, 5, bestows it upon *Lucelle* by Le Jars; Frères Parfaict, III, 454, and La Vallière, I, 189, select *Bradamante* as the original tragi-comedy.

single personage like Iokebed or Thobie, or in the accomplishment of some object, as is the case in *L'Homme iustifié par Foy, La Gaule, Bradamante, Polyxene, L'Ombre de Garnier Stoffacher.*

The choice of subject is influenced by the author's purpose of instructing or amusing his audience. In the *moralités* the end is so essentially didactic that the events are largely neglected; the biblical plays, while pointing a moral, introduce into the piece action that is frequently dramatic; the tragi-comedies of *romanesque,* or farcical plot, reach the audience through the emotions without attempting instruction of any sort. So the plots are religious or historical in the didactic tragi-comedies and fictitious in the rest. The Bible is the source of *L'Homme iustifié par Foy, Les Enfants dans la Fournaise, Iob, Thobie, Iokebed, Le patriarche Abraham; La Gaule* and *Garnier Stoffacher* are declared by their authors to be historical, although the history with which they are concerned is treated allegorically. On the other hand, the *romanesque* tragi-comedies are based on obviously fictitious narratives, the *Orlando Furioso, Amor Costante,* a *novella* of Bandello, and the *Jerusalemme Liberata.*[1] The slight plot of *La Nouvelle tragicomique* is probably an invention of its author.

In the last-named play, the mainspring of the action is avarice, which appears subordinately in *Lucelle, Bradamante,* and *Thobie.* It is love in the *romanesque* plays, and religion in the biblical tragi-comedies and in the majority of *moralités.* Love enters subordinately into *Thobie,* as does religion into *Polyxene.* Religion struggles against pride in *Les Enfants dans la Fournaise,* hypocrisy in *L'Homme iastifié par Foy,* and Satan and his assistants in the latter play, *Iob, Thobie, Iokebed,* and *Garnier Stoffacher.* Patriotism, which dominates religion, though working in unison with it, in *La Gaule* and *Garnier Stoffacher,* is seen in the *intermède* of *Caresme prenant* "touchant quelques abus de ce temps," in the frequent expression of desires for peace by personages in *Polyxene,* and in the prologue of *Iob,* where the author speaks of his theme, as a

[1] If *Sophronie* be included here; see above, page 69.

> "Sujet bien conuenable à la saison passee,
> Qui depuis quelques ans a la France oppressee :
> Et dont ie prie à Dieu que le temps à venir
> Par contraires effets oste le souuenir."

Particularly worthy of note are the expressions of patriotism, and of admiration of France found in *Bradamante*; as, when the heroine of the play declares,

> "Mais le pais natal ha ne sçay quelle force,
> Et ne sçay quel appas qui les hommes amorce
> Et les attire à soy." [1]

Nymes says of the Saracens,

> "Ils sont assez puissans pour leurs terres defendre,
> Mais non pas pour oser contre vous entreprendre,
> Pour la France assaillir, mere des Cheualiers,
> Mere des bons soudars, qu'elle enfante à milliers." [2]

Leon adds a foreigner's praise by speaking of "vostre France, en Cheualiers feconde, Et feconde en vertus." [3]

The tragi-comedy was, indeed, able to appeal to the patriotism of the audience to an extent denied the classical tragedy, by reason of the fact that the scene in plays of the former *genre* could be laid in the country in which they were represented. In the biblical plays, it is true, the Orient is naturally chosen for the scene of action, but in *La Gaule, Lucelle, Bradamante, Le Desesperé Caresme prenant,* and *La Nouvelle tragicomique* the scene is laid in France, just as the action of *L'Ombre de Garnier Stoffacher* takes place in Switzerland, and that of *Polyxene* in Savoy and neighboring lands. That the audience responded to this feature of the tragi-comedy, along with its other popular characteristics, is shown by the number of recorded representations of tragi-comedies, by the extensive geographical distribution of the *genre* in France, and by the variety of professions represented by its authors.

It is well established that *Genièvre, Iob, Iokebed, Bradamante,*[4] *Garnier Stoffacher, Le patriarche Abraham, Polyxene, Le Desesperé, Caresme prenant, Amour Vaincu,* and *Aymée* were actually repre-

[1] II, 3, lines 584–86. [2] I, 2, lines 141–4. [3] III, 3, lines 860–1.

[4] Recorded representations of this play took place in the seventeenth century.

sented. *L'Homme iustifié par Foy*, *Les Enfants dans la Fournaise*, *La Gaule*, and *Lucelle*, evidently written for representation, were also probably produced on the boards. We know that performances took place in the sixteenth century at Fontainebleau, Poitiers, Antwerp, Geneva, Montbéliard, Rouen, Bordeaux, and Aix-en-Provence. The plays were published at Paris, Geneva, Poitiers, Antwerp, Rouen, Tours, Lyon, Harlem, Toulouse, and Niort. If *Les Enfants dans la Fournaise* was acted, the event probably took place in Béarn, for the author lived there and dedicated his play to Jeanne d'Albret. The tragi-comedy was, therefore, known in nearly all parts of France. That it appealed to various classes is shown by the fact that its authors included Barran, a preacher; Behourt, Heyns, and Jean-Georges, schoolmasters; Du Chesne, a physician; Bonet and La Fons, lawyers; Le Jars, the King's Secretary of the Chamber; Papillon, a retired captain; Garnier, Sainte-Marthe, and Mlle des Roches, who occupied themselves largely with literary pursuits.

Another characteristic of the tragi-comedy that gave it wide appeal was the varied rank of its characters. Contrary to subsequent usage, tragi-comedies might now be altogether *bourgeois*, as are *le Desesperé*, *Caresme prenant*, *La Nouvelle tragicomique*, and *Thobie*. The principal personages are *bourgeois* in *Lucelle* and *Iokebed*, but persons of high rank are found in subordinate rôles. *Les Enfants dans la Fournaise*, *La Gaule*, *Bradamante*, and *Polyxene* are primarily aristocratic, though *La Gaule* admits the *tiers état* and soldiers, and the three other plays present attendants of inferior rank, as do classical tragedies.

As the dramatic art in France was not yet sufficiently developed to create rôles thoroughly consistent with life, the study of character in these plays is, as a rule, crudely done. The personage often embodies only a single quality, after the manner of the abstractions that enter into many of these plays. He thus lacks a sufficient number of emotions to rouse a psychological struggle within himself. The audience sees in him the personification of a single virtue or vice, rather than the complex composition of the individual. Occasionally, however, a personage is found in such a situation that his action is dependent, not on external forces, but on the conflict of emotions that takes place within him. An eminent example of such a psychological struggle is seen in Roger's debate as to whether he should fight against Bradamante,[1] where the hero hesitates between his love and his oath. In the same play,[2] Beatrix displays in conversation with Bradamante a hesitation between the maternal love that prompts her to allow her daughter to marry Roger and her ambition that makes her prefer Leon as son-in-law. Similarly, Sarra struggles against her love of Thobie[3] for fear of causing his death, Polyxene wavers between yielding to Mandosse and remaining faithful to her husband,[4] and the midwives in *Iokebed*[5] debate the question of saving the young Hebrews at the cost of disobedience and deception. These passages, however, take up but a small portion of plays that are more largely concerned with the events themselves, than with the mental processes that bring them about. There is nothing to compare with the heroic struggle in the mind of Chimène. On the other hand, opportunities of expressing psychological study are neglected; as, when *Nabochodonosor* shows no hesitation in declaring himself divine, Carpony in directing his daughter's murder, or Polyxene's husband in condemning her to be burnt.[6] The struggle in Sidrach's mind between human and divine guidance is ended almost as soon as it begins.[7]

A number of types are found in these plays. The protagonists of *La Gaule* and *L'Homme iustifié par Foy* have utterly weak characters, swayed by all those with whom they come into contact. With them may be compared *Gent-Israëlite* in *Iokebed* and *La Paix* in *L'Ombre de Garnier Stoffacher*. The worthy hero, whose virtues are *bourgeois* rather than warlike, is represented by Ascagne in *Lucelle*, Charles in *Le Desesperé*, and Thobie in the play that bears his name. The invincible warrior is exemplified by Roger in *Bradamante*, Mandosse in *Polyxene*, and Garnier in *L'Ombre de Garnier Stoffacher*. To these two varieties of hero

[1] *Bradamante*, III, 5. [2] *Ibidem*, II, 3. [3] *Thobie*, IV, 6.
[4] *Polyxene*, II and III. [5] *Iokebed*, IV, 5.
[6] See above, pages 50, 62, 67. [7] See above, page 50.

correspond the *bourgeois* class of heroines that includes Sarra, Lucelle, and Iokebed, and the aristocratic, represented by Bradamante and Polyxene. The villain is a rare type, except in such abstractions as *Concupiscence, Volupté, Gloutonie, Cruauté, Le fol amour,* or such personages as Rabby and Bellone, abstractions under another name. *Nabochodonosor* is scarcely a villain, as he offers to pardon the three children for their first offense, and honors them at the end of the piece. Carpony is hardly a serious character. The only true villains are Pancalier in *Polyxene* and Furcifer in *La Nouvelle tragicomique,* who are seen little on the stage.

Nabochodonosor has been mentioned[1] as the first representative of the tragi-comic type of king that will be frequently met in the seventeenth century. Charlemagne presents a somewhat similar character, with less pride and greater weakness of purpose. All his actions are suggested by others. Charles plays too small a part in *La Gaule* to be criticized. Thermuth in *Iokebed* is an amiably uninteresting princess. Leon, with his timidity, generosity, and frank admiration for Bradamante is a more sympathetic character than men of sterner virtues. The fact that he is not made ridiculous by the contrast of his character with that of Roger is an indication of the dramatic skill of the author of *Bradamante.*

The *bourgeois* and his wife are usually well drawn. Carpony and Thobie *le pere* are typical of their class, to which, on account of his love of money and desire for high rank, may be added Aymon, father of Bradamante. Similarly Beatrix, however aristocratic in origin, shows the family affection and lack of high ideal that characterizes the *bourgeoise.* Still more appropriately depicted is the character of Anne, the simple housewife, unmoved by the unpractical altruism of her husband and son. Among other personages are to be noted Griffon, the lawyer, akin to Pathelin and Sganarelle; Magis, the magician, who belongs to a type especially frequent in the *tragi-comédie pastorale;* Claude, the apothecary, restorer of Lucelle and Ascagne; Raguel, the divine agent, who may be compared to the abstract virtues. Attendants and mes-

[1] See above, page 52.

sengers are also introduced into these plays. The latter type is found evidencing classical imitation in *Lucelle*, *Bradamante* and *L'Ombre de Garnier Stoffacher;* the former occurs in the first two of these plays, in *Les Enfants dans la Fournaise*, *Iokebed*, *Polyxene*, *Le Desesperé*, *Thobie*, and *La Nouvelle tragicomique*. Of especial importance among such personages are Philippin, the irrepressible wag, in *Lucelle*, who plays the part of the valet after Italian example; the scolding maid in *Thobie;* and the rôle of *confidante* that shows classical influence, exemplified by Hippalque in *Bradamante*, Eubolie in *Polyxene*, and Marguerite in *Lucelle*. Other minor personages are added in many of the plays, so that the total number of characters is large in comparison with the usage of the classical stage. Thus, *Polyxene* has nineteen persons besides the chorus, while *Caresme prenant* has twenty-nine in all. Usually, however, the number is smaller, amounting in *Garnier Stoffacher* to only four, in addition to the three choruses.

There seems to have been no restriction as to the number of personages that appeared on the stage at a time, or that took part in the conversation. The dialogue is used more extensively than in contemporary classical plays, a fact that has been noted by Faguet in comparing *Bradamante* with tragedies written by the same author.[1] Monologues are occasionally employed to excess in tragi-comedies, however; as, in *Polyxene*, *Iokebed*, and especially *Garnier Stoffacher*.

While the subject of most of these tragi-comedies is essentially serious, comic elements are admitted into certain plays. The character of Aymon in *Bradamante* is distinctly humorous. The *Satellites* introduce a grim humor into *Les Enfants dans la Fournaise*. *Caresme prenant* includes a farce. Several personages in *Lucelle*, particularly Philippin, show decided humor. In all of these, however, such passages are subordinate to the serious portions of the play. The only extant tragi-comedy that is an exception to this is *La Nouvelle tragicomique*.

The *dénouement* in all these plays is happy for the persons principally concerned. *L'Homme* and *Le Voluptueux* in *L'Homme*

[1] *Tragédie française*, 215.

iustifié and *Caresme prenant* finally attain salvation; the three children escape from the furnace; La Gaule, Iob, and Iokebed are freed from their troubles; peace is brought by Garnier Stoffacher; Lucelle, Bradamante, Thobie, Polyxene, and Charles of *Le Desesperé* are fortunately married. Even in *La Nouvelle tragicomique* the lawyer and his wife are reunited at the end.

In form the tragi-comedies show some variation from classical usage. A marked division into five acts, with subdivisions into scenes, is the rule, to which the following exceptions are found: the division into acts in *Les Enfants dans la Fournaise* is indicated only by the presence of the choruses; in *La Nouvelle tragicomique* no such division is made; in *La Gaule* there are only four acts; in *Garnier Stoffacher* only three; in none of these four plays are there subdivisions into scenes. The Alexandrine is the meter employed in *Bradamante*, *Le Desesperé* and *La Nouvelle tragicomique*, and in all but lyric portions of *Iob*, *La Gaule*, *Thobie*, and *Polyxene*. In *L'Homme iustifié* and *Les Enfants dans la Fournaise* verses of ten and eight syllables are employed instead of Alexandrines, except in the prologue and epilogue of the latter play. No apparent distinction is made in the use of the two kinds of verse. The former play shows verses of six syllables, furthermore, in the ninth scene of the first act, perhaps in order that the lightness of the meter may correspond to the pleasures that *L'Homme* anticipates in yielding to *Concupiscence*. Verses of eight syllables are used in *Caresme prenant*. *Lucelle* and *Iokebed* employ prose. Lyric passages in these plays occur in the choruses and in cantiques, which are written in verses of six, seven, and eight syllables, showing considerable variety in rime order. The choruses in *Les Enfants dans la Fournaise* employ all three meters, using the six-syllable verses only in connection with others of greater length. The same usage is seen in *La Gaule*, except that no verses of seven syllables are found. In *Iob* and the *Thobie* of Mlle des Roches the lyric portions are written in verses of seven syllables; *L'Ombre de Garnier Stoffacher* has choruses in eight-syllable verse, *Iokebed* a *cantique* in six, while *Polyxene* uses both these meters.

The style of these verses, both lyric and dramatic, has been shown by citations made in this chapter to be frequently puerile and rarely imbued with poetic qualities. This fact, coupled with weakness of dramatic conception, has prevented the tragi-comedy of the sixteenth century from furnishing more than two plays of literary pretensions. These are the *Lucelle* and *Bradamante*, plays that compare favorably with the classical tragedies produced in France during this century, however inferior they are to those of a later date. The *genre* as a whole, furthermore, is shown to have appealed to the people by the comparatively large number of plays known to have been represented and by the fact that it was adopted by Alexandre Hardy, whose work was written primarily for representation before a popular audience.

It is, indeed, as the link between the non-comic theater of the middle-ages and this work of Hardy that the tragi-comedy of the sixteenth century is historically important. The stages of the dramatic development are readily traced. In the looseness of structure that violates the classical unities and shows a frequently illogical succession of scenes, united by some general interest, these theaters of the middle ages, the sixteenth, and early seventeenth century, are largely the same. So are they also in the seriousness of the subject and the possible, but not necessary, addition of the comic. In other respects, there is a noticeable development. The medieval subject is almost always religious and frequently historical; the sixteenth century tragi-comedy is often religious and historical, but shows plays that have neither of these qualities; in the theater of Hardy and his contemporaries the predominant variety of subject is neither religious nor historical. Again, personages of various social classes appear in the three theaters, but in the first and second the aristocrat can be entirely omitted from a play, while in the third his presence is the rule. The *dénouement* in the Middle Ages, while usually happy, may be the reverse; in the tragi-comedies it is always happy. In form, the medieval theater shows no classical influence, while the tragi-comedies of the sixteenth century, by their use of Alexandrines, chorus, or division into acts,[1] follow

[1] I do not include in this statement *Les Aveugles*, a mere prose translation of a foreign original.

classical models; in the seventeenth century the division into acts and the use of Alexandrines is extended to almost all cases, though by the usual omission of the chorus there is a reversion to the medieval position.

It is evident, therefore, that by means of the tragi-comedy of the sixteenth century, the medieval plays, especially the *mystères* and *miracles*, developed into Hardy's popular dramas. With him the *romanesque* form of tragi-comedy triumphed definitively over other types of the *genre* that continued to be written sporadically. It will be shown in the next chapter how this was accomplished, with the resulting predominance of the tragi-comedy on the French stage, a position lost to it only by the advent of the classical tragedy of Pierre Corneille.

CHAPTER III.

THE TRAGI-COMEDY OF THE SEVENTEENTH CENTURY BEFORE ROTROU AND CORNEILLE (1600 TO 1628).

While all the types of tragi-comedy written in France during the sixteenth century are continued in the period from 1600 to 1628,[1] they show a great change in their relative importance. During the sixteenth century five tragi-comedies are known which resemble the *moralité*, and six the *mystère* of biblical plot, but only four can be called *romanesque*. From the following period, as far as Rotrou, twenty-eight *romanesque* tragi-comedies are known, but only eighteen of all other classes of tragi-comedy, including those based on lives of saints, of which no examples are preserved from the sixteenth century. Furthermore, the *romanesque* tragi-comedy of Hardy and his contemporaries was attracting the Parisian public to the Hôtel de Bourgogne, while the other forms of the tragi-comedy were being acted by school-children at provincial colleges, and, since the coming of Hardy to Paris (1593), exerted little influence upon the development of the French drama. Thus it is that the religious and farcical tragi-comedies were published altogether in the provinces, while the *romanesque* tragi-comedies appeared chiefly at Paris.

Considering the decided preponderance of the *romanesque* over other forms of the tragi-comedy, I have divided the plays treated in this chapter[2] into two classes, according to the absence or presence in them of *romanesque* elements. As the plays that

[1] This date marks the end of Hardy's career as far as his extant works are concerned, the beginning of Rotrou's work and of the influence of the Spanish drama upon the French. In the following year appeared Corneille's first play and Scudéry's first tragi-comedy.

[2] For a list of these plays, their authorships, dates, bibliography, etc., see Appendix B, II, below.

possess such qualities are more numerous and of greater importance than those that do not have them, they will be more fully discussed than the comparatively unimportant tragi-comedies, classified as *non-romanesque.*

I. The Non-Romanesque Tragi-Comedy.

A. Analyses.

As the plays belonging to this class resemble closely the religious and farcical tragi-comedies of the sixteenth century, they may, like their prototypes, be divided for analysis according to their resemblance to medieval *genres*. The *moralité, mystère, miracle,* and farce, as tragi-comedy, will consequently be discussed in succession.

1. The Moralité as Tragi-Comedy.

Of the three extant plays belonging to this division *L'Amour divin* (1601) and *Zo'anthropie* (1614) express religious views after the manner of *L'Homme iustifié par Foy,*[1] while *L'union Belgique* (1604) inclines to the political *moralité,* of which types have been found in *La Gaule* and *Garnier Stoffacher.*[2] As the first two have been analyzed by Sainte-Beuve and La Vallière,[3] respectively, a brief account of their plots will suffice.

L'Amour divin presents in allegorical form the fall and salvation of the human race. *Le Roy* places his daughter, Physique, in a garden under Lucerin's guard. She is much pleased until she is told by her guardian:

> "Vous ne pouuez en somme
> Vous guarantir du mal si ne cueillez la pomme
> Qui est sur le pommier, dont le fruit deffendu
> Ne peut pas par vos mains ia estre despendu,
> Iouissez donc du bien qui ore se presente."

But when she has eaten the apple, she is exiled and Lucerin

[1] See above, p. 37. [2] See above, pp. 40 and 44.
[3] For references, see Appendix B, II.

cursed. Her brother, Amour Divin, however, aided by Eleone and opposed by L'Astree and Verité, consents to suffer and die for her, thus restoring her to the royal favor. Even L'Astree and Verité are won over at the end.

Zo'anthropie, a longer composition than the preceding, is appropriately called by La Vallière "la plus ennuyeuse que j'aye encore lue." Like the preceding play it is concerned with man's salvation, even introducing Amour Divin and Verité, but it is still more abstrusely allegorical. Nineteen abstractions, provided with Greek names, take part in the play. The virtues and vices strive to win Anthrope (*l'homme*) by fighting against one another. Anthrope is induced by Cupidon to love Zoé (*La Vie humaine*), who gladly bestows her favors on him. A digression is made to describe the courtship of Pseude (*Fausse Religion*) by Oecomene (*le monde*). Asthenee (*L'infirmité, vieux sorcier*) now attacks Anthrope and his friend, Andrie (*la virilité*), leaving them nearly dead. When Anthrope has been rescued by Metanoee (*la Penitence*), he is saved by the virtues and married to Aïdie (*la Vie eternelle*). Zoé is left lamenting the loss of her lover, while the vices quarrel and the virtues discuss immortality.

The *Miroir de L'union Belgique* furnishes an allegorical treatment of contemporary history in a polemical spirit, of which the fanatical protestantism may be detected in the list of personages: *L'union Belgique; L'Homme Partial; La Religion; Le Iesuite; L'Espagnol, Fleau du Monde; La Feinte Paix; Soul-de lard, moine; Satan en habit de Iacobin; Le bon Patriot; Le Duc Albert; L'Historiographe; Messager; Pere-Pillart, Prestre; L'Infante, Femme du Duc Albret; Le Conte Maurice de Nassau.*

Satan, rejoicing at the woes of *L'union*, cries:

> "Quoi, elle veut des-ja sus mes faits disputer
> Et maintenir les Loix d'un Calvin et Luther
> Faisant milles ergos jusqu'a blamer en somme
> Les plus rusez abus du Pontife de Rome." [1]

He adds an interesting anachronism in

> "De nostre grand Dieu Mars, il la faut ruiner."

---

[1] I, 2.

After an argument between *Partial* and *bon Patriot* against and for "les povres huguenaux," a council is held by Satan, Iesuite, and Albert, lately arrived from Spain, to devise means for subduing *L'union.* Next, *Historiographe* describes the defeat of the Armada. The news of Spanish reverses afflicts Iesuite and Satan, who console themselves by reflecting that,

> "Tel n'est mort qui combat, ou bien qui est malade.
> L'issue d'un bancquet n'est point à la salade," [1]

but they exclaim:

> "Que ses gœux se riront de nos croix et reliques,
> Dont avions charmez nos soldats Catholiques!" [1]

A feigned peace, proposed by Iesuite and approved by Albert, is offered in vain to the shrewd *union.* The war breaks out again, but is ended by the victory of Maurice de Nassau over Albert and his Spaniards.[2]

2. The Biblical Mystère as Tragi-Comedy.

This division contains two plays on the story of Jacob (1604 and 1609); one concerned with the *Purification du temple de Jérusalem après la profanation faite par Antiochus* (1613);[3] *Daphnis, célébrant l'ascension du Christ* (1618); and *Sephoe* (1626), if Mugnier is correct in his conjecture that the name of this play refers to *Séphora,* wife of Moses.[4] The last three plays have been lost. The subject of *Jacob ou Antidolatrie,* an unimportant play, six folios in length, is taken from the Bible and church fathers. Its object is to show "par quelz moyens, s'est augmenté le culte et le service d'un seul Dieu du tout l'univers, par la seule famille de Jacob, et d'Abraham, le Diable y resistant par tous les Roys Idolâtres de ce temps là."

[1] III, 4.

[2] The battle referred to took place at Nieuport, July 2, 1600, only four years before the play was printed.

[3] Cf. Apocrypha, First Maccabees, IV.

[4] For the bibliography of these plays, see Appendix B, II.

A more important play on the same subject is *Jacob* by Anthoine de la Puiade (1604), written at the command of "la Royne Marguerite, Duchesse de Valois," the only one of these pieces that can claim a more than scholastic vogue. The author believes that he attains in the tragi-comedy a religious mean between the tragedy and the comedy, for, after declaring in his prologue that his work has nothing of "seuere enflé, comme en la Tragedie," nor "d'un Plaute gaudisseur l'outrageuse insolence. . . . Les tours de passe-passe et ruses d'un Terence," he states his position as follows:

> "Au vulgaire ignorant nous ne desirons plaire,
> Son humeur nous desplait, et nous luy desplaisons.
> Nous ne mendyons pas d'un rude populaire
> Une vaine loüange aux mots que nous disons.
> Mais c'est pour esgayer nostre grande Princesse."

The author has provided careful stage directions, choruses, and a "Musicien ioüant du luth et chantant." The first part of the tragi-comedy, written in a pleasingly natural style, shows decided dramatic qualities, in spite of its close adherence to the biblical narrative. In the fourth and fifth acts, on the other hand, the number of incidents in the story becomes too large for the author's dramatic skill, so that the play degenerates into a rapid succession of loosely connected scenes.

At the beginning of the play, Isaac enters with a staff in his hand, supported by Esau and Rebecca. When his wife has retired to the other end of the stage, Isaac promises to bless Esau, if he will bring him venison. The men retire, leaving Rebecca to soliloquize upon her desire to aid Jacob, who now enters, to be told his mother's plans. When he has been persuaded to deceive his father, he leaves the stage with his mother, whereupon Esau enters to inform the audience of his skill in the chase, which enables him to kill even the elephant. The chorus concludes the act by explaining that this is an allegory, in which Esau represents the Hebrews, Jacob the Church and Christ.

The second act follows closely the biblical account of the blessing of Jacob and his escape. The author has wisely introduced into his play the pathetic words of Esau, when he hears of his brother's trickery:

> "Mon pere donnés m'en une toute semblable
> Benissés vostre Aysné."

Isaac replies with characteristic weakness:

> "Ie ne puis autrement.
> Ton frere est ja benit, mais bien que finement
> C'est une grand prudence à luy d'auoir soustraite,
> La benediction que i'auoy toute preste,
> Pour en benir celuy qui s'offriroit à moy
> Et que ce soit Jacob, Dieu le veut, ie croy." [1]

Esau now curses his brother, but the chorus defends him sophistically, "pour auoir mis de Dieu le vouloir en effect."

The third act forms a digression in the play, as it is entirely concerned with the marriage of Esau to the daughter of Nabajot. In the fourth act Jacob enters, to lie down and sleep while the musician sings his vision as follows:

> "Iacob voit par une eschelle
> D'anges une troupe belle,
> Et descendre et remonter,
> Eschelle dont le mystere,
> Luy presage que son frere,
> Ne le pourra surmonter." [2]

The "Musique" now prophesies the blessings in store for Jacob, who awakes and tells what he has seen in the vision.

A second digression is made by a brief scene between shepherds and shepherdesses, which shows pastoral influence. In the next scene they point out Rachel to Jacob, who is well received by his relatives. The courtship follows, seven years pass by, and the marriage is arranged in a single scene. The shepherds celebrate the wedding in musical stanzas:

> Chantons en ce iour bien-heureux,
> Iacob le Pasteur amoureux
> De Rachel belle Pastourelle,
> O belle Pastourelle belle. [3]

---

[1] II, 1. [2] III, 1. [3] III, 3.

The ease with which periods of time could be passed over in such a drama as this, is shown in the fourth act, when Rachel gives Bala to Iacob, *exeunt omnes*, Iacob returns to be presented with Zylpha by Lya, whereupon Rachel enters with Bala's two children, followed by Lya with those of Zylpha, so that Jacob now finds himself the father of four children, who were not yet begot at the beginning of the scene. The rest of the play dramatizes faithfully the remainder of the biblical narrative down to the return of Jacob to his own land. The inartistic succession of disappearances and reappearances of the actors continues to mar the representation.

This play is particularly interesting from the light it throws upon the stage decoration used at this time in southern France. A *toile* covered the back of the stage, for Esau and Jacob are directed to retire behind it and Isaac to enter from behind it.[1] These passages indicate, furthermore, that one end of the *toile* represented a forest, toward which Esau and Jacob retire. As there is no mention of the presence of *mansions*, and as the chorus is obliged to inform the audience of Jacob's arrival at Bethel, it is likely that this feature of the medieval *mise en scène* was absent here. The actor progresses from one place to another by leaving the stage and returning, instead of walking from *mansion* to *mansion*, as was done on the older stage. Further attention is paid to the decoration by the stick, chair, and bed for Isaac,[2] and the *aigneaux et brebis* that follow Rachel on the stage.[3]

3. The Miracle as Tragi-Comedy.

The *miracle*, which draws its plot from the life of a saint, rather than from the Bible, is represented in this period by the following seven plays: *Saint Etienne* (1605), treating of the first king and christianizer of Hungary; *La Clotilde* (1613), concerning a miracle wrought by Saint Léonard de Limousin, friend of Clovis and Clotilde; *Henry et Kunegonde* (1616), based on the

[1] II, 1; III, 1; I. [2] I and II, 1. [3] III, 2.

deeds of Henry II, Emperor of Germany, and his wife Kunigunde; *Sainte Aldegonde* (1622), which takes its name from the Abbess of Maubenge, who lived in the seventh century; *Ignace de Loïola* (1622), in honor of the canonization of the founder of the Jesuits; *La vie et mort du glorieux Saint Lambert* (1628), which has to do with the seventh century bishop of Maestricht, who converted a part of the Netherlands and was said to have been murdered by emissaries of Pepin's second wife, whose marriage he had opposed; *Richecourt* (1628), in which the *dénouement* is accomplished by Saint Nicholas.[1]

With the exception of *La Clotilde* these plays were all written and printed in Belgium, Luxemburg, and neighboring towns of France. They were brief, priestly compositions, played by school-children and without influence on the tragi-comedies of Paris. I shall analyze two of them, thus, I hope, sufficiently showing the nature of the plays that belong to this class.

La Clotilde presents little of interest in subject, structure, or style. Clovis tells of his conversion by his wife Clotilde and the divine aid received in battle. Having defeated his enemies, he meditates pursuit of the Visigoths, against which Sigibert advises him, remarking with political sagacity worthy of the French classical tragedy:

> "Le salut des vaincus qu'un desespoir possede
> Est de n'esperer plus ne salut ne remede :
> On a veu tant de fois le vaincu prendre cœur
> Quand on le desespere, et vaincre son vainqueur." [2]

Clovis, however, convinced that God's will coincides with his own, decides to pursue the enemy, commanding that his determination be kept from Clotilde, as she is "enceinte de huict mois." In the next act, however, Clotilde persuades Clovis to take her with him on the expedition. When the king goes hunting, Clotilde fears that he has abandoned her and faints into the arms of her *nourrice*. A page, going to inform the king of his wife's

[1] For the bibliography of these plays see Appendix B, II.

[2] I, 2.

condition, makes known the whole matter to Saint Leonard, who lives in the wood where the king hunts. When Clovis returns home, he finds that the physician has despaired of Clotilde's life and advises an operation to save the child. Clovis wishes to pray to Pluto and Proserpine. Clotilde laments:

> "Ie voy le vaisseau prest, et le nocher Charon
> Qui tient la perche en main pour passer l'Acheron.
> I'entends comme il m'appelle, et comme des la riue
> Il me tançe, et me dict que ie suis trop tardive."[1]

Saint Leonard, arriving opportunely, rebukes them for their heathen expressions, makes them repent, and teaches them how to pray. In the fifth act the physician informs the audience of the miracle wrought by Saint Leonard in so praying for Clotilde, that she was not only cured, but happily delivered of a son. Clovis and Clotilde thank God and offer a bishopric to Saint Leonard, who declines the honor, but accepts as much land as "i'en entourneray durant la nuict obscure," which shall be to him and his, untaxed forever. The play ends with preparations for the foundation of a monastery upon this tract of land.

Still more scholastic in character is *Richecourt*, represented and printed in 1628. The argument states that the play celebrates events that took place toward the year 1240, when the Duke of Lorraine led an army to Palestine, where he was defeated and his follower, Richecourt, captured. The latter's miraculous escape from prison by the aid of Saint Nicholas forms the *dénouement* of the play. In the first act a *Chrestien de Iudee* and a *Trouppe chrestienne de Iudee* mourn over the unhappy condition of the Holy Land, while awaiting aid from France. The chorus comforts them with the hope of victory. A *Maistre de camp Turc* expresses his hatred of the Christians, whom he calls upon his followers to attack, while the chorus bids *Sion* lament.

In the second act Richecourt enters with his men, crying:

> "Que fais-tu, mon trenchant,
> Qui le prophane sang ne vas point espanchant
> En enyurant le pré? Encor le More encore

[1] IV, 3.

> Va bravant nostre nom, l'Otomannique More
> Se panade de nous. Or ce glaive d'acier
> I'empourpreray du sang de cest Othoman fier,
> Et le verray tranchant distiller de ses veines."

The act is continued by the threats of Nemesis, Alecto, and Mors, who, with the exception of Mors, employ Latin exclusively. After a chorus of soldiers have expressed their martial ardor, a battle is fought, which ends in the defeat of the Christians and the capture of Richecourt. The *Bachas* decide to imprison him, while the chorus of angels welcome the souls of the dead Christians and the furies carry off the Turks, slain in battle.

After a digression in which Mors takes away an old man who wishes to live and neglects one who wishes to die, Richecourt is represented, calling on Saint Nicholas for aid, despite the taunts of his captors. By a series of cleverly constructed echo rimes the saint promises his aid to Richecourt, when he begs to be freed from captivity :

> "Pour revoir de Nancy la belle et riche cour.
> Echo : Richecour.
> Richecourt : Entend-je pas le son de quelque voix humaine ?
> Ou si mon geolier par icy se pourmeine,
> Qui se gabe de moy ? ô Dieu ! ou si c'est toy,
> Ou bien si l'echo vient consoler mon esmoy ?
> Echo : moy.
> . . . .
> Richecourt : Chere voix, que veux tu ? helas ceste esclavage
> Me sera de la mort l'infortuné passage.
> Echo : tu n'es pas sage."

This dialogue continues till the hero learns that he will soon be rescued from prison. The next act finds him, accordingly, before the *Chappelle du Prieuré au Bourg de S. Nicolas de Port*, of which the doors are miraculously opened for him, to the astonishment of the sacristan and prior. A third miracle is performed when the iron chains of his prison drop from him. It is these chains, which "se voyent encores en l'Eglise du dict Sainct," that furnish the pious proof of the authenticity of the miracle.

4. The Farce as Tragi-Comedy.

This class of tragi-comedy is the farthest removed from the *romanesque* type of the *genre.* The few plays that belong to it may be called tragi-comedies as they are survivals of the medieval stage with happy *dénouement* and a partially classical form, shown by the use of Alexandrines or the division into acts. There are only four of them in both sixteenth and seventeenth centuries, of which one, *La nouvelle tragicomique,* has already been discussed.[1]

The *Tragi-Comedie de la rebellion ou mescontentement des Grenouilles contre Jupiter* is based on the fable of the frogs who asked a king of Jupiter. La Vallière[2] remarks that "il devoit être cependant assez plaisant de voir des Acteurs, croassant dans un marais, en sortir pour monter à l'Olimpe, et en habit de grenouilles, plaider leur cause devant Jupiter et toute sa Cour." The moral of the piece inculcates the patient acceptance of monarchical rule:

> "Et tels que sont les Rois que l'Eternel nous donne,
> Il leur faut obéir et chérir leur personne."

In still lighter vein are the *Tragi-Comedie plaisante et facecieuse intitulée La Subtilité de Fanfreluche et Gaudichon et comme il fut emporté par le Diable,* a pure farce based on the Italian models, in which Fanfreluche plays the rôle of Pulcinella; and the *Tragi-Comedie des enfans de Turlupin, où l'on void les fortunes dudit Turlupin, le mariage d'entre luy et la Boulonnoise, et autres mille plaisantes ioyeusetez qui trompent la morne Oisiveté,* a play that is chiefly interesting on account of the introduction of Henri Legrand, the famous actor, under his sobriquet of Turlupin.

B. Characterization.

The small reputation gained by the *non-romanesque* tragi-comedies written between 1600 and 1628 is shown by the fact that out of eighteen plays, nine are anonymous and the others were

[1] See above, p. 70. For the bibliography of the other three plays see Appendix B, II.

[2] I, 453.

written by men of whom little more than the name is known. Anthoine de la Puiade "Conseiller et Secretaire des finances" of Marguerite de Valois, is known as the author of *La Christiade, La Mariade,*[1] and other religious poems. François Auffray, *Gentilhomme Breton,* may be the same as Auffray, *Chanoine de Saint Brieuc,* who translated *Hymnes ou cantiques sacrez à la gloire de Dieu.*[2] Anthoine Lancel, Amédée, and Candide were schoolmasters. Iean Prevost, a lawyer of Basse-Marche, wrote *Le Bocage, L'Apothéose de Henri IV,* and several tragedies. Denis Coppée and Iean Gaulché are known to have been born toward 1570 at Huy[3] and Vitry-le-Croisé,[4] respectively. Simplicien Gody, the probable author of *Richecourt,* was a monk of the *Congrégation de Saint-Vanne,* who wrote *Odes sacrées* (1629), a Latin tragedy called *Humbertus* (1633), and other poems.[5]

The plays were published at Bordeaux, Poitiers, Rouen, Troyes, and several towns in Belgium. Most of them were acted by children at schools of the Jesuits, Barnabites, or Benedictines, situated in Savoy, Belgium, and northeastern France.

La Clotilde appears to have been acted by a *confrérie* from the author's introductory statement, "Je l'entrepris et dressay à la sollicitation du sieur Chalart, bourgeois de Saint-Léonard."[6] The *Jacob* of La Puiade, written for Marguerite de Valois, and probably acted before her, shows no connection with a school. The occurrence of the name, Turlupin, indicates that the *Enfans de Turlupin* was acted. *Zo'anthropie* is shown to have been acted by mention of the audience and by the printing with the play of "vers présentés à quelques Messieurs de l'assistance."[6] The only remaining plays are *L'Amour divin* and *L'union Belgique,* of which there is nothing to show that the first was acted, but the second is provided with a prologue and epilogue addressed to the audience, which do not, however, prove that the play was

[1] Paris, 1604, and Paris, 1605.

[2] Saint-Brieux, 1623.

[3] Faber, IV, 267.

[4] Louis Morin, *Théâtre à Troyes, Bulletin historique et philologique,* 1901, p. 25.

[5] Beaupré, *Richecourt, Tragi-Comédie,* note at the end of the reprint, Saint-Nicolas-de-Port, 1860.

[6] Cf. Lanson, *Revue d'hist. litt.,* x, 224–25.

acted, as they may be the result of literary imitation. In any case, it is evident that nearly all, if not all the tragi-comedies of this *non-romanesque* group were acted, a fact that shows the popularity of the *genre* even in forms that must have seemed antiquated in the seventeenth century.

In all these plays, except the farces, appears a religious spirit which unites them to the tragi-comedies of the sixteenth rather than to others of the seventeenth century. The primary object of the plays is, accordingly, instruction instead of amusement, the usual goal of the tragi-comic author. In accordance with their religious and didactic spirit, the sources of the plays are taken from the Bible, including the Apocrypha, dramatized directly or allegorically; from medieval history, distorted for pious ends when saints are concerned; and from contemporary history, allegorically treated.[1]

The strong feeling of patriotism pervading *L'union Belgique* becomes local pride in *La Clotilde, Saincte Aldegonde, Lambertiade,* and *Richecourt,* the subjects of which concern the deeds of the authors' saintly compatriots. The author of *Richecourt* puts into the mouths of the Turks praise of the "Gaulois triomphans," for

> "Ils s'estendent puissans par tous les champs du monde
> A guise d'un torrent, qui ravisseux inonde
> Sur les guerets voisins."[2]

The plays show little merit in construction, violating not only the unity of action, but by digressions even the unity of interest. In the fifth act of *L'Amour divin* digressions occur in conversations between the protagonist and two of his sisters; in *Jacob,* the third act is given up to Esau's courtship, with which Jacob has nothing to do; in *Richecourt* a scene that has no connection with the plot of the play is acted by Death and two old men. The lack of restriction as to place and time is best shown by *Jacob,* where the action lasts over twenty years, and by *Richecourt,* the scene of which is laid in Palestine and Lorraine.

[1] *L'union Belgique,* the only play based on contemporary history, may be compared with *Garnier Stoffacher, La Gaule,* and *Fernandus Servatus.*

[2] I.

The treatment of character is slight in most of these plays and can scarcely be said to exist in the farces. The abstractions, most fully represented in *L'Amour divin* and *Zo'anthropie*, are in *L'union Belgique* largely replaced by types that approach them closely; as, *Le Iesuite, L'Espagnol, Le bon Patriot, L'Historiographe.* The personages in these *moralités* are still near the medieval vices and virtues, with the weak protagonist, here seen in *Physique* and *Anthrope.* The consistent character of these personages is lacking in the treatment of Richecourt, who suddenly changes from a blustering warrior to a pious monk. Some skill is shown in the impetuous character of Clotilde in the play that bears her name. Perhaps the best scenes are those at the beginning of *Jacob*, where the patriarchal family is well described after the biblical model. The rank of the personages is allowed the variation characteristic of tragi-comedies. Kings appear in *L'Amour divin, Saint Etienne, La Clotilde, Henry et Kunégonde;* a physician in *La Clotilde;* shepherds in *Jacob.* Besides the personages that fall into the three social classes thus represented, are found the abstractions, which defy such classification.

The style of the plays has as little to recommend it as the treatment of character found in them. Prosaic and platitudinous in *L'Amour divin* and *La Clotilde*, it becomes inflated in *Zo'anthropie* and *Richecourt.* In *Jacob* it is less pretentious and consequently more agreeable, displaying at times a pleasing naïveté. A shepherdess declares:

"Non Berger ce n'est pas toy
Que i'ayme et que ie prise:
Cesse ton entreprise,
Tu es trop laid pour moy:
Car i'ayme un beau Pasteur,
De qui ie suis entreprise,
Qui m'a rauy le cœur." [1]

In contrast with these lines stand the following:

"Tel est digne dit-on que celui porte trompe
Qui trompe le trompeur lequel un autre trompe" [2]

---

[1] III, 2.

[1] *L'union Belgique*, II, 1

> "Richecourt ! bien plustost pauvre-court, qui ne peux
> Esgaller à tes maux ton discours souspireux." [1]

The *précieux* spirit of these lines is further evidenced by the large amount of Latin used in *Richecourt* and by the ponderous compound adjectives of such expressions as "Mores porte-carquois," "bras gaigne-lauriers," "tranche-fer acier," "cœur souffle-feux," "l'astre guide-nef." [2]

Despite the didactic spirit of many of the plays, there seems to have been a desire for variety in the minds of some of the authors, which is manifested by the occasional use of lyric verse-forms and comic passages. Thus, the chorus in *Jacob* recites verses of eight syllables, alternating lines of twelve and six syllables, and a strophe composed of lines of eight, six, and twelve syllables. In *Richecourt* the chorus of Christians uses six-syllable verse; that of angels and *vaincus* eight-syllable verse; that of *bourgeois*, twelve- and eight-syllable verse; that of soldiers the following complicated measure:

> "Le Monarque d'Orient
> Se riant
> De nostre Mars, est en calme;
> Allons, courons, foudroyons,
> Et noyons
> Au sang ce voleur de palme,
> Don, don, don, don, don, à l'assaut;
> Pour le ciel mourir il nous faut.
> Çà, çà, soldats
> Armez vos bras, etc." [3]

The chorus in *La Clotilde* is only a band of men, who first appear in the last act, when they speak in Alexandrines. *Zo'anthropie* has no chorus, but shows metrical variety in an eight-syllable dialogue between *Le bon Genie* and Philothee [4] and in Zoé's lamentation after she has lost Anthrope.[5] *Jacob*, besides frequent prose passages, departs from the Alexandrine in the seven-syllable speech of the musician and in the shepherds' use of six- and eight-syllable lines.[6] The latter form recurs with

[1] *Richecourt*, IV. [2] *Ibidem*, I and IV.
[3] II. [4] IV, 2. [5] IV, 4. [6] I and III, 1.

musical accompaniment upon the patriarch's return to Bethel.[1] In *Richecourt* a further metrical variety is shown by Mors, who recites couplets of twelve-, ten-, eight-, six-syllable verses. The echo rimes of this play have been quoted.[2] They are found again in *Zo'anthropie*.[3]

Such metrical variety is in keeping with the usage of the *romanesque* tragi-comedy and probably added to the popularity of the *genre*. Short verse forms are freely employed for musical passages, represented by a chorus, a lamentation, or a communication from angels or Death. The usual meter of the plays, however, is the Alexandrine, but verses of ten syllables are employed in *Enfans de Turlupin*. This play and the *Rebellion des Grenouilles* show further irregularity by a division into four acts instead of the usual five acts. *Purification du temple de Jérusalem* has only three acts.

The *dénouements* of these plays are happy, as the stories are brought to a successful termination, as far as the happiness of the protagonist is concerned. Even the *Lambertiade* forms no exception to this, for the saint's death cannot be considered an unhappy event, as the author's object is to show the heavenly reward won for the saint by his holy life and pious death.

Comic scenes are not confined to the farcical tragi-comedies, but appear also in *L'union Belgique, Zo'anthropie*, and *Richecourt*. In the first of these occurs the following dialogue between two priests:

"Pere Pillart: Ha Salve Domine frere en Dieu soul de lard.
Soul-de-lard: Gratia Domine Pasteur Pere-pillart.
P. P.: Soul-de-lard qu'avés vous?
S.-d.-l.: Ie pantelle de joye,
D'autant que l'Archeduc pour nostre bien s'employe.
. . . .
Allons faire bouillir nostre Marmite grasse.
Sus resjouissons nous malgré les roupieux,
Car d'ici à cent ans nous serons morts ou vieux." [4]

The comic elements in *Zo'anthropie* appear in a coarse dialogue

[1] v, 1. [2] See above, p. 93. [3] v, *Scène dernière*. [4] IV, 6.

between Phronime and Idoneon,[1] and in the account of the rescue of Oecomene from the water, whence he comes up "chargé de pots de terre et d'argent."[2] A grim humor is shown in the dialogue between Death and two old men in *Richecourt*, which furnishes a good example of the mingling of the serious and the comic:

"La Mort: Dea! i'ay cy rencontré un vieillard en desbauche.
Deuxiesme Vieillard: Ie ne suis pas si vieil, n'estant point soustenu
D'aucun noüeux baston.
L. M.: Te voy-ie pas chenu,
Et le poil imitant la blanchissante laine
Et la neige qui chet en hyuer sur la plaine?
D. V.: C'est mon, si tu avois des lunettes au né
Tu verrois bien que i'ay le poil enfariné
Du moulin, non de l'aage: et pourtant tire arrière.
L. M.: Non, non, il faut passer, et boucler ta carrière.
D. V.: Ou il m'en coustera la vie, ou ie verray
Plus de trente soleils, et à mon saoul boiray.
O! que ie ne suis pas encor prest de te suivre,
Tandis que ce flacon me fera ioyeux viure.
L. M.: Tu as beau reculer, et esperer du temps,
Le moment est venu qui bornera tes ans.
D. V.: A bon ieu?
L. M.: C'est bon ieu, et mon ieu quand ie frappe.
C'est trop tergiuersé; ça, ça que ie t'attrape.
D. V.: Si tost.
L. M.: Tout de pas allons.
D. V.: Si brusquement?
Auray-ie pas pour boire au moins quelque moment?
L. M.: Autant que i'en mettray à faire ma faulchée.
D. V.: Ie meurs, ie meurs, ie meurs.
L. M.: Ainsi va ta fusée."[3]

This review of the *non-romanesque* tragi-comedy indicates that it existed between the years 1600 and 1628 as a belated survival of the sixteenth-century tragi-comedy, of which it retains the sources, construction, and form. While the sixteenth-century plays are of value as furnishing the link between the medieval play and the *romanesque* tragi-comedy of the seventeenth century, these late, *non-romanesque* plays exert no such influence and are

[1] II, 2. [2] V, *Scène dernière.* [3] III.

consequently of interest only as showing the persistence of a dramatic form that had been the true expression of an earlier age, but made small appeal to an audience of the seventeenth century. The recurrence of such plays decreases with the progress of the century, for the last *moralité* called a tragi-comedy appeared in 1614, the last *mystère* in 1609. The *miracle* flourished throughout the period, but only as a school composition, absolutely without influence in Paris. Very different is the history of the *romanesque* tragi-comedy, which is now to be considered.

II. The Romanesque Tragi-Comedy.

Between the years 1600 and 1628, the *romanesque* type of tragi-comedy not only became the predominant form of the *genre*, but was raised by Hardy and his contemporaries to the position of the most popular and extensively written form of dramatic production in France. As Hardy wrote some seven hundred plays and about half his extant plays are called tragi-comedies,[1] it is probable that between three and four hundred tragi-comedies came from his pen alone. He was followed by several writers, Du Ryer, Mairet, Schelandre, Pichou, and others, who, while not equalling his fertility, surpassed him in the excellence of individual plays and prepared the way for the notable success won by the *genre* between 1628 and the middle of the century.

In the following pages the tragi-comedies written by these authors[2] will be analyzed, their sources given, and their structure discussed. As Hardy's plays have been fully treated by Rigal,[3] their discussion here will be brief. After the analyses of his works will have been given in the order of their publication, those of the tragi-comedies written by his contemporaries will follow chronologically. The characterization of the more general qualities

[1] Hardy places the number at six hundred some years before his death. Rigal estimates the total at seven hundred. If *Aristoclée* be classed as a tragedy and the eight *journées* of *Theagene et Cariclée* as eight plays, the number of his extant tragi-comedies is twenty-one, out of a total of forty-one extant plays.

[2] For the bibliography of these plays see Appendix B, II.

[3] In *Alexandre Hardy.*

possessed in common by several or all of the tragi-comedies will not be taken up until all of the individual plays have been analyzed.

A. Analyses and Sources.

Theagenes and Chariclea, the Greek romance of Heliodorus, is the source[1] of eight plays of five acts by Alexandre Hardy, which, together, form the eight *journées* of his *Theagene et Cariclée*. In the first *journée* the Egyptian, Calasire, aids the lovers, after whom the play is named, to fly from Delphi and its high-priest, Charicle, who wishes to marry his supposed daughter, Cariclée, to another than Theagene. Shipwrecked on an island, Calasire and the lovers are captured by pirates, whose chief prepares to wed Cariclée. Another pirate, however, persuaded by Calasire of Cariclée's love, seeks to take her from the leader. In the fight that ensues all the pirates are slain except one, who is promptly despatched by Theagene.

A second band of pirates, arriving in the next *journée*, capture the lovers, who represent themselves as brother and sister. Thiamis, leader of the band, gives them to Gnémon for safe keeping until he can find a temple in which to marry Cariclée. When he is defeated in battle, he seeks to kill Cariclée, but mistakes another woman for her, so that she escapes. In the third *journée* Theagene is captured by the soldiers of Orondate, a governor under the king of Egypt, while Cariclée escapes with the aid of Gnémon to Nausicle, a friend of Calasire. In the fourth *journée* Calasire is reunited to Cariclée, but Theagene is recaptured by Thiamis, now seeking to regain the priesthood of Memphis. But Calasire shows that he is the father of Thiamis, resumes his position as priest, and reunites Theagene and Cariclée.

In the fifth *journée* Arsace, wife of Orondate, falls in love with Theagene and imprisons him for refusing to yield to her demands. In the following *journée* she seeks to have Cariclée burnt, but the

[1] Through Amyot's translation, *Histoire Aethiopique de Heliodorus* (Paris, 1547). Cf. Rigal, *Alexandre Hardy*, 435. In the same work the sources of Hardy's other tragi-comedies are also established. For references see Appendix B, II.

flames flee from her. The lovers, led away to Orondate, are captured by soldiers of Hydaspes, king of Ethiopia. This monarch conquers Orondate in the next *journée* and decides to sacrifice Theagene and Cariclée to the gods. In the eighth *journée*, however, Cariclée proves by tokens in her possession that she is the daughter of Hydaspes, exposed in infancy because her white skin offered so great a contrast to her father's Ethiopian hue that her mother had feared to acknowledge her as her daughter. Now she is welcomed by her parents, but Hydaspe still wishes to sacrifice Theagene. After various persons have protested against this barbarity, ambassadors arrive opportunely from Thessaly, seeking their lost prince. Theagene, thus proved to be of royal blood, is set free and married to Cariclée.

This play, or series of plays, furnishes an excellent example of the system employed in tragi-comedies, in which a story is dramatized *ab ovo,* without unity of action and consisting of a series of episodes, united by interest in the welfare of the lovers. The time that elapses during the progress of the story is about two years, of which individual *journées* are assigned from a few days to several months. The scene is laid at Delphi, in Egypt, and on an island between these two localities. In the individual *journées* it is less extensive, but is never confined within classical limits.

Hardy's first three tragi-comedies after *Theagene et Cariclée* hold, by reason of their mythological and half-tragic subjects, a mid-position between his tragedies and other tragi-comedies. Their author seems to have realized that they might be placed in either *genre,* for in *Procris* he writes *tragedie* at the top of the alternate pages and in the argument, though in the heading of the play and of the argument he writes *tragi-comedie.* Similarly, *Alceste* and *Ariadne Rauie* are called tragedies at the tops of the pages and in the headings of the arguments, but tragi-comedies in the titles. The chief objection to considering them tragi-comedies is furnished by their mythological plots, which occur in no other tragi-comedies except the *Travaux d'Ulysse* (1631). Rigal cannot be criticized for classifying them apart from both tragedies and tragi-comedies.

The plot of *Alceste* has been given above,[1] where it was compared with the play of Euripides which treats the same subject. In *Procris* Aurore seeks to induce Cephale, the hunter, to forsake for her charms his wife, Procris, daughter of the King of Athens. He agrees to do so, provided his wife is proved unfaithful. Disguised as a traveller, he visits Procris, whom he finds indignant at the neglect she is receiving from her husband. He wooes her and, after succeeding in making her waver in her fidelity, reveals his identity, only to heap reproaches upon her. He now indulges Aurore's desire, but is seen by an ox-herd, who informs Procris and brings her to the place where Cephale awaits the goddess. Seeing a movement in the bushes, Cephale shoots an arrow and hits Procris, who dies in his arms, insisting that he is not to blame. Full of remorse, he is prevented from suicide by Aurore, whose love will comfort him now that the only obstacle to its gratification has been removed.

Ariadne Rauie begins with a council, held by Minos to take measures for the pursuit of his daughters and Thesee. The scene is changed to the island of Naxos, where Phalare persuades Thesee to transfer his affections from Ariadne to her sister, Phœdre. Thesee and his new love then leave the island, on which Ariadne laments her abandonment and attempts suicide. She is comforted by Bacchus, however, who marries her upon his return with Pan and Silene from the conquest of the East.

The sources of these three plays are found in Euripides's *Alcestis* and in Ovid's *Ars Amatoria*, *Metamorphoses*, and *Heroides*.[2] The double plot and consequent violation of the unities in *Alceste* have been noted above.[3] The action in *Procris* is also double, as it is concerned with the fate of Procris for her own sake, as well as with the accomplishment of the desires of Aurore and Cephale. The second scene of the first act, furthermore, violates the unity of action, for it consists of a dialogue between Thiton and Pritame, which plays no part in the development of the plot. In *Ariadne Rauie* there are three independent actions, concerned, respectively,

[1] P. 18.

[2] For references see Rigal, *Alexandre Hardy*, 401, 410.

[3] P. 18.

with the council of Minos, the desertion of Ariadne by Thesee and Phœdre, and the rescue of Ariadne by Bacchus. The unities of place and time are similarly violated, for the time of *Procris* and *Ariadne Rauie* is several days, of *Alceste* several months, at least; the place of *Procris* is the house of Cephale and several localities in a forest; of *Ariadne Rauie*, Crete and Naxos; of *Alceste*, Sparta, Thessaly, and Hades.

From Lucian's *Toxaris* Hardy drew the plot of *Arsacome*, in which Leucanor, *roy du Bosphore*, chooses a husband for his daughter, Masée, from among princes of the neighboring countries. To promote their suits, Adimache and Tigrapate boast of their wealth, valor, and renown, but Arsacome, who is loved by Masée, only of his two trusty friends. Adimache is chosen by the king, who laughs Arsacome to scorn. When the latter, however, retires to Scythia and tells his two friends of his humiliation, they prove that they are more valuable than the possessions of Arsacome's rivals, for one slays Leucanor, while the other aids Masée to escape from her father's palace to the arms of Arsacome, to whom she is quickly married. The time of the action is several months; the scene is laid in Bosphore, Scythie, and the land of the Malliens; the unity of action is violated chiefly in the manner in which the play follows the story, dramatizing the king's choice of Adimache as well as the deeds of Arsacome's friends. The unity of the play suffers through the absence of a protagonist, a title that cannot well be applied either to Arsacome, or to his two friends, who, more than he, bring about the *dénouement*.

Cornelie is based on Cervantes's *Novela de la Señora Cornelia.*[1] The heroine, from whom the play takes its name, has been seduced by Alphonse, Duke of Ferrara, who intends to marry her, but hesitates till after a child is born. By her maid's mistake the infant is given one night to Dom Iuan de Galboa, whose friend, Dom Anthoine Isunça rescues Cornelie, wandering from home for fear of her cousin, Bentivole. The mother and child are reunited at the home of the two friends. Meanwhile Dom Iuan rescues Alphonse from the vengeance of Bentivole and learns

[1] *Novelas exemplares*, IV.

from Cornelie the story of her love for Alphonse. Visiting the latter, he finds him anxious to marry Cornelie and easily makes peace between him and Bentivole. The happiness of the lovers is delayed, however, by the flight of Cornelie, who still fears Bentivole, to a hermitage, where she is subsequently discovered and married to Alphonse. The unity of action is violated by the double nature of the plot, concerned with the separation and reunion of mother and child as well as of the two lovers, by a digression in the fourth scene of the fourth act, and by the fresh complications introduced toward the end of the play by the flight of Cornelie. The duration of time is at least a number of days; the scene is laid in various localities in and near Bologna.

Hardy again made use of Cervantes in *La Force du Sang*, derived from the *Novela de la Fuerza de la Sangre.*[1] Alphonse, a Spanish hidalgo, carries off and ravishes Leocadie. He is shortly afterward sent by his father, Dom Inigue, to travel in Italy and France, where he feels remorse for his crime and would atone for it. Meanwhile Leocadie gives birth to a boy, who, seven years later, is knocked down in a crowd and rescued by Dom Inigue. The latter sees the family likeness in his newly found grandson and subsequently establishes his identity, when the boy's mother recognizes the room in which she has been ravished. Dom Inigue and Leocadie's parents arrange a marriage between her and Alphonse, who now returns from his travels to consent gladly to the union. Two actions are dramatized in this play: the first concerned with the commission of Alphonse's crime, the second with its atonement. The scene is laid in both Spain and Italy. The time is about eight years.

In *Felismene*, a tragi-comedy based on the *Diana* of Montemayor, Dom Felix, sent by his father from Spain to Germany in order that he may not marry the beautiful, but humbly born Felismene, with whom he is in love, is followed by this young woman, who disguises herself as a page and enters into the service of her lover. She is employed by him to arrange an interview with Celie, a German Princess, whom Dom Felix now loves. Celie rejects

[1] *Novelas exemplares*, II.

Felix's proposals, but falls in love with Felismene in her disguise as a page and dies of grief when she finds that the latter does not return her passion. Felix is accused of murdering Celie, while Felismene is unable to explain the true situation to him, for fear that he may suspect her of having murdered her rival. She accordingly becomes a shepherdess, and has the good fortune to rescue Dom Felix from his enemies by means of her darts. He at once arranges to marry his rescuer. The numerous episodic adventures that occur in this play destroy the unity of its action. The time is several months. The scene is laid in Spain and Germany.

Dorise is based on the *Histoires des Amants volages*[1] of François de Rosset. Salmacis and Licanor, Persian nobles, love Dorise, beautiful, but poor. She and the wealthy Sydere love Salmacis, who is obliged to go on a journey. Licanor and Sydere take advantage of his absence by telling Dorise that he has boasted of having possessed her. Convinced that Salmacis has thus slandered her, Dorise tears up his letter, an action that, when told him, makes him retire to a hemitage. Licanor now succeeds in winning the hand of Dorise, while Sydere, by the aid of a *magicienne* obtains that of Salmacis. The unity of action, as well as that of interest, is here violated by the double nature of the plot, which relates the fortunes of four lovers instead of two, and by the introduction of the *magicienne*, a *deus ex machinâ.* The scene is laid in the houses of the lovers and in a hermitage some distance away. The time is a number of days, at least.

Fregonde is derived from Diego Agreda's *Doce Novelas morales y ejemplares.*[2] The marquis de Cotron, after an unsuccessful attempt at seducing Fregonde, wife of Dom Yuan, conquers his passion and secures the husband a military command. Moved by Dom Yuan's praise of the marquis, Fregonde regrets her coldness toward the latter and intimates to him her change of heart. The marquis, however, resists her advances, but shortly afterward, when Dom Yuan is killed in battle by the Turks, he renews his

[1] Paris, 1619.
[2] Valencia, 1620. Translated into French by J. Baudoin, Paris, 1621.

suit and readily wins Fregonde, moved by her own inclination and the command of her husband's ghost. The action is divided into three parts, the marquis's courtship of Fregonde, the latter's courtship of the marquis, and the incidents following the death of her husband, an event similar to the action of a *deus ex machinâ*. Furthermore, a digression is made in the third scene of the third act, which does not advance the action. The scene is laid at Naples and on the coast of Calabria. The time is a month or more.

Hardy drew upon Boccaccio[1] for the plot of *Gesippe ou les Deux Amis*, which concerns the friendship of the Athenian Gesippe and the Roman Tite. The former, about to be married to Sophronie, insists on yielding the girl to his friend, when he finds that the latter loves her. Tite, after some remonstrance, consents to pass the night with her in Gesippe's stead. In the morning Sophronie is horrified to discover the imposture, but Gesippe continues his demonstrations of friendship by arranging a marriage between Tite and Sophronie, who leave Athens for Rome. After some time Gesippe, greatly reduced in fortune, seeks aid from Tite, who fails to recognize him when they meet at Rome. Gesippe, thinking that Tite despises him, retires to a cave to die. In the cave two robbers quarrel over stolen property and one of them slays the other. Gesippe, arrested for the crime, declares himself guilty, but, when brought before the senate, he is recognized by Tite, become senator, who seeks to rescue him by declaring the murder to be his own deed. The ensuing contest in generosity is ended by the guilty robber, who confesses his crime before the senate. Gesippe is released, enriched by Tite, and married to the latter's sister. That all may be happy, the robber is pardoned by virtue of his voluntary confession. The action of this play is evidently double, as it is concerned, first, with Gesippe's sacrifice and Tite's marriage, then, with the adventures of Gesippe at Rome. The time must extend over some years, the place includes Athens and Rome.

[1] *Decameron*, x, 8.

Giraldi Cinthio[1] furnished the source of *Phraarte,* in which the son of the King of Macedon loves Philagnie, daughter of Cotys, King of Thrace. War is declared between these two countries because of an attempt made by two women, agents of Cotys, to poison Philippe of Macedon. His son Phraarte, by freeing the women from prison, secures their influence with Philagnie, who now allows him to possess her. Philippe, victorious over Cotys, takes from him all but one city, in which the latter is besieged by Phraarte, captured, and imprisoned for the supposed murder of Philagnie. She, however, with her new-born infant has taken refuge at a peasant's house. On hearing of the Macedonian victory, she hastens to Phraarte, who receives her joyfully, frees her father, and gives him back his kingdom. The lovers are married and Phraarte is acknowledged heir to the throne of Thrace. The events in this play are ordered as in a novel, with the story told from the beginning. The action is double, concerned with the courtship of Philagnie and her restoration to Phraarte. The time is a year or more. The scene is laid at various localities in Thrace and Macedon.

The plot of *Elmire* is drawn from the *Deuxiesme volume des Méditations historiques de M. Philippe Camerarius,* translated from Latin into French by Simon Goulart.[2] The Comte de Gleichen, imprisoned in Egypt, refuses to accept his liberty at the price of turning Mahometan, but consents to escape with Elmire, daughter of the Sultan, who loves him and whom he agrees to marry, if the Pope will grant him an indulgence to have two wives. Meanwhile the comtesse, left in Germany, resists the solicitations of the marquis de Bade and remains faithful to her husband. When Gleichen reaches Rome, he has no difficulty in obtaining his indulgence, and marries Elmire. On his return to Germany the two wives become devoted friends, each insisting on yielding Gleichen to the other. He arranges, however, to divide his time

[1] *Cent excellentes nouvelles de M. Jean Baptiste Giraldy Cynthien . . . Mis d'Italien en François par Gabriel Chappuys Tourangeau.* Paris, 1584.

[2] Lyon, 1610. Rigal, *Alexandre Hardy,* 239, has shown that the story is not told by Camerarius, but added by the translator, who got it from André Honsdorf, *Théâtre d'exemples.*

equally between them. In this story two plots are interwoven concerning the bigamy of Gleichen and his wife's resistance of the marquis de Bade. The time is about a year. The scene is laid in Egypt, Italy, and Germany.

Hardy returned to Cervantes in *La Belle Egyptienne,* which is derived from the *Novela de la Gitanilla.*[1] Dom Iean de Carcame joins the gipsies in order to marry Precieuse, one of their number. He easily surpasses his rival Clement, but is troubled by Carduche, a wealthy *bourgeoise,* who wishes to marry him. When he refuses her on the ground that a gipsy cannot marry a woman of another race, she accuses him of theft and pretends to find jewels in his wallet. In the disturbance that follows, Iean kills a soldier who has struck him, is arrested and taken before a judge, who fortunately turns out to be the father of Precieuse, stolen by the gipsies when a child and now recognized by marks on her body. Iean reveals his identity, finds that the judge is a friend of his father, is released and married to Precieuse after a mock-sentence of death has been passed upon him. There is little dramatic unity in this play, as the incidents of the story are narrated one after another with small regard to a central action. The incident of Clement's rivalry has nothing to do with the development of the plot. The scene is laid near Madrid and Seville and in Estramadura. The time is several months.

The first *romanesque* tragi-comedy of the seventeenth century extant from another pen than Hardy's is *L'Aymée, jeu tragecomique* (1601), a slight composition, written to be played after a banquet, if one may draw any conclusions from the opening lines:

> "Apres ceste table levée
> Où les tiens ont beu à qui mieux."

The lack of incidents and total absence of intrigue make this play a very exceptional tragi-comedy, which shows in its lyric measures and the character of its personages the influence of the pastoral, although no shepherds are introduced into it. The plot is probably due to the author's invention.

[1] *Novelas exemplares,* I.

The author states in his dedication that his aim is to contrast *l'amour sainct* with *l'amour charnel*, an object that is scarcely obvious from a reading of the play. Content is assured by a dream and by an echo that his love for Aymée, Diane's nymph, will be successful. Le Désespéré, on the other hand, laments extravagantly his unsuccessful love of this nymph. After Antoine, Content's valet, has humorously complained of his task of announcing to Aymée his master's visit, the lovers discuss philosophically the true nature of love and Content sings the praises of Aymée. Le Désespéré, rejected by Aymée, stabs himself, crying:

> "Sus donc, qu'un poignard m'ouvre au besoin la poitrine,
> La Parque me domine,
> Malheureux, je me jette aux ondes d'Achéron,
> Mais heureux, je verray et Styx et Phlegéton." [1]

Antoine discovers the suicide and buries the body. Diane fears that ill luck may come from this death, but Aymée reminds her that

> "Rien de mauvais n'arrive à ceux qui vivent bien
> Et ceux qui craignent Dieu d'ailleurs ne craignent rien." [2]

Songs by nymphs and the *paranymphe* follow in praise of love and marriage, accompanied by Antoine's more practical observations on the same subjects. After Content and Aymée have celebrated the power of love, an epithalamium is recited, and Aymée declares:

> "Par un baiser je t'ai donné mon âme:
> Par un baiser ta lèvre me le rend." [3]

The play is ended by Antoine "fort de ce qu'il a veu et ouy à la porte."

Although there is scarcely any plot to this play, the unity of action is violated by the incident of Le Désespéré, which does not influence the love-affair of Content and Aymée. The statements regarding the location and duration of the action are not clear, but it seems to take place in several neighboring localities and to last for several days, at least.

[1] III, 3. [2] IV, 1. [3] V, 3.

The next tragi-comedy is the *Lucelle* (1607) of Jacques Duhamel, a versified reprint of the *Lucelle* of Louis Le Jars.[1] As it follows its model closely, occasionally curtailing or expanding scenes, but not materially altering the plot or treatment, it is unnecessary to give its analysis here.

Two years later appeared *L'Ethiopique* by Octave-César Genetay, a play that is, like Hardy's *Theagene et Cariclée*,[2] based on the romance of Heliodorus. The play does not show the direct influence of Hardy's drama.[3] It is much more classical than this, for it has a chorus, a prologue, only five acts, a scene laid in a single town, and an action that covers a short space of time. The play begins with the meeting of Sisimetre, who had given Chariclée, when an infant, to Charicles at the command of her mother, Persine, Queen of Ethiopia, and Charicles, come to Egypt in pursuit of the same Chariclée, who has grown to womanhood and eloped with Theagene, Prince of Thessaly. Charicles relates the story of her flight, which here inspired the first *journée* of Hardy's drama. Sisimetre replies with the information that she and her lover have been condemned by Hydaspe, King of Ethiopia, to be sacrificed to the gods. Sisimetre now informs Chariclée that she is the daughter of Hydaspe and that her mother had wished her exposed lest her white complexion should cause her legitimacy to be suspected. He promises to save her with her lover. The third act is taken up with preparations for a combat between Theagene and a giant. Persine, informed that Chariclée is her daughter, rescues her from prison and learns of her wanderings, which had furnished the plot of six *journées* in Hardy's drama. The chorus, which ends each act, here discourses on the difference between

[1] See above, p. 62. [2] See above, page 102.

[3] That it is not based on Hardy's work is shown by the transliteration of the heroine's name, which is Cariclée in one and Chariclée in the other, both of which are due to the Greek writing with the letter *chi;* also by episodes that appear in Heliodorus and Genetay, but not in Hardy: as, for example, when Chariclée is offered in marriage to Merœbe in Heliodorus and Genetay, while that prince does not appear in Hardy; or when the giant, presented by ambassadors and barely mentioned in Hardy, is presented by Merœbe and treated at some length in Heliodorus and Genetay.

white and black races, promulgating the law of reversion to previous types:

> "Et si quelqu'un vient à naistre
> De teint qui soit different
> Il le tient de quelque ancestre
> Qui l'a eu tel apparent." [1]

Hydaspe, greatly pleased at the discovery of his daughter's identity, wishes to marry her to his nephew Merœbe, but he is determined to sacrifice Theagene, who has just overthrown the giant and a bull. He regrets that the sacrifice is necessary, adding:

> "Mais quoy? la loy le veut et mon vœu solennel,
> Et faut que vous soyez immolé sur l'autel:
> Prenez pourtant bon cœur; vostre mort honorable
> Sera de temps en temps entre nous memorable." [2]

Charicles now arrives, demanding vengeance on Theagene for carrying off Chariclée. He is well received and assured of Theagene's approaching end. Chariclée begs for his life and, when Hydaspe continues inexorable, follows her lover into the fire, which has been prepared to test his chastity. The flames flee from the virtuous couple, an event which so startles Hydaspe that after learning from Sisimetre that human sacrifice is a superstitious practice, he frees Theagene. When told that he is of royal blood, he marries him to Chariclée, satisfying his nephew with another spouse.

This play is more compact and more smoothly written than Hardy's long drama, but it is less dramatic, consisting of recitations and a hurried *dénouement*. The unity of action is violated by the digressions concerned with the giant and Merœbe and by the long narrations of previous events in the story of the lovers. The action does not last more than a few days and is confined to the city of Meroé.

A second tragi-comedy was published in 1609, called *Marfilie* or, in the edition of 1628, *L'Innocence Descouverte*, the plot of

[1] IV.   [2] V.

which seems remotely connected with the story of Hippolytus and Phædra, with the vindication and escape of the former, conformably with the usage of the tragi-comedy. The use made of a drug, supposed to be a poison, and the prominent rôle of the valet suggest the influence of *Lucelle*.[1] In the first act Marfilie, wife of Phocus, a Roman knight, confesses to her *nourrice* her love for her stepson, Fabrice. To the remonstrances of the *nourrice* she replies that "l'amour n'a point de loy," citing the classic examples of Myrrha, Phædra, Biblis, and others. Seeing that her passion cannot be conquered, the *nourrice* arranges a meeting between Fabrice and her mistress by pretending that the latter is sick. A physician declares that she suffers from "une humeur bilieuse" and prescribes as follows:

"Vous prendrez tout premier ce petit apozeme,
Puis dessus vostre cœur sera cet epitheme,
Usez de ce iulep alternativement,
Ces sirops esteindront vostre feu vehement, etc."[2]

The valet, Thomas, parodies these lines with others of insistant vulgarity. Fabrice now receives a declaration of love from Marfilie, which he rejects with horror. Immediately after, however, he pretends to be willing to comply with her requests, in order to cure her. The situation is relieved by the timely arrival of Phocus. Fabrice soliloquizes on the wickedness of women, citing historical examples, when Marfilie enters, lamenting her sufferings with great *préciosité*:

"Playe, non, ains un feu brusle incessamment,
Un feu non, un vautour me livre ce tourment,
Un vautour, non, ie faux, une rage amoureuse,
Rage, non, ains plustost une vie ennuyeuse,
Vie, non, ains plustost une cruelle mort,
Mort, non, elle ne peut, son dard n'est assez fort
Pour faire tant de mal, ou bien c'est ce me semble
Playe, vautour, feu, rage, et vie, et mort ensemble."[3]

When Fabrice rejects her proposals, she cries

"Lares, larues, lutins, lemures et demons,"

[1] See above, p. 62. [2] II. [3] III.

which Thomas parodies with,

> "O iambons, cervelas, bouteilles et flacons."

Resolved to revenge her rejection by poisoning Fabrice, she sends Thomas to the physician for "la froide cigüe, le caustique arcenic, ou le prompt sublimé." The valet, arrived at the physician's house, gives a long account of the "cul musicien" in a passage that seems to have obtained some celebrity.[1] After bantering the physician for some time, he obtains a drug, which, he is told, is the required poison. When this is put into wine to destroy Fabrice, it is drunk by Anthoine, Marfilie's son, who at once becomes unconscious. Marfilie, now in great distress, is advised by the *nourrice* to accuse Fabrice of murdering his half-brother.

A court scene is next represented, in which two *conseillers* generalize at length on justice, while Thomas suggests:

> "Disons tant seulement que tout ainsi qu'on voit
> L'aiguille du Nocher tendre tousiours vers l'ourse,
> La main d'un aduocat tend tousiours vers la bourse." [2]

Phocus demands vengeance for Anthoine's murder. Against Fabrice's protest of innocence, the *nourrice* offers a detailed testimony of the poisoning. The judge, convinced of his guilt, is about to sentence him to death, when the physician arrives with information regarding the purchase of the drug. Anthoine is now revived. Marfilie, after confessing her crime, is banished with Thomas and the *nourrice*; Fabrice is released and reunited to his father.

The unity of action is here violated by the comic elements introduced chiefly in the rôle of Thomas. The place is limited to a single city, of which several localities are represented. The time is probably not longer than a few days.

In the following year appeared *Genevre*, an undramatic play, based on the *Orlando Furioso*,[3] that has been fully analyzed by Th. Roth.[4] Ariodan declares his determination to kill himself

[1] Cf. Soleinne, I, No. 941. [2] V. [3] IV, stanzas 56–72; V; VI, stanzas 2–16.
[4] For references, see appendix B, II.

from despair at the infidelity of Genevre, daughter of the King of Scotland. His brother, Lurquain, accuses Genevre of licentious conduct and the King reluctantly agrees to put her to death, if she be proved guilty. The question is to be decided by a duel between Lurquain and Genevre's champion, who presents himself in armor, so that he is unrecognized. In the midst of the combat Renaut de Montauban arrives, separates the two men, and proves Genevre's innocence and the guilt of Polynesse and Dalyde, whom Ariodan had thought to be Genevre when she received Polynesse into her chamber. Polynesse is condemned to be burnt. Genevre's champion, removing his armor, shows that he is no other than Ariodan, escaped from the sea, in which he had sought death. The marriage of the reunited lovers is at once arranged. The unity of action is here violated by the interposition of Renaut, who has taken no part in the first four acts of the play and consequently serves as a *deus ex machinâ*. The time is at least a month. The scene is laid in several localities near the court of the King of Scotland.

The story of the Widow of Ephesus, which has furnished a popular theme in fable literature since Phædrus[1] was dramatized in 1614 by Pierre Brinon under the title of *L'Ephesienne, tragicomédie.* In the argument the author states that his source is found in the Satires of Petronius Arbiter,[2] whose brief narrative is greatly elaborated in the play. Astasie *la Vefve* laments her husband's death and resolves to follow him to the grave, replying to the remonstrances of her friends:

> "Il ne sera point dit que iamais Astasie
> Non, qui luy donneroit le Sceptre de l'Asie,
> Ait oublié celuy qu'elle avoit en si cher;
> Pour luy ie veux fuir et le monde et la chair,
> Et sa triste demeure à mes plaisirs éleuë
> Sera le lieu fatal de ma mort resoluë."[3]

[1] For references to various versions, see A. C. M. Robert, *Fables Inédites*, II, 430, Paris, 1825; 2 vols.

[2] Cf. Petronii Satirae et Liber Priapeorum, 77–79, edited by Franciscus Buecheler, Berlin, 1882.

[3] I.

Teleme, the *servante*, commends this resolution and agrees to follow her mistress. The magistrate, Dicaste, unable to turn Astasie from her purpose, leaves her bidding adieu to her city, her friends, and her life. A chorus of Ephesian virgins praises her constancy. In the next act Frontin leads before Calepe, governor of the city, a detachment of soldiers in charge of a captured pirate captain. After describing the capture, he is ordered to hang the pirate and guard his body, exposed on the gallows. The next act shows Frontin guarding the body and complaining of this unwelcome duty in a passage that seems to express the true feeling of the author and the soldier:

> "Et puis suyvez la Cour ! faites service aux grands !
> Donnez à leurs plaisirs vostre force et vos ans !
> Embrassez leurs desseins d'un zele tout extresme !
> Méprisez vos amys ! méprisez-vous vous-mesme !
> Courez mille hazards pour leur ambition !
> A la premiere humeur, la moindre impression
> Qu'ils prendront contre vous, vous voila hors de grace,
> Et cela seulement tous vos bien-faits efface."

Seeing a light in a tomb hard by, he approaches it and finds Astasie and Teleme, who tell him the reason of their presence there. He argues against the widow's resolution, convincing Teleme that life is worth living and making an agreeable impression on Astasie, although she does not change her purpose. As day approaches, Frontin retires, but returns the next night with food and drink and declares his love to Astasie. Urged by him and Teleme, she says:

> "Baille donc que ie mange afin de te complaire.
> Ha, que c'est chose douce à un corps affamé
> D'avoir dequoy manger !
> Frontin: Plus douce d'estre aimé
> A un cœur qui languit recuit de mille flames !
> Astasie: Mais est-il vray Frontin qu'on aime tant les femmes?" [1]

After further argument, Frontin swears to marry her and she replies:

[1] IV,

> "Ie ne peux refuser cét honneur desirable
> De plus dignes que moy l'auroient bien agreable:
> Le bon-heur m'a voulu que perdant mon tresor,
> Un autre m'est offert plus precieux encor." [1]

While Astasie and Frontin are enjoying in advance the marital privileges, pirates carry off the body of their leader from the gallows. Frontin, upon leaving the tomb to arrange his marriage, discovers the loss of the body and laments his fate, for he will be put to death as soon as his negligence becomes known. But the widow comforts him, advising that the body of her dead husband be substituted for that of the pirate:

> "Car puisque mon Destin veut cette extremité
> Que de deux corps aimez ie perde l'un ou l'autre,
> Celuy de mon mari ià deffunct, ou le vostre,
> Pour ne perdre le vif que le Ciel m'a rendu
> Ie bailleray le mort qui m'est desia perdu."

They accordingly place the body on the gallows, thus saving Frontin and removing all obstacles to their marriage.

The unity of action is here nearly observed except for the second act, which, concerned with the account of the pirate's capture and the command to hang him, might have been omitted from the play without affecting the progress of the principal action. The scene is laid in and around Ephesus. The time is about a week.

The story of Apollonius of Tyre, known in various versions, was drawn from the *Gesta Romanorum cum applicationibus*, chapter 153, to be dramatized as *Les Heureuses Infortunes*, a tragi-comedy by Bernier de la Brousse (1617).[2] The details of the story are largely followed with accuracy, though some are omitted and others expanded for dramatic purposes. The long narrative, from the incest of Antiochus to the reunion of Apollonius's family is dramatized in two *journées* of five acts each. Little delicacy is

[1] IV.

[2] For the text of the *Gesta Romanorum* and a study of the versions of the story, see S. Singer, *Apollonius von Tyrus*, Halle, 1895. Several French versions are mentioned by A. H. Smith, *Shakespeare's Pericles and Apollonius of Tyre*, 41–3, Philadelphia, 1898. Neither of these authors mentions *Les Heureuses Infortunes*.

shown in the treatment of Antioque and his daughter in the opening act. The king glories in his crime, defying the gods:

> "De leur feu, de leur fer, mon cœur n'a nul soucy
> Qu'ils commandent au ciel, moy ie commande icy."[1]

His daughter laments her unfortunate position. At the end of the act the duc d'Apamée presents himself before the king, only to die for failing to guess the riddle, which gives to the man who solves it the hand of Antioque's daughter. But Apollonie guesses this riddle, as Antioque tells his attendant:

> "Il a leu dans mon ame, et tiré de mon cœur
> Le doux amour, qui fait que ie ne vis qu'en peur.
> Quels dieux l'ont inspiré? qui prompt à ma ruine
> Luy auroit descouvert le fonds de ma poictrine?"[2]

He seeks to kill Apollonie, but the latter escapes, only to be shipwrecked and rescued by a fisherman. No attempt is made at introducing the humorous and realistic conversation of the fishermen, found in the corresponding part of *Pericles Prince of Tyre.* Arrived at the court of Altistrate, King of Pentapolis, Apollonie gains his favor and the love of his daughter, Lucine, whose music-teacher he becomes. She rejects noble suitors and insists upon marrying Apollonie, finally winning her father's consent. The subsequent news of Antioque's death and the accession of Apollonie to his throne is celebrated by the lovers in lyric measures:

> "Soit que tu sois dans les Cieux
> Dieu des dieux
> Ou en ta Crete ennoblie
> Entens de nostre chanson
> Le doux son
> Et iamais ne nous oublie, etc."[3]

The couple now take ship for their new kingdom. A last scene is added to this first part of the drama to show that the fisherman, who had saved Apollonie and been forgotten by him, is finally rewarded.

[1] I, 1. [2] II, 1. [3] V, 1.

Fifteen years elapse between the first and second parts, a departure, the author declares in his preface, from the "forme absoluë de la Tragedie." The story is recommenced at the point where Dorade expresses to her husband her envy of Tharsie, the daughter whom Apollonie has left in their charge with much treasure, and her desire to do away with her in order that their daughter may inherit this wealth. The husband's objections are silenced by his crafty wife, who engages a slave, Theophile, to kill the girl. The attempted murder of Tharsie and her rescue by pirates are not acted, as they are in *Pericles,* but are related by Theophile in a lengthy monologue. He tells Dorade that he has slain the girl and asks for his liberty, the reward that she has promised him. She replies:

> " Quoy? meschant, liberté pour un meurtre commis
> Il n'en faut point parler; et si tu m'en accuse,
> I'ay assez de moyens pour me servir d'excuse.
> Fay comme auparavant, si ie t'oy plus prescher
> Hault ie te feray pendre, ou tout vif escorcher."[1]

Meantime Tharsie, sold to the keeper of a brothel in *Metelin,* is told that she must help in the business. By the aid of Athanagore, Prince of Lesbos, whom she wins over to a virtuous life when he visits her for other purposes, she succeeds in making a living by music, astrology, and mathematics, till her father Apollonie, informed by Dorade that she is dead, arrives in despair off the coast of Lesbos. Athanagore sends Tharsie to divert him, but, after guessing her riddles, Apollonie orders her out of his presence, whereupon she laments, calling herself by her name. This leads to her recognition and restoration to her father. After marrying her to Athanagore, Apollonie proceeds to Ephesus in obedience to a dream, and is reunited to Lucine, who had been living in a convent there since the birth of Tharsie. Another scene shows Dorade hearing through her husband's dream of the punishment in store for her crimes.

The violation of the unities in this play is too obvious to need notice. The play includes four stories: the incestuous relations of

[1] Part II, II, 1.

Antioque and his daughter; the marriage of Apollonie and Lucine; the story of Tharsie; the reunion of Apollonie and Lucine. Each part takes up several months at least, while a period of fifteen years elapses between them. The scene of the first part is laid at Antioch and in Pentapolis, that of the second at Tarsus, Mitylene, and Ephesus.

In 1618 appeared *Aretaphile*, the first play of Pierre Du Ryer. The manuscript in which the work has been preserved states that it was received with much applause and called *sa pièce* by the duc d'Orléans. A further proof that it was acted is that it appears in the *Mémoire*[1] of Mahelot, which gives the decoration that it needed when acted at the Hôtel de Bourgogne:

"Il faut, au milieu du théâtre, un palais caché ou il ayt un tombeau et des armes, de la bougie, des larmes, du soucy, deux piramides ardantes. Au devant de ce palais, un autre palais pour un roy. A un des costez du théâtre, une grande tour, et de l'autre costé, une chambre fermée, des tablaux, une table, des flambeaux dedans la chambre. Au troisiesme acte, il se faict une nuit. Il faut deux menottes ou chaisnes, deux fiolles, un chapeau de fleurs, une ficelle où l'on attache une lettre."

The plot of the play is taken from Plutarch's *Virtues of Women*[2] with changes in personages and incidents. It has been incompletely analyzed by La Vallière, and by his follower, K. Philipp, in a recent dissertation.[3] The scene is laid in Libya, where Aretaphile is wooed by Philarque, son of the king, and his cousin, Nicocrate. She dismisses the latter and goes with the former into the garden to hear the birds sing. The king arranges a marriage between his son and Aretaphile, reflecting that,

"Malgré la tombe, ou le destin nous livre
Nôtre posterité nous peut faire revivre." [4]

Nicocrate, however, determines to prevent this union and soon informs the audience of his succession to the hand of Aretaphile and the throne of her father:

[1] Fol. 35 Vo and 36.

[2] No. XIX. Cf. *Plutarchi Scripta Moralia*, I, 315, Paris, 1868.

[3] For references, see Appendix B, II. [4] I, 7.

> "Les Dieux sont Rois au Ciel, je le suis ici bas,
> Qu'ils gouvernent la haut la pluye et le tonnerre,
> Pour moy j'aurai le soin de gouverner la terre"[1]

He rejoices in his cruelty and punishes a *sacrificateur* who warns him against it. When his mother informs him that Aretaphile has attempted to give him poison, he shows his cruelty by forcing a captive to drink the liquid in question and thus proving its deadly effect.

Aretaphile, imprisoned while awaiting trial for this attempt, is visited by her lover, Philarque, who passes her a letter by means of a cord, when he is obliged to retire by the approach of soldiers. Summoned before her husband, Aretaphile replies to his reproaches, "l'innocence et l'amour méprisent le danger," explaining that the poison was a love potion, which she gave him for fear that he loved another. As soon as she is released, she plots again to destroy Nicocrate, who, she discovers, has fallen in love with her sister, Belise, who loves and is loved by his brother, Cleandre. By showing Cleandre a letter from Nicocrate, Belise incites him to have the latter murdered, when he comes to visit her that night. After this has been accomplished, Clearque succeeds to the throne, proving to be as cruel as his brother. But Philarque now arrives with an army to demand his father's kingdom. Clearque surrenders and begs for mercy. Philarque pardons him and marries Aretaphile.

In this plot, Du Ryer has departed from his model in the interest of *romanesque* elements and a happier *dénouement*. In Plutarch, Philarque, called Phaedimus, is married to Aretaphile before the usurpation of Nicocrate and is slain by the latter. The army which he leads against the tyrant is led, in Plutarch, by Anabus, a neighboring prince. Belise is, in the original version, the daughter, and not the sister of Aretaphile. The latter, after the overthrow of the tyrants, retires to private life, in Plutarch, instead of remarrying, as she does in Du Ryer. The play lacks unity of action, for the acts succeed one another without close connection, while the incident of the poisoning does not advance the action.

[1] II, 1.

The time is some months, possibly years. The scene is laid in several localities of a city and on a battle-field.

Les Amours du Seigneur Alexandre et d'Annette (1619) may be compared with *L'Innocence Descouverte*[1] in the vulgarity of the language and the prominent comic rôle of the valet. Alexandre, a young aristocrat, loves and is loved by Annette, who introduces him into her room at night. His servant, Lambert, left at the door, hears the wife of a shoemaker complaining of the blows she has received from her husband and comforts her by leading her away to his room. Meanwhile Annette's father breaks into his daughter's room to take vengeance on the lover, who escapes in spite of him. Furious at missing Alexandre, the father bids a valet kill Annette, but instead of executing this barbarous order, the valet provides her with men's clothes, disguised in which she escapes to her uncle's house, which she enters as a servant. Her father, however, dies of disappointment, so that she is enabled to reveal her identity to her uncle and to marry Alexandre. The unities are violated in this play by the digression concerning the valet and the shoemaker's wife, by the number of days that elapse during the progress of the play, and by the various parts of the town in which it takes place. The source of the play is unknown.

The author of *Les Amours de Philandre et Marisee* (1619) seems to have called it both tragedy and tragi-comedy, for the latter term is used in the title, the privilege, and at the tops of the pages, while the author writes in his dedication to Honoré d'Urfé concerning "ce ieu tragique" and refers to the play in his *au lecteur* as "ceste Tragedie." The subject is, indeed, eminently tragic, but the representation of the reunion in Heaven of the separated family gives the play a happy *dénouement*, so that it is possible to look upon it as a tragi-comedy.

Philandre, lamenting his ill success in love, is sent by Destin to Avignon, where a bride is promised him. The chorus deplores Destin's power. Philandre wins the affection of Marisee, but is obliged to leave her to succeed to an inheritance at Nîmes. Marisee's uncle is seeking in the third act to arrange a marriage

[1] See above, page 103 *seq.*

between her and Prince Rectival, when the news comes that the girl has eloped with Philandre, whereupon the uncle exclaims:

"O Priamide cœur! ô traistre! ô inhumain!
As-tu soubs mots pipeurs enleué de ta main
L'Helenine beauté de ma niepce tant chere?"[1]

Pursuit is vain. The uncle hears, after ten years, that the lovers have married, fled to Scotland, and are now the parents of four children. Philandre complains to his wife of their poverty, which he resolves to remedy by returning to Provence for their fortune. He takes with him his oldest son, Fleury, leaving the rest of the family behind.

In the fifth act Marisee learns from her uncle that Philandre has abandoned her for another woman. She decides to kill herself and her children, whom she convinces that death is preferable to life. Meanwhile Philandre has determined to rid himself of his oldest son, but, when on the point of killing him, is prevented by hunters, who come upon him in the forest. He escapes, but is condemned in his absence to be hanged and burnt, while Fleury is told to go on a pilgrimage to thank *Marie à Lorette* for his preservation. Twenty years later he starts on this journey and meets his father, turned hermit. He forgives him and they embrace. Not long after, Philandre falls sick and is visited by the spirits of his wife and dead children, who announce his approaching death and assure him that he has been saved by their prayers. They are thus happily reunited after a curious speech of Philandre upon his death-bed, a speech so constructed as to form with the initial letters an anagram on the name of the author of the play.

This artificial ending is in keeping with the exaggerated style in which other parts of the work are written. The unities are violated in many ways. Three plots can be seen in the marriage of Philandre and Marisee, his desertion of her, and their reconciliation. The action lasts over thirty years and takes place in Scotland and several localities in southern France.

[1] III.

The second play by Du Ryer is *Clitophon* (1622), known to have been acted from its occurrence in *L'Ouverture des jours gras*[1] (1634), which mentions it among pieces to be seen at the Hôtel de Bourgogne, and from the elaborate account of its *mise en scène* given by Mahelot,[2] which includes a handsomely decorated temple to Diana, two prisons, a garden, a mountain with a tomb on it, a cave, a sea, half a ship, blood, sponges, a skin, flowers, turbans for Turks, a dark lantern, trumpets, chains, etc. The source of the play, *Cleitophon and Leucippe*,[3] the Greek romance of Achilleus Tatius, has been followed with only a few changes. The play begins at Tyre, where Lucippe is dwelling with her mother and has fallen in love with Clitophon. The latter's father is opposed to his marriage to Lucippe, as he wishes him to wed Calligonne, but a former lover of Lucippe now comes from Byzantium and carries off Calligonne, mistaking her for Lucippe. Alarmed by the news of this catastrophe, Lucippe's mother determines to leave the city with her daughter, whereupon Clitophon persuades the latter to elope with him to Alexandria, after some hesitation on her part:

"Lucippe: L'amour doit aprouver une telle entreprise
Mais l'honneur me deffend ce qu'amour autorise.
Clitophon: Si tu veux toutesfois nôtre commun bonheur
Tu dois te rendre sourde aux conseils de l'honneur."[4]

Shipwrecked on the coast of Egypt, the lovers are captured by the soldiers of a tyrant, Busire, who orders them to be sacrificed to the gods. Clitophon, separated from Lucippe, succeeds in escaping to Charmide, King of Alexandria, now at war with Busire, but only to see Lucippe sacrificed on a mountain out of reach of his aid. His lamentations over this disaster are interrupted by Satyre, Lucippe's servant, who leads him to the mountain, opens the tomb, and shows his mistress alive and unhurt. They explain that the sacrificer was Menelas, father of Satire, and that he had saved Lucippe by fixing a skin, full of blood, on her breast, which

[1] See E. Fournier, *Variétés historiques*, II, 345–55.
[2] *Mémoire*, fol. 47 vo. and 48.
[3] See *Erotici Scriptores*, 27 *seq.*, edited by G. A. Hirseling, Paris, 1856.
[4] I, 9.

he opened with his knife in the sight of the soldiers, making them believe that the flowing blood was Lucippe's. The deception was not difficult, as no one came nearer than the foot of the mountain during the supposed sacrifice. After this event Lucippe had been placed in the tomb, whence she is now taken.

The lovers take refuge with Charmide, declaring that they are brother and sister. He receives them only too well, desiring to add Lucippe "au nombre de mes femmes." She escapes this fate by an opportune duel between Charmide and Busire, in which both are killed, but she is shortly afterwards carried off by pirates and is believed dead by Clitophon and Satyre. They pursue the pirates as far as Ephesus, where they meet a wealthy widow, called Melite, who at once falls in love with Clitophon. At her house they find Lucippe, so changed in appearance that her lover fails to recognize her. Brought there by the pirates, who perished in a dispute over her, she has succeeded in escaping to the woods, and is living as a shepherdess on one of Melite's farms.

The lovers are about to be reunited when Tersandre, Melite's husband, appears, having escaped from a shipwreck in which he has been supposed dead. Hearing of his wife's passion for Clitophon, he has him imprisoned and seeks to win Lucippe for himself. Clitophon, informed of her assassination, wishes so strongly to die that he accuses himself of her murder, but, before he is executed, Lucippe reappears after her third supposed death to tell of her taking refuge in a temple, in order to escape the importunities of Tersandre. Then she is finally united to Clitophon, while Tersandre is pardoned on his wife's interposition.

Besides shortening many of the philosophical discussions and explanations of his prose source, Du Ryer has made certain changes to suit the views of his audience and to heighten the *romanesque* qualities of the piece. Thus, Calligonne is made the cousin instead of the half-sister of Clitophon; Lucippe is sacrificed, and not ripped open; Clitophon meets Melite in Ephesus instead of Alexandria and does not marry her; the oracular test of Lucippe's virtue is omitted. As it stands, however, the play has as little unity as the romance. Five distinct actions are evident, which end in the heroine's escape from her mother at

Tyre, from the sacrificial block, the King of Alexandria, the pirates, and Tersandre. The scene is laid in Tyre, Egypt and Ephesus. The time must cover a year or more.

A striking contrast to this play is furnished by Troterel's *Pasithée* (1624), a tragi-comedy of few incidents and only eight personages, of whom four are allegorical. Cleostene, returning from a journey to wed Pasithée, is informed by his friend, Ceraminte, that his suit is supported by her *confidante*, Philoxene, but that she appears favorably inclined to another suitor. On his arrival, however, Pasithée receives him well and the marriage is arranged. But Fortune, learning that Cleostene has defied her, proves her power by pursuading Pasithée to renounce the world and enter a convent. Cleostene, in great distress, arranges an interview with Pasithée, but is unable to alter her purpose.

"Pasithée: Ie vous serviray plus estant dans ce lieu saint,
Que si ie demeurois dedans le monde feint.
Cleostene: Si chacun s'enfermoit dedans un monastere,
Le monde deviendroit un desert solitaire:
I'estime grandement le vœu de chasteté,
Mais le saint mariage a plus d'utilité." [1]

But Destin, taking pity on Cleostene, sends Cupidon to shoot Pasithée with his darts, which he does during Cleostene's second visit to the convent, thus inducing Pasithée to agree to marry her lover. When Fortune opposes this union, she is captured by Mercure and Cupidon, brought before Destin, and condemned to be imprisoned till after the wedding of the lovers, which soon takes place.

The absence of intrigue indicates that the play has no source, but is due to the author's invention. Despite its lack of incident, the piece violates the unity of action, for the incident of Pasithée's second lover, mentioned in the first act, has nothing to do with the plot, and the solution of the drama is made by the introduction of a *deus ex machinâ*. The time extends over a number of days. The scene is laid at the home of Pasithée, in the parlor of the convent, at a place some distance from these localities in which the action begins, and in the places inhabited by Destin and Fortune.

[1] III, 2.

The plot of *Chriseide et Arimand* (1625), the first play of Jean Mairet, is taken from the third book of Honoré d'Urfé's *Astrée* (1610). According to Bizos,[1] the play has undergone the influence of Théophile's *Pyrame et Thisbé* (1617). Mairet himself called it a *péché de sa jeunesse* and was not responsible for its publication. That it was acted is shown by its appearance in Mahelot's *Mémoire*.[2] As Bizos has given a full analysis of the play, I shall be brief in discussing it. At the beginning the lovers are in prison some distance apart, Arimand as a prisoner of war, Chriseide because she refuses to forsake Arimand and love King Gondebaut. Their servant, Bellaris, succeeds in helping Chriseide to escape at night from a window by means of a rope and in conducting her to an inn, where he leaves her to return to Arimand, changes clothes with him, and takes his place in prison. Arimand finds Chriseide and is soon rejoined by the faithful Bellaris, who has succeeded in escaping from prison. They set out for Vienne, but chance upon King Gondebaut, who recaptures Chriseide. She refuses to marry the king, and, when he endeavors to force the marriage, seizes a knife and swears on the *Tombeau des Amans* her fidelity to Arimand:

> "Ie ne puis receuoir un autre feu dans l'ame,
> Ferme iusqu'à la mort dans ce premier dessein,
> Et preste à me porter ce coûtau dans le sein,
> Si l'on me veut tirer du Tombeau que i'embrasse." [3]

Arimand now arrives, surrendering himself and demanding,

> "De me donner le don promis au delateur
> Du chef de l'attentat dont ie suis seul l'auteur." [4]

The reward demanded is the liberty of Chriseide, to which the king is forced to consent, assuring Arimand that he shall be put to death at once. Chriseide promises to die with him, but Bellaris takes the guilt of Chriseide's escape upon himself and demands Arimand's liberty as his reward for giving himself up. The king is again forced by his oath to agree, but is resolved to revenge

[1] For referenee see Appendix B, II.
[2] 54 vo. and 55. [3] v, 3. [4] 54 vo. and 55.

himself on Bellaris. But the priest pleads for him and so moves the king by pointing out these examples of self-sacrifice that his heart is softened, he pardons them all, and unites the lovers in marriage.

While this play is, like other tragi-comedies of the period, full of incidents that are introduced for their own sake rather than to advance the action, there is, nevertheless, an unusually logical arrangement of material, so that the scenes grow out of each other and nearly produce unity of action. The *dénouement* is reached by the pity excited in the king's breast by the self-sacrifice displayed by the lovers and Bellaris, which was made possible by the king's offer of a reward to the man who would bring him whoever accomplished Chriseide's escape. This circumstance gives the escape of the lovers an integral part in the development of the play. It does not have the episodic nature of incidents that occurred, for example, in *Clitophon.* This tendency to unity is to be looked for in Mairet, who by his *Silvanire* and *Sophonisbe,* did as much as anyone else to establish the unities in France. The unities of time and place, however, are here violated, for the scene is laid in several distinct localities of France, in two prisons, a palace, and a forest, while the time must have covered a number of days.

In 1625 Pichoû obtained the privilege to print his *Folies de Cardenio,* a tragi-comedy drawn from *Don Quixote.*[1] Dorothée, finding that Fernant has transferred his affections from her to Luscinde, retires to the forest to lament, while Fernant persuades Luscinde's father to grant her to him, although she loves Cardenio and is loved by him. Her father forces Luscinde to come before a *Sacrificateur*[2] to be married to Fernant, who promises to marry her, after which the following scene occurs :

"Sacrificateur : Puisque vous connaissez sa fidele amitié,
Ne desirez-vous pas le nom de sa moitié?
(Cardenio paraist derriere la tapisserie)

---

[1] Part I, chaps. XXIV and XXVII-XXX.

[2] Fournier, *Théâtre,* 263, notes that the laws against the representation of priests on the stage forced Pichou to use this term, although the scene of the play is laid in modern Spain and a monastery is alluded to in the same scene.

Luscinde : Ouy.
Cardenio : Ha ! desloyauté qui trahis mes services
Qu'un seul mot me condamne à d'estranges supplices
(Il sort du theatre)." [1]

Luscinde faints and is found to have a knife concealed in her bosom with a paper stating that she intends to kill herself rather than be unfaithful to Cardenio. When revived, she refuses to wed Fernant and soon after escapes to a monastery to mourn the loss of her lover. Cardenio, believing that she has ceased to love him, retires to the desert and goes mad from grief.

In this state he is met by Don Quixote and Sancho, who try to protect him from his imaginary enemies. But Cardenio pays little attention to Don Quixote, beats his follower, as the "rival injurieux à l'honneur de mon sort," and disappears in the forest. He next encounters the curate and the barber seeking Don Quixote and mistakes the second of these for Luscinde :

"Ne m'oste pas le bien de te parler icy,
Et rend d'un seul regard mon martyre adoucy.
Permets que ie te baise.
Le Barbier : O ! la folle cervelle,
Monsieur ie suis Barbier, et non pas Damoiselle." [2]

After a number of pleasantries, Cardenio leaves them and soon returns to his senses. He meets Dorothée, who informs him of Luscinde's fidelity. Meanwhile Fernant with two companions captures Luscinde, whom Don Quixote tries in vain to rescue, crying :

"O Dieux ! c'est Sagripant qui ravit Angelique,
Quitte infidelle Roy, ce dessein tyrannique,
Ie suis l'appuy des bons, et l'effroy des peruers,
Dom Quichot de la manche, honneur de l'univers." [3]

Shortly afterwards, Cardenio meets them at an inn and is reunited to Luscinde. Fernant and he are on the point of coming to blows, when Dorothée intervenes, pursuading Fernant to return to his former love for her, so that both couples are content.

This double intrigue with a corresponding *dénouement* destroys the unity of action, which is further prevented by several scenes

[1] II, 4. [2] IV, 2. [3] IV, 7.

concerned with Don Quixote that form amusing digressions from the principal plot. The scene is laid in the forest, at a monastery, a tavern, the home of Luscinde and apparently at that of Dorothée. The time is probably a month or more. That the play was acted is evident from its appearance in the *Mémoire*[1] of Mahelot.

In 1608 Jean de Schelandre had written, under the anagram Daniel d'Anchères, *Tyr et Sidon Tragedie ou les Funestes Amours de Belcar et Meliane*, a *romanesque* tragedy in which the heroine is executed by her father's orders. Twenty years later he rewrote the play in two *journées* with a happy *dénouement*, a subordinate plot, and comic scenes, calling it *Tyr et Sidon, tragi-comedie.* Leonte, Prince of Tyre, and Belcar, Prince of Sidon, are captured by their enemies in a war between these cities. Leonte, allowed on parole the freedom of Tyre, succeeds in winning the love of Philoline, the young wife of Zorote, a jealous *bourgeois*. By the aid of his page, disguised as a girl, he seduces Philoline, but Zorote, learning his wife's dishonor, hires ruffians, who kill the prince. The wounded Belcar, whose virtuous conduct is contrasted with Leonte's libertinage, is restored to health at Tyre by the daughters of the king, who fall in love with him. Since he prefers Meliane, her older sister, Cassandre, plans with her *nourrice*, Almodice, to make him transfer his affections to herself.

Now, when the king of Tyre hears of his son's death at Sidon, he determines to revenge him by executing Belcar; but that prince is released from prison by the influence of Meliane, in order that she may fly with him by boat to Sidon. Almodice, however, introduces into the boat with him Cassandre instead of Meliane. When Belcar discovers this treachery, he will have none of Cassandre, who in despair stabs herself and leaps into the sea. Her body is carried ashore, where it is found by Meliane, come to the beach to drown herself, when she thinks that Belcar has deserted her. Suspected of murdering her sister, she is rescued by the timely arrival of Almodice, captured by the Tyrian admiral and forced to tell how Cassandre met her fate. Meanwhile it has been proved that Zorote is alone guilty of Leonte's murder, so that, as he is

[1] Fols. 55 vo. and 56.

handed over to the King of Tyre, the latter has nothing against Belcar. Urged by his advisers, by Belcar and Meliane, he consents to the marriage of these lovers.

M. Rigal,[1] following M. Édouard Droz, posits Ronsard's *Franciade* as the source of this play, showing the resemblance between the love affair of Belcar and that of Francus, loved by two princesses, one of whom is aided by her *nourrice* and kills herself from jealousy of the other. As there is no suggestion, however, in the *Franciade* of Leonte's adventures and as the setting and many of the incidents are different from those of *Tyr et Sidon*, it seems that Schelandre did not derive from the *Franciade* more than a general suggestion as to the conduct of his plot. Two distinct actions are seen in this play, the unhappy adventures of Leonte and Philoline and the happy fortunes of Belcar and Meliane. Digressions are added concerning the war and the household of Zorote. The scene of the action is laid in various localities in Tyr and Sidon and in the territory between the cities. The time is some months.

Agimee ou L'Amour extrauagant, Tragi-Comedie (1628), with its shepherds and shepherdesses, its princes and princesses disguised as such, its kisses, mild duels, and double *dénouement*, is a *tragi-comédie pastorale,* despite its title, and is consequently not to be treated here. Rotrou's *Hypocondriaque,* published in 1631 and probably written in 1628, does not come within the scope of this chapter, which is concerned only with the tragi-comedies written by predecessors of that author.

La Tragedie des Amours de Zerbin et d'Isabelle, Princesse fugitive[2] is a *romanesque* play, based on the *Orlando Furioso,* the qualities of which are those of the tragi-comedy, although it is called a tragedy. It has been analyzed at length by La Vallière.[3]

B. *Characterization.*

It is probable that nearly all the *romanesque* tragi-comedies treated in this chapter were acted; as, with the exception of

[1] In Petit de Julleville's *Langue et Littérature,* IV, 227.

[2] Troyes, 1621, anon.

[3] *Bibliothèque,* I, 536–38.

Genevre and *Pasithée,* they are essentially dramatic in composition. Hardy's plays were certainly acted, for he was the professional playwright of the Hôtel de Bourgogne. His *Felismene, Cornelie,* and *Belle Egyptienne,* furthermore, are mentioned in the *Mémoire* of Mahelot, who seems to have been the *mécanicien* of that theater. The presence in this *Mémoire* of *Aretaphile, Clitophon, Chriseide et Arimand,* and *Folies de Cardenio,* shows that they also were acted. *Aymée* is shown by its preface to have been acted after a banquet, probably in a château. All these plays were published at Paris or Rouen, except *Aymée, Les Heureuses Infortunes, Alexandre et Annette,* and *Philandre et Marisee,* which appeared at Poitiers, Troyes, and Lyons, and Du Ryer's two plays, which exist only in manuscript.

The authors of these tragi-comedies are, with the exception of Hardy, Du Ryer, and Mairet, almost unknown. Hardy, who may be considered in some respects the founder of the modern French stage, is remembered as the badly paid playwright of Valleran Lecomte's troupe, during its provincial travels and when it was established at the Hôtel de Bourgogne. He is the first professional dramatic author who turned his attention to the tragi-comedy, and the first author to give this *genre* a position of popular equality with the tragedy of classical imitation. He was followed by Pierre Du Ryer and Jean Mairet, of whom the former, supposed to have been the son of the poet, Isaac Du Ryer, obtained the positions of *secrétaire du roy* and *historiographe de France,* was twice married, was admitted to the Academy, and died in 1658. His cheerfully endured poverty forced him to continuous literary labors, which produced twenty-one plays and a large number of classical translations.[1] Mairet, born at Besançon in 1604, protected at Paris by the duc de Montmorency and the comte de Belin, won fame by his *Sylvie* (1626) and *Sylvanire* (1630), and was largely responsible for the introduction of the unities into the French theater by his use of them in *Sophonisbe* (1634). His correspondence with Corneille on the question of the *Cid* made him notorious. He died in 1680.[2]

[1] For a list of these, see K. Philipp, *Du Ryers Leben,* 14.

[2] See Bizos, *Étude,* and Dannheisser, *Studien.*

A few details have survived regarding other authors of *romanesque* tragi-comedies. André Mage, sieur de Fiefmelin, wrote various poems beside his *Aymée,* which were collected in a *Polymnie.*[1] Jacques Duhamel was an advocate of Normandy.[2] Claude Billard, seigneur de Courgenay, Bourbonnois, brought up in the household of the duchesse de Retz, was *conseiller et secrétaire des commandements de la reine Marguerite de Valois.* Besides eight plays, he wrote an epic, *L'Église triomphante,* and other poems.[3] Jean Auvray (cir. 1590–1633), an advocate in the parliament of Rouen, besides plays, wrote *Oeuvres saintes* (1628) and a collection of poems of various kinds, called the *Banquet des Muses* (1623 and 1627).[4] Pierre Brinon translated Buchanan's *Baptiste* and *Jephté.* Bernier de la Brousse of Poitou wrote poems and three plays in addition to his tragi-comedy.[5] Gilbert Giboin declares himself to be *harpeur, arithmeticien, et maistre escrivain* at Molins in Bourbonnois. Pierre Troterel, sieur d'Aves, *écuyer,* was the author of ten dramatic works in various *genres.*[6] Pichou came to Paris from Dijon, was protected by the prince de Condé, brought out three tragi-comedies and a pastoral, which met with much success, and was assassinated in 1631, when about thirty-five years old.[7] Jean de Schelandre (cir. 1585–1635) from the neighborhood of Verdun, fought as a captain under Turenne and wrote *La Stuartide* (1611) and other poems besides his tragi-comedy.[8] These facts show that the authors came from various parts of France and that tragi-comedies, though still composed by men of affairs, were coming to be more extensively written by professional playwrights like Hardy, Mairet, or Pichou.

The sources of the plays treated have been stated with their analyses, as far as they are known. Euripides furnishes the principal plot of *Alceste* and perhaps the subject of *L'Innocence Descouverte,* but it is upon the later and more romantic writers of

[1] See Appendix B, II.
[2] La Vallière, I, 279.
[3] Frères Parfaict, IV, 109 *seq.* ; La Vallière, I, 391.
[4] La Vallière, I, 424 ; Brunet, I, 575.
[5] Frères Parfaict, IV, 171 ; La Vallière, I, 477.
[6] La Vallière, I, 372.
[7] Isnard, preface to Pichou's *Filis de Scire,* Paris, 1632.
[8] *Bibliothèque elzévirienne. Ancien Théâtre,* VIII, 6.

Greek and Latin that the tragi-comedies are chiefly based. Plutarch, Lucian, Ovid, and Petronius are followed in five tragi-comedies, while the erotic Alexandrian writers, Heliodorus, Achilleus Tatius, and the author of the Apollonius legend furnish the theme of twelve *journées* of five acts each, which are printed as four plays. Italian sources are found in the works of Boccaccio, Ariosto, and Giraldi Cinthio; Portuguese in the *Diana* of Montemayor; Spanish in the tales of Agreda and Cervantes, from the latter of whom four tragi-comedies are derived; French in Honoré d'Urfé's *Astrée*, Ronsard's *Franciade*, Rosset's *Amants Volages*, and Goulart's version of Honsdorf's *Théâtre d'exemples.*

The dramatic unity of the plays varies greatly. In *Dorise, Alexandre et Annette, Aretaphile, Folies de Cardenio,* and *Tyr et Sidon,* the interest is divided between two couples instead of being concentrated upon one. Similarly, there are two closely connected plots in *Procris* and *Elmire.* Numerous digressions occur; as, for example, the episodes of Clement in *La Belle Egyptienne,* the giant in *L'Éthiopique,* Don Quixote in the *Folies de Cardenio.* In addition to plays in which a subordinate is woven in with a principal plot, are found tragi-comedies in which one plot succeeds another; as, for instance, in *Les Heureuses Infortunes, Gesippe,* or *Philandre et Marisee.* The unity of action may be further violated by the introduction of a *deus ex machinâ,* which constitutes a new element in the play, not produced by what has preceded. This undramatic device has been avoided by Hardy in all his tragi-comedies except *Theagene et Cariclée, Ariadne,*[1] and *Dorise,* where the rôle is played by Thessalian ambassadors, Bacchus, and a *magicienne,* respectively. The ambassadors of Hardy's *Theagene et Cariclée* do not reappear in Genetay's dramatization of the same theme, but there is a *deus ex machinâ* in the rôle of Renaud in *Genevre* and of Destin in *Pasithée.* Greater unity of action is shown in *La Force du Sang* and *Arsacome,* but both of these plays depart from classical usage by dramatizing the story *ab ovo.* The most serious effort towards unity of action is seen in *Chriseide et Arimand.*

[1] The rôle of Hercule in *Alceste* forms too integral a part of the play to be considered that of a *deus ex machinâ.*

The scene of these tragi-comedies may be laid in a single town or in places that are long distances apart. It may include Sparta, Thessaly, and the infernal regions, as does *Alceste*, or Syria, Libya, and Asia Minor, as does *Les Heureuses Infortunes;* a single country may contain it, as in *Fregonde* or *Pasithee;* or a single town, as in *L'Éthiopique;* but the scenic dimensions are never those of the classical stage. Similarly, the time varies from thirty years in *Philandre et Marisee* to a few days in *Ariadne* and *L'Innocence Descouverte.*

In this disregard for the classical unities there is no appreciable difference between the usage of Hardy and that of his contemporaries. The greatest freedom is evident in the tragi-comedies. Even the approach to unity that is at times visible is due rather to the nature of the source than to the dramatic theories of the author. To compensate this lack of classical unity, there is ordinarily a unity of interest in the fortunes of the protagonists, though this is at times obscured by digressions or subsidiary plots.

The love of a man and a woman is the emotion upon which the action is based in these tragi-comedies. Even Gesippe, whose friendship conquers his love, is moved to his sacrifice by Tite's love of the woman. The passion is varied, including the "chastes amours" of Theagene and Cariclée or of Clitophon and Lucippe, the marital affection of Admete for Alceste, the legitimatized bigamy of the comte de Gleichen, the unsatisfied love of the marquis for the married Fregonde, the passion that leads to the seduction of Cornelie, to the adultery in *Procris* and the first *journée* of *Tyr et Sidon*, and to the incest, desired in *L'Innocence Descouverte* and accomplished in *Les Heureuses Infortunes.*

Friendship is as important as love in *Gesippe, Arsacome*, and *Alceste.* It is to be noted, also, in *Fregonde, Chriseide et Arimand*, and *Cornelie.* A religious *motif* is obvious in *Philandre et Marisee.* Instead of attempting innovations in the accepted philosophy and social conventions, the authors change past conditions to fit the state of French society, as when Clitophon's fiancée is changed from his half-sister to his cousin. The bigamy allowed in Elmire does not evidence a revolt from European custom, for it is permitted by the Pope.

Another symptom of social conservatism is found in the aristocratic expressions that are in keeping with the high rank of the leading personages. The reader learns that "un Prince bien-né a tousiours le dessus encontre un terre-né."[1] In *Genevre* the father of the heroine refuses to believe that she has been seduced, for "elle est trop bien nee."[2] *Noblesse oblige* inspires Lucine, when she says:

> "Les filles des grands Roys, patrons d' honneur tres amples,
> Aux filles de bas lieu doivent servir d'exemples."[3]

Further aristocratic and monarchical sentiments are seen in:

> "Les Rois ne meurent point, puisque ce sont des Dieux
> Que le vouloir du Ciel établit en ces lieux."[4]

> "En un esprit bien né la charité doit luire."[5]

> "Par la race des rois les peuples sont en paix."[6]

A further conservatism is shown in patriotic allusions:

> "Ces Paladins, que la Gaule feconde
> Feit jadis renommer aux quatre coins du monde."[7]

> "La Gaule se presente en peuples plus feconde
> Que l'Espagne beaucoup: qui semble un autre monde,
> Peuples ciuilisez, conuersables, courtois
> Qui n'ont rien d'arrogant comme nos Iberois."[8]

Chriseide et Arimand and *Philandre et Marisee* furnish patriotic elements by the location of their scenes in France, but, as a foreign country lends romantic interest to a play, one more frequently finds the scene placed in such countries as Scotland, Spain, Italy, Greece, Egypt, Syria, or Persia.

Other *romanesque* elements are furnished by dreams, ghosts, disguises, recognitions, duels, shipwrecks, captures by pirates, human sacrifices. Such elements are at times introduced, when unnecessary to the development of the plot, merely to appeal to the imagination of the audience. Thus, the ghost of Fregonde's

[1] *Éthiopique*, III. [2] II, 2. [3] *Heureuses Infortunes*, Part I, IV, 1.
[4] *Aretaphile*, V, 1. [5] *Tyr et Sidon*, *J.* I, II, 1. [6] *Ibidem*, *J.* II, IV, 6.
[7] *Cornelie*, II, 1. [8] *La Force du Sang*, II, 3.

husband bids her wed her lover,[1] though she has not sought her husband's advice during his life in regard to her relations with the other man. When Clitophon arrives in Egypt, it is after a shipwreck, though he was bound for that country and could have arrived there without such a catastrophe. Two brothers are induced to fight a duel in *Genevre,* though the *dénouement* is not brought about by this event, but by the arrival of Renaud.

The happy ending is characteristic of these plays. In *Procris* the happiness consists in the removal of obstacles to the love of Aurore and Cephale, in *Philandre et Marisee* to the salvation of the protagonist, in *L'Innocence Descouverte* to the vindication of the hero, in *Alceste* to the restoration of a wife to her husband. In the other plays it is produced by the removal of all obstacles to the marriage of the hero and heroine, to which is added a family reunion in *Elmire* and *Les Heureuses Infortunes.* In *Gesippe,* though a marriage occurs at the end, the chief happiness lies in the restoration of Gesippe to his fortune and the friendship of Tite. A double *dénouement* occurs in *Dorise* and the *Folies de Cardenio.* In *Tyr et Sidon* the subordinate plot, which concerns the love of Leonte and Philoline, ends tragically, but the principal plot results in the marriage of Belcar and Meliane.

In most of these plays the comic element is of slight importance. Hardy neglects it altogether in seven tragi-comedies and gives it a subordinate place in the others. In his *Theagene et Cariclée* the heroine jests about her disguise.[2] A humorous situation is found in *Alceste,*[3] where Admete's parents, after extravagant protestations of their love for him, decline to die for him when the opportunity is offered. The last act of *Ariadne* is enlivened by Pan's broad jokes. Into *Cornelie*[4] a courtisane is introduced with farcical effect. A witty page appears in *Felismene.* In *La Belle Egyptienne* a humorous situation is made by the mock condemnation of the hero[5] and in the reception of gratuities by the *garçon egyptien*[6] and the *vieille egyptienne*[7]:

"Clement : Helas ! quelles douleurs incroyables i'endure
Vieille : Ouy, mais tu ne dis mot quant au principal point,
Que plus que tes douleurs la pauureté me point."

[1] *Fregonde,* V, 1. [2] *J.* IV, IV, 4. [3] II. [4] IV, 4. [5] V, 5. [6] II, 2. [7] III, 2.

The small number of comic passages found in Hardy shows that such elements, spoken chiefly by subordinate personages, formed no integral part of his work. His example was followed by the majority of his contemporaries. *L'Éthiopique*, *Genevre*, *Les Heureuses Infortunes*, and *Pasithee* show no humorous passages. In *L'Ephesienne*[1] the widow's servant exhibits a coarse wit in comparing Frontin to a skilled anatomist. A witticism is intended when, after Aretaphile has cried to her lover :

> " J'entends quelques soldats qui font la ronde ici.
> Mon ame sauvez vous,"

he replies :

> " Et si ie suis vôtre ame
> Puis-je sans vous tuer, sortir d'ici madame." [2]

Melite, the supposed widow, is humorously discussed in Clitophon.[3] Soldiers, joking over their drinks, are introduced into *Philandre et Marisee.*[4] The host of the tavern in *Chriseide et Arimand*[5] adds some humor to the play. The second *journée* of *Tyr et Sidon*, which represents the form of the play that appeared in 1608, is entirely serious except for a soldier's jest at the close.

These plays follow Hardy's usage, but in six others the humor occupies a larger, though always a subordinate place. Aymee introduces a humorous valet, a rôle already seen in Le Jars's *Lucelle*[6] and repeated in Duhamel's play on the same subject. *Innocence Descouverte* is also full of a valet's jokes, which are usually coarse and often obscene. A similar vein of humorous vulgarity is seen in *Alexandre et Annette.* In *Folies de Cardenio* much fun is made out of the encounter between Cardenio, the curate, and the barber, and the sayings of Don Quixote and Sancho. The first *journée* of *Tyr et Sidon* contains amusing scenes between the jealous Zorote, an early Sganarelle, and his sister, a supposed prude ; also between his wife's lover and attendants.

[1] IV. [2] III, 3. [3] IV, 5. [4] II.
[5] III, 1 and IV, 3. [6] See above, p. 62.

The coarse humor of such passages is in keeping with the freedom of speech used by lovers to express their desires and the scabrous scenes that occur in some of the plays.[1] Some of the later tragi-comedies show such elements in a much smaller degree than those written towards the beginning of the century. *Pasithée* and *Chriseide et Arimand* are free from vulgarity.

The events in the tragi-comedies are commonly the result of entirely exterior circumstances, or of the action of an individual, moved by love, parental affection, friendship, hatred, or other passion. A conflict of passions in the mind of a single personage is rare, but occurs in the following cases: Procris wavers between fidelity to her husband and the solicitations of a supposed stranger;[2] Felismene soliloquizes as to whether or not, in her disguise as page, she should aid the love of Felix for Celie;[3] after a struggle Tite yields to Gesippe's offer of his place in Sophronie's bed;[4] Lucippe hesitates to elope with Clitophon.[5] In the last two cases, the passion conquers the sense of honor, a moral laxity that is still more apparent in the conduct of Arimand in allowing his faithful servitor to take his place in prison, believing that it will probably mean the man's death:

"Arimand: Dieux! que mon ame icy souffre de violence,
L'amour et le deuoir me tiennent en balance,
Si ie m'en vay sans luy c'est une lacheté,
Si ie demeure aussi, c'est une cruauté.
Amour, pitié, deuoir, Bellaris, ma Maistresse
Voyez un peu comment vostre respect me presse." [6]

Had such situations been artistically elaborated and given more prominent positions in the tragi-comedies, Corneille's psychology might have been anticipated. As it is, the personages in these plays are commonly swayed by simple emotions, the treatment of which makes no great demand on the author's dramatic ability.

The hero is usually a brave and handsome youth, endowed with most desirable manly attributes; as, Theagene, Apollonie,

[1] Cf., for example, *Procris*, III, 2; *Ariadne*, III; *Felismene*, IV, 2; *Dorise*, III, 2; *Gesippe*, III, 1; *Heureuses Infortunes*, I, I, 1; *Innocence Descouverte*, I; *Tyr et Sidon*, *J.* I, IV, 9.

[2] *Procris*, II, 2.

[3] *Felismene*, III.

[4] *Gesippe*, II, 2.

[5] *Clitophon*, I, 8.

[6] *Chriseide et Arimand*, III, 1.

Ariodan, Clitophon, or Belcar. The moral weakness of Arimand, just noted, is visible in the heedless love of Alphonse d'Este and Phraarte, which becomes brutality with the hero of *La Force du Sang*, and inconstancy with Cephale in *Procris*, Thesee in *Ariadne*, and Felix in *Felismene*. The Comte de Gleichen in *Elmire* and Admete in *Alceste* are already married when the play begins. It is to be noted that Hardy has made the character of Admete more sympathetic than it is in Euripides by causing Alceste's sacrifice to take place without his knowledge or consent.

While the hero's wisdom equals his other virtues in the case of Apollonie or the Comte de Gleichen, it frequently needs to be supplemented by the advice or assistance of a friend. Calasire and Gnemon play this rôle in *Theagene et Cariclée*, Hercule in *Alceste*, Loncate and Macente in *Arsacome*, Dom Juan and Dom Anthoine in *Cornelie*, Ceraminte in *Pasithée*, Ariste in *Aretaphile*. The aid comes from a go-between, Phalare in *Ariadne*, and Timadon in *Tyr et Sidon;* a page in *Felismene*; a faithful servant in *Chriseide et Arimant* and *Clitophon*.

Among the heroines, Alceste shows exalted altruism, Carícleé and Tharsie a high degree of chastity, Chriseide and Luscinde of fidelity, Marisee of forgiveness. Felismene exhibits much ingenuity in overcoming obstacles to her love. Other heroines do not work out their problems, but are carried along by the course of events; as, in the case of Leocadie, Elmire, and Lucippe. Procris is a sympathetic character, made by an unworthy husband to waver in her fidelity to him and receiving an unmerited fate. She has no rebuke for her husband when he has shot her, but submits with pitiful weakness, saying:

"Mon cœur ie te voye auant que trépasser,
Que i'aye encor vn coup cét heur de t'embrasser.
Cephale: M'embrasser scelerat, m'embrasser homicide,
O cruauté du sort! ô Deité perfide!
Procris: Ma ialousie est cause, et non toy du malheur,
Ne rengrege donc point de plaintes ma douleur."[1]

Cornelie, Philognie, and Dorothée are further examples of heroines whose fidelity is not altered by their lover's neglect.

[1] v.

A low estimate of woman's position is shown in *Gesippe*, when the protagonist substitutes his friend for himself as Sophronie's betrothed and as her husband. Gesippe is evidently actuated by a lofty spirit of self-sacrifice, but he does not seem to realize that Sophronie should be consulted in the matter. Along with the heroine are found women unsuccessful in their love, as Cassandre in *Tyr et Sidon* and Celie in *Felismene*; and women who aid the heroine in her love, as the *nourrice* and *suivante* that occur in many of the tragi-comedies, playing the rôles of mere adviser or of efficient go-between. Especially noticeable in the last capacity are Almodice and Tharside in *Tyr et Sidon.*

Other prominent personages are kings, often proud and pompous, with no keen perception of what the future has in store. Pharnabaze in *Tyr et Sidon,* Philippe in *Phraarte,* Gondebaut in *Chriseide et Arimand* are good examples of this type. A milder sovereign is the virtuous Abdolomin of *Tyr et Sidon,* sincerely distressed by the evils brought upon his country in time of war. When a king is captured, he does not forget himself. Cotys yields nothing to Phraarte, when threatened with death. Orondate replies proudly to Hydaspe's reproaches :

"Un peril affranchy défie un grand courage
D'en affranchir un autre et oser davantage.
Hydaspe : Un peril affranchy doit tout homme prudent
Garder qu'il ne retombe en un pire accident.
. . . .
Tu te sçavois pour nous de nombre incompetant.
Orondate : Ouy, mais ie m'estimoy de courage bastant." [1]

The lovers are opposed by various persons, as Arsace, the passionate wife of Orondate in *Theagene et Cariclée,* or a calculating villain, as Dorade in *Les Heureuses Infortunes.* A rival appears in Nicocrate in *Aretaphile,* Phœdre in *Ariadne,* Adimache in *Arsacome,* the marquis de Bade in *Elmire.* A stern parent interferes to send away the hero on a journey or refuse the heroine to a lover who is not considered her equal, cases that occur in *Felismene, Dorise, Theagene et Cariclée,* and *Philandre et*

[1] *Theagene et Cariclée, J.* VII, III, 1.

Marisee. On the other hand, paternal affection is displayed in *Force du Sang* and *Tyr et Sidon.*

Minor personages are added from various social classes, a courtesan in *Theagene et Cariclée* and *Cornelie*, slaves in *Tyr et Sidon* and *Les Heureuses Infortunes*, a barber in *Folies de Cardenio*, a jailer in Phraarte, a *bourgeoise* in *La Belle Egyptienne* and *Tyr et Sidon*, shepherds in Felismene, *archers* in *Gesippe*, a physician in *Force du Sang*, judges in *Innocence Descouverte*, *Clitophon*, and elsewhere. It is thus evident that all social classes may be represented in these plays from kings to peasants. The leading personages, however, belong to the aristocratic,[1] leisure classes, and are at times of royal blood; as, in *Phraarte*, *Les Heureuses Infortunes*, *Aretaphile*, *Tyr et Sidon.*

The stylistic qualities of these plays are of a low order. Hardy's work, written hurriedly to meet a popular demand, is involved, exaggerated, and frequently obscure. There is a lack of taste in the speeches of his personages, whose emotions are rarely expressed with accuracy. Although his contemporaries wrote with greater care, their style is rarely fluent. Lines are padded, sentiments concealed by a wealth of classical allusions, or refined under the influence of the rising *précieux*. Of numerous examples that may be cited, the following suffice to show the bad taste of the authors:

> "Le bouton degoutant des larmes de l'Aurore
> Plus auide n'attend le Soleil à s'éclorre,
> Les petits Oisillons dans le nid affamez,
> Vn repas incertain de leurs parents aymez,
> La Tourtre sa moitié par le bois écartée,
> Le Pilote vn bon vent à sa Nef arrestée,
> Que fiévreuse d'amour i'attens ce beau pourtrait,
> Cét aymable voleur qui mon ame soustrait." [2]

> "Terreurs d'Acheron, geines epouventables
> Du Cocyte fumeus, aux ombres lamentables:
> Embrazements cruels du nuiteus Phlegeton,
> Foudres, rages, effrois de la fiere Alecton, etc." [3]

[1] The only exception seems to be found in *L'Ephesienne*, where the rank of the widow is not stated. The governor of the province is, however, introduced.

[2] *Felismene*, I, 2.

[3] From Ariodan's invocation, *Genevre*, I.

A *nourrice* thus reminds her mistress of her age:

> "Madame, le flambeau de ce grand Univers
> Trace l'oblique enceint de ses globes diuers
> Pour la fois quarantiesme, et Cerés la feconde
> Par quatre fois dix ans panche sa tresse blonde,
> Depuis qu'à l'œil du Ciel vos yeux ont emprunté
> Les esclairs foudroyant de leur viue Clarté,
> Et qu'avez attiré de vos leures iumelles
> Le nectar nourricier de mes ieunes mamelles." [1]

Clitophon, finding Lucippe alive in a coffin, exclaims:

> "Ha que ie suis ravie
> De trouver au cercueil une seconde vie." [2]

Meliane, lamenting the loss of her lover, cries:

> "O mer! amère mère à la mère d'Amour." [3]

Yet by the side of such absurd *préciosité*, graceful lines occur. The same Meliane, when about to be killed, says to the executioner:

> "Pauvre homme, pleures-tu? te desplaist-il à toy
> De suivre mon desir et le plaisir du roy?" [4]

In *Ariadne* Phœdre recites the following lines, which, though commonplace, offer a pleasing contrast to Hardy's usual style:

> "Le soldat ne sçauroit parler que de la guerre,
> Le pasteur des troupeaux, le rustre de la terre,
> Des vents le marinier, et les amans touiours,
> De voix, où de penser parlent de leurs amours." [5]

A higher degree of excellence is reached by Du Ryer and Pichou:

> "Que la plus belle loy que l'amour puisse avoir
> C'est de n'en avoir point, et de n'en point sçavoir." [6]

> "Si je suis Roy d'un peuple, elle est Reine sur moy." [7]

> "Le plus rude trépas
> Sous un Prince cruel a toujours des apas." [7]

> "La femme est un roseau qui branle au premier vent,
> L'image d'une mer et d'un sable mouvant." [8]

[1] *Innocence Descouverte*, I.
[2] *Clitophon*, III, 2.
[3] *Tyr et Sidon*, *J.* II, IV, 3.
[4] *Ibidem*, V, 2.
[5] III.
[6] *Aretaphile*, I, 10.
[7] *Ibidem*, II, 1.
[8] *Folies de Cardenio*, II, 2.

Such speeches, however, tend to become platitudes, which are of common occurrence in these plays, furnishing, perhaps, one reason of their popularity, if one may judge by the applause that greets the trite on the contemporary stage. A dialogue is sometimes carried on by a series of platitudes; as,

"Sisimetre:	Donter sa passion c'est chose vertueuse.
Charicles:	Il faut en cause iuste une ame courageuse.
S.:	La colere sied mal à l'homme malheureux.
C.:	La fortune n'a rien sur un cœur genereux.
S.:	L'affligé doit en tout user de patience.
C.:	A l'affligé ne faut user de violence, etc." [1]

However artificial such a dialogue may be, it shows a dramatic advance from the ponderous monologues that had been the bane of the French sixteenth-century tragedy, and were imitated by early tragi-comedies. Hardy uses the monologue especially in *Procris* and *Ariadne,* writing the fourth act of the latter in one long soliloquy. When he wrote his later plays, he seems to have realized the superior dramatic qualities of the dialogue. The plays of his contemporaries show corresponding changes, from the lengthy monologues of *Genevre* to the rapid dialogues of Du Ryer.

The classical influence, which is partly responsible for the excessive use of the monologue, predominates in the divisions of the play. All of these tragi-comedies are divided into five acts. The subdivision into scenes is the rule, but exceptions occur in acts of *Procris, Ariadne, Alceste, L'Éthiopique, Genevre, L'Ephesienne, Philandre et Marisee.* Du Ryer, on the other hand, is prodigal of scenes, dividing both *Aretaphile* and *Clitophon* into no less than fifty-eight.

Another advance is in the suppression of the chorus, which survives only in *L'Éthiopique, L'Ephesienne, Genevre,* and *Philandre et Marisee.* In the last two plays it occurs after all the acts except the fifth; in the others, after all the acts. It serves in these cases to comment upon the action without mingling in it. Hardy's tragi-comedies show a lyric chorus in the third act of

[1] *L'Éthiopique,* I.

Arsacome, where soldiers recite seven strophes on the insecurity of kings, while Loncate is murdering Leucanor, and in *Theagene et Cariclée,*[1] where inhabitants of Memphis offer a hymn to Isis and pirates sing at the nuptials of their leader. Elsewhere Hardy's chorus has become a non-lyric *troupe,* comparable to the Roman mob.

Apart from *Alexandre et Annette,* which is written in eight-syllable verse, and *Aymée,* composed in verses of six, eight, ten, and twelve syllables, the tragi-comedies are written in Alexandrines, except in the case of certain lyric passages that occur in nine of them. Hardy uses shorter verse forms only in the choral passage just mentioned. In *Genevre* the choruses are written in verses of seven and eight syllables, and Ariodan's long final speech is in eight-syllable verses. The choruses in *L'Éthiopique* are in verses of six, seven, and eight syllables; in *L'Ephesienne* and *Philandre et Marisee* in verses of eight syllables. In the first part of *Les Heureuses Infortunes* are three erotic songs, the first two in eight-syllable, the third in six- and three-syllable verse.[2] *Clitophon,* when imprisoned for the supposed murder of Lucippe, laments in strophes of alternating lines of twelve and six syllables, the lines riming with the next of the same length.[3] In the *Folies de Cardenio* a love letter is written in eight-syllable verses, and two erotic soliloquies[4] in verses of eight and twelve syllables, of which the first has almost the same strophic form as the *Stances* in *Polyeucte,* while the second shows nine verses of eight syllables, followed by a single Alexandrine. Finally, in *Tyr et Sidon* a page sings a song, in verses of eight syllables with a refrain, praising peace and love as opposed to war. The possibility of using these lighter measures shows a stylistic improvement upon Hardy's classical monotony of form. But this classical influence is still predominant in the tragi-comedy, for the lyric measure, outside of the choruses, is used only in occasional letters or songs of an erotic nature and in soliloquies expressing sadness or joy.

[1] *J.* v, i, 2 and *J.* i, v, 3.

[2] Cf. above, p. 119.

[3] *Clitophon,* v, 2.

[4] ii, 1; iii, 2; iv, 6.

The qualities discussed in the preceding pages are those of the tragi-comedy when definitively established in France. A structural freedom which violates all unities but that of interest in the fate of the leading personages, a *romanesque* and non-historic plot, a happy *dénouement*, personages of mixed rank, of whom the principal individuals are aristocrats, classical division into acts, and use of Alexandrines in the main parts of the plays, are the dominant characteristics of the *genre.* The religious tragi-comedy has now been relegated to provincial schools and monasteries, while the *romanesque* has become the most popular dramatic *genre* on the French stage. The rising generation of playwrights turn their attention largely to it. Du Ryer, Mairet, Rotrou, Scudéry, Boisrobert, Quinault, and others write many tragi-comedies during the following thirty years, which carry on the principles established for the *genre* by Hardy and his contemporaries. With the last publication of Hardy's plays (1628) the history of the tragi-comedy in France during its time of development is complete. To show the extent of the influence exerted by these plays, I shall, however, give in a final chapter a brief account of the subsequent history of the *genre.*

CHAPTER IV.

SUBSEQUENT HISTORY OF THE TRAGI-COMEDY.

To show the influence exerted by the tragi-comedies of Hardy and his contemporaries on those that followed in the next period (1628–1636), a list of tragi-comedies, beginning with Rotrou's first play (1628) and ending with Corneille's *Cid* (1636) has been added as Appendix B, III. From the eight years that lie between the representations of these two plays, fifty-three tragi-comedies are extant, a larger number than that of the extant tragi-comedies of the preceding twenty-eight years.[1] That this *genre* had now become the most popular in France is shown by an examination of the *Mémoire* of Mahelot, a document that gives a list of plays acted at the Hôtel de Bourgogne from about 1633 [2] to 1636, some of which were written during this period, others in the preceding decade, or even earlier. Of the seventy-one plays listed, twenty-two,[3] including twelve assigned to Hardy are lost, so that it is not

[1] It does not follow that a larger number of tragi-comedies were written in the later than in the earlier period, for the bulk of Hardy's work was produced between 1600 and 1628, including without doubt numerous tragi-comedies that have been lost.

[2] Rigal (*Alexandre Hardy*, 682) posits 1631 instead of 1633, basing his conclusion on the dates of the second, fourth, and sixth plays mentioned in the *Mémoire*. Since he wrote, however, Stiefel (*ZFSL*, XVI, 22–3) has shown that the first of the three plays, Rotrou's *Occasions perdues*, was written in 1633 instead of 1631, as the Frères Parfaict state. As this is the first play in the list of which the date is known, the *Mémoire* cannot have been begun before 1633.

[3] I include among these Auvray's *Madonte*, mentioned, without name of author, in the *Mémoire*, folios 17 vo. and 18. Rigal (*Alexandre Hardy*, 687) is in doubt as to whether this play is meant, or one by Pierre Cottignon, mentioned by Beauchamps, II, 96; while Dacier (*Mémoire de Laurent Mahelot*, discussion of folios 17 vo. and 18), blindly following the statement of the Frères Parfaict (IV, 494) that Auvray's play was not acted, declares that "il s'agit de Pierre Cottignon." No one who reads Auvray's *Madonte*, however, can doubt that this is the play indicated by Mahelot, for not only do the general details of the *mise en scène* described by the latter fit this play, but there are special correspondences, as when Mahelot

known to what *genre* they belonged. Of the remaining forty-nine, two are tragedies, eleven comedies, five pastorals, four *tragi-comédies pastorales,* and twenty-seven tragi-comedies. It seems, therefore, that at the Hôtel de Bourgogne, the leading French theater, more tragi-comedies were acted from 1633 to 1636 than plays belonging to all the other dramatic *genres* put together.

The tragi-comedy was now written by the leading dramatists, Rotrou, Du Ryer, Mairet, and Scudéry. Corneille contributed *Clitandre* (1632) to the *genre* and called his *Cid* a tragi-comedy in its early editions, though its classical elements subsequently induced him to publish it as a tragedy. All but three of the extant tragi-comedies were published at Paris, where the great majority of them must have been acted. Their sources were much the same as those used by Hardy and his contemporaries. The Odyssey, source of *Les Travaux d'Ulysse,* is the only classical work followed, but the *Orlando Furioso,* the *Amadís,* Cervantes's *Novelas Exemplares,* Gomberville's *Polexandre,* Barclay's *Argénis,* and, especially, the *Astrée* of Honoré d'Urfé, supplied the plots of many tragi-comedies. Rotrou's *Occasions Perdues* (1633) is the first tragi-comedy to show the influence of the Spanish drama, from which source he had drawn the plot of his comedy, *La Bague de l'Oubly,* in 1628.

As may be supposed from such sources, the plays are thoroughly *romanesque,* based on love and employing in detail disguises, resemblances, duels, poisonings, suicides, and other measures, with which the reader of earlier tragi-comedies is thoroughly familiar. Further interest is added by a spirit of adventure, particularly visible in the *Travaux d'Ulysse,* by a delineation of loyalty to a monarch in the *Vassal Genereux,* by appeals to patriotism, shown in the frequent location of the scene in France, and by such occasional passages as that found in *Argenis et Poliarque,* v, 2:

> "La valeur se nourrit dans le sein de la France,
> Elle a tousiours faict voir que ses moindres guerriers
> Arracheroient à Mars ses plus riches lauriers."

---

writes, "l'acte deuxiesme, un mouchoir ensanglanté, une bague," both of which articles are used in Auvray's *Madonte,* in the third scene of the second act; and "il faut un rondache ou il y ayt un tigre peint," referring to the hero of this play "qui porte pour sa marque un tigre en son bouclier," (v, 3).

The only *non-romanesque* tragi-comedies written during these years are two school plays, of which one, the lost *Triomphe d'Octave César* (1631), is historical, the other, *S. Sebastien Martyr* (1635), is religious. In these the purpose is the instruction of the audience, as it is again in *L'Inconstance Punie.* The main purpose elsewhere is to arouse the curiosity of the audience by a series of romantic adventures and exaggerated expressions of emotion, although morality may be inculcated subordinately; as, in *Madonte* or the *Trompeur puny.*

So little regard is paid in these pieces to the unities that many of the plays have nearly the structural looseness of the romances from which they are derived. Distinct plots are dramatized successively in one play; as, for example, in the *Travaux d'Ulysse* and the *Trompeur puny.* They may be interwoven with one another, as they are in *La Sœur Valeureuse, Ligdamon et Lidias,* or *L'Orizelle.* Rotrou is especially given to the latter usage, which leads him to a triple *dénouement* in *Les Occasions perdues* and *L'Heureuse Constance.* The unity of place is similarly violated, so that, for example, the scene of *Argenis et Poliarque* is laid in France and Sicily; that of *L'Indienne Amoureuse* in Florida and Peru. The time in which the action takes place is usually several months.

The personages represent various social ranks, with aristocrats in the leading rôles. Kings are frequently introduced, as in *Argenis* and *Orizelle; bourgeois,* as in *La Bourgeoise;* the lower classes, as the butcher in *Lisandre et Caliste,* or the coachman in *Agarite.* The *dénouement* is happy, even in *L'Inconstance Punie,* where the heroine's sisters perish, but she escapes death and is united to the hero. The comic elements are purely subsidiary and usually take up a small part of the play,[1] but in *L'Ospital des Fous* they are of frequent occurrence, though subordinate to the main plot. The division into five acts and subdivision into scenes continue throughout the period. The use of Alexandrines is the rule, to which exceptions occur, especially in *L'Inconstance Punie,* where the verse forms of the dialogues are

[1] Cf., for example, *Madonte,* I, 3 or *Argenis,* II, 2.

repeatedly varied. In other plays short verse forms are used, especially for love letters, soliloquies, and hymns.[1]

Similar dramatic qualities are found in the tragi-comedies that continued to appear, still in large numbers, after the representation of the *Cid*, at the end of 1636. It was by means of a tragi-comedy, *L'Amour tyrannique* (1638, printed 1639), that Scudéry sought to rival the *Cid.* It was in tragi-comedies that Richelieu tried to show that his genius was dramatic as well as political. Under his direction a tragi-comedy, *L'Aveugle de Smyrne,* was written by the collaboration of Corneille, Rotrou, Boisrobert, L'Etoile, and Colletet; and another tragi-comedy, *Mirame,* was composed by Desmarests for the opening of the "grande salle du Palais Cardinal." Such authors as Rotrou, Mairet, Du Ryer, Mareschal, Scudéry, and Boisrobert, who had written tragi-comedies before 1636, continued to write them after that date. Their example was followed by a number of younger authors, among whom the most prominent were Desfontaines, La Calprenède, Desmarests, Chevreau, Gillet de la Tessonnerie, Baro, Colletet, Gabriel Gilbert, d'Ouville, Scarron, and Quinault. By the side of the *romanesque* dramas of these authors, the religious tragi-comedies of the school continued sporadically the medieval tradition, for one finds in Savoy a *Sainte-Barbe, vierge et chrestienne* of 1654,[2] and in Belgium *La Bonne et Mauvaise Croix, ou Saint André* of 1665.[3]

Toward 1650, however, the number of tragi-comedies that appeared each year was decreasing and by 1660 had become very small, if one may judge by those of which the names have been preserved. With the *Psyché* of Corneille, Molière, and Quinault (1671) and the *Parfaits Amis* of Chappuzeau (1672) the *genre* practically ceases to exist, although sporadic examples of the use of its name recur during the following centuries.[4] The causes of this decay are not far to seek.

[1] Compare, for example, *Pyrandre et Lisimène,* I, 4; *L'Infidelle Confidente,* IV, 4; *Omphalle,* V, 3.

[2] See Mugnier, *Théâtre en Savoie,* 97.

[3] See Faber, IV, 346.

[4] The following plays may be cited in illustration of this recurrence:

Monsieur le maréchal de Luxembourg au lict de la mort, tragicomédie en cinq actes . . . MDCC. Bibliothèque Nationale, MS. *fr.* 2957, fol. 232.

In the first place the popular taste had reacted from the spirit of the early seventeenth century, which had found expression in the *romanesque* tragi-comedy, as well as in the *précieux* Hôtel de Rambouillet and in the romances of Honoré d'Urfé and Madeleine de Scudéry. The Parisian public, grown weary of the multiplicity of incident and exaggerated portrayal of character, found in the tragi-comedy, turned from that *genre* to the truer representations of life that they found on the classical stage. It is after the appearance of *Horace* and *Polyeucte* that the tragi-comedy begins to decline, not long after the successes of Molière and Racine that it ceases to exist.

But in addition to the change in the taste of the Parisian public and the increasing popularity of the classical stage, the tragi-comedy suffered from certain changes in its own composition and in the use of the terms, tragedy and comedy, which brought about its confusion with these *genres*. As early as Mairet's *Chriseide et Arimand* (1625) tendencies toward unity of plot existed in tragi-comedies. In his *Silvanire*, a *tragi-comédie pastorale*, and his *Virginie*, a tragi-comedy, Mairet continued these tendencies, which were carried further by Desmarests in *Mirame*, a tragi-comedy which preserves the classical unities. At the same time psychological struggles, which had formerly held a distinctly subordinate place in tragi-comedies, became important in the *dénouements* of *La Fidelle Tromperie* and *Agésilan de Colchos* and formed the essence of the plot of Rayssiguier's *Celidee*. Thus it is that the unity and psychology of the *Cid* did not prevent its being called a tragi-comedy, a title that fitted well its *romanesque* plot and happy *dénouement*.

Le Berger d'Amphise tragi-comédie (1727) by Delisle de la Drevetière, Bibliothèque Nationale, MS. *fr*. 9311.

L'Ambitieux et l'Indiscrette tragi-comédie (1737) by Néricault Destouches, *Oeuvres dramatiques*, vol. VI (Paris, 1758).

Le Nottaire extravaguant, tragi-comédie (undated, but probably latter half of the eighteenth century). Bibliothèque Nationale, MS. *fr*. 9248.

Les Constipés d'Asnières ou la Découverte de l'émétique, parade tragi-comique (1840), by T. Thibaut, Bibliothèque Nationale, MS. *fr*. 9248.

Scarron, comédie tragique, by Catulle Mendès, Paris, 1905.

While the tragi-comedy was thus approaching the tragedy by a greater unity of plot and a more careful study of the emotions, another barrier that had separated the two *genres* in France, the nature of the *dénouement,* was removed by Corneille, when, following the example of Euripides, he showed in *Cinna,* and partially in *Horace,* that a tragedy could have a happy *dénouement,* a usage approved by d'Aubignac, as already noted.[1] Thus, the more serious tragi-comedies, which showed an approach to classical unity and psychology, came to be called tragedies, in spite of their happy *dénouement.* The *Cid,* first known as a tragi-comedy, was called a tragedy along with *Polyeucte* and *Rodogune.*

On the other hand, certain tragi-comedies, as *L'Ospital des Fous,* approached the comedy by an increase in the comic element, as did others by a *bourgeois* spirit that enters more especially into *La Bourgeoise* and *L'Esperance Glorieuse.* The term *comédie,* moreover, was now applied to translations of the Spanish *comedia* and related plays, which differed little in their essential qualities from the lighter forms of the tragi-comedy. Thus some tragi-comedies were confused with comedies, as others were with tragedies. The two terms that had the sanction of Greek and Latin usage were gradually extended to occupy the intermediate ground formerly held by the tragi-comedy. Thus French dramatists, answering the demands of their age, either ceased to write tragi-comedies, or called them by another name. As an independent *genre,* the tragi-comedy ceased to exist.

Such is the history of the French tragi-comedy. Drawing its substance from the medieval drama and its form from the Greek and Roman stage, it united these elements after the example of the *genre* in other European countries and came into existence in 1552. During the sixteenth century it represented a number of medieval *genres,* connected by their partially classical form and happy *dénouement.* One variety, the *romanesque,* showed its superior qualities, becoming with Hardy in the seventeenth century the only active form of the tragi-comedy. Before the establishment of the classical tragedy this *romanesque* tragi-comedy became the most

[1] See above, p. xvii.

popular and extensively written dramatic *genre* in France. But its preëminence was brief, for, encroached upon by the closely related tragedy and comedy, and out of harmony with the classical spirit of the time, it fell into disuse and, toward 1672, ceased to have a more than sporadic existence.

Unless the *Cid* be considered a tragi-comedy, the *genre* left behind no great literary monument, since it neglected the study of character and passion for the *romanesque* and the melodramatic, thus attaining a large popularity, but making no permanent or universal appeal. But the tragi-comedy holds an important position in the history of the French stage, serving as a connecting link between the theater of the middle ages and that of the classical period, and by its influence making it possible for Corneille's tragedy to succeed where Jodelle's had failed. It preserved the popular qualities of the medieval drama, modernized them, and passed them to the classicists, thus establishing itself as an integral part of the most continuously excellent of national theaters.

APPENDIX A.

NON-FRENCH TRAGI-COMEDIES WRITTEN BEFORE 1582.[1]

1494.—*Fernandus Servatus. Tragicomoedia* by Carlo and Marcellino Verardi. Acted and printed at Rome. Reprinted at Strasburg in 1513.[2] The dedicatory epistle to Cardinal Mendoza refers to a representation of the play in his presence.[3]

1501.—*Tragicocomedia de iherosolomitana profectione illustrissimi principis pomeriani* by Johann von Kitzscher. Leipzig.[4]

[1] See above, page 24 *seq.*

[2] The reprints mentioned by Creizenach (*Geschichte*, II, 10, n.) were of the *Historia Baetica* only and not of both dramas, as he incorrectly states.

[3] Hain, *Repertorium Bibliographicum*, No. 15943, Stuttgart, 1826-38, 4 vols.; Ginguené, *Histoire littéraire d'Italie*, VI, 16-17; Soleinne, *Dictionnaire*, I, no. 172; Chassang, *Essais dramatiques*, 140-1; Brunet, *Manuel*, V, 1128; D'Ancona, *Sac. Rap.* II, 155-6; Creizenach, *Geschichte*, II, 9. The edition dated Aug. 16, 1494, is cited by Hain, *Repertorium*, II, 474. Another edition, without place or date, is bound with the *Historia Baetica* of Carlo Verardi, which was acted in 1492 and printed in 1493. On this account these dates have been incorrectly assigned to *Fernandus Servatus*. Now, this play commemorates the attempted assassination of King Ferdinand of Spain and his recovery from the wound received at the time. As the attempt was made on Dec. 7, 1492, and as the king was not restored to health until three weeks later, it is impossible that the play could have been written and produced at Rome before 1493. Furthermore, as it is dedicated to Pedro Mendoza, who died Jan. 11, 1495, it must have been written before 1495. As the year 1493 has nothing in support of it except the fact that the *Historia Baetica* was published that year, while 1494 is endorsed by Hain, the latter date must be assigned to the play.

[4] Soleinne, *Dictionnaire*, I, no. 275; Brunet, *Manuel*, III, 671; Creizenach, *Geschichte*, II, 34.

1502.—*Celestina. Tragicomedia de Calisto y Melibea.* Authorship unknown, but assigned to Fernando de Rojas. Probably written about 1483; first extant edition published at Burgos, 1499; first called *tragicomedia* in the edition of Seville, 1502. Numerous reprints before 1582 at various towns of Spain, at Venice, Milan, Genoa, and Antwerp.[1]

1513-1533.—Nine *tragicomedias* in Portuguese and Spanish by Gil Vicente: *Exhortaçaõ da Guerra, Côrtes de Jupiter, Dom Duardos, Fragoa de Amor, Templo de Apollo, Nao de amores, Triumpho do Inverno, Romagem de Aggravados, Amadis de Gaula.* Collection published at Lisbon, 1562.[2]

1530.[3]—*Tragicomedia del Epicuro napoletano. intitulata la Cecaria, nuovamente aggiuntovi un bellissimo lamento del Gelcso. Con la Luminaria non più posta in luce.* Antonio Marsi is the author's name. Venice. It had been printed at Venice in 1525, 1526, and 1528 as *Dialogo di tre Ciechi* without being called *tragicomedia.* It was reprinted seventeen times at Venice once at Milan and once at Naples by the year 1575.[4]

[1] Gallardo, *Ensayo,* IV, 241; Brunet, *Manuel,* I, 1715 and Supp., I, 229; Barrera, *Catálogo,* 298; *Biblioteca de Autores españoles,* III, 12; R. Foulché-Delbosc, *Revue Hispanique,* VII, 28-80 and IX, 171-99; Konrad Haebler, *ibidem,* IX, 137-70.

[2] Gil Vicente, *Obras,* II, 181-532 (edited by J. V. Barreto Feio and J. G. Monteiro, Hamburg, 1834, 3 vols.); Braga, *Historia da Litteratura. Theatro no Sec. XVI,* 10-207; Creizenach, *Geschichte,* III, 191 *seq.* Of these plays *Exhortaçao* is in Portuguese; *Aggravãdos* and *Côrtes de Jupiter* (also called *Al parto de la Reina*) are in Portuguese, with the exception of some thirty lines of Spanish in each; *Duardos* and *Amadis* in Spanish; the four others in both languages.

[3] D'Ancona would place here a *Comedia overo Tragedia* by Bartholomeo Ugoni, "che sarebbe il primo saggio di Tragicomedia." Published without date or place, it is found bound with a work dated 1521. D'Ancona, *Origini del Teatro in Italia,* II, 217. Cf. Salvioli, *Bibliografia,* 811. With this may be compared the beginning of *La Rapresentione* [sic] *di S. Theodora,* published 1554, where "*incomincia la commedia o vero tragedia.*" Cf. D'Ancona, *Sacre Rappresentazioni,* II, 324.

[4] Salvioli, *Bibliografia,* 701-2; *Scelta di curiosità letterarie, I Drammi Pastorali di Antonio Marsi,* Vol. II (*Bologna,* 1888); De Gubernatis, *Storia universale della letteratura,* I, 384; Brunet, *Manuel,* II, 1016; Soleinne, *Dictionnaire,* III, Nos. 4130 and 4131; Riccoboni, *Histoire du Théâtre italien,* 148; *Crescimbeni, Comentarj,* II, 185.

1535.—*Tragicomoedia ex Daniele prophetâ contrà idolatriam* by Joannes Carbonirosa Kirchoviensis or by Xystus Betulius of Augsburg. Bâle.[1]

1537.—*Susanna Comoedia Tragica* by Xystus Betulius (Sixt Birk). Augsburg. Reprinted at Cologne and Zurich 1538; Cologne 1539; Augsburg about 1540 and 1564; Zurich 1541; Bâle 1541, 1547, and 1564. Reprinted recently by Johannes Bolte in *Lateinische Litteraturdenkmäler,* VIII, Berlin, 1893.[2]

1539.—*Tragicomedia alegórica del Paraíso y del infierno. Burgos.*[3 4]

1540 (?).—*Iudith. Drama comicotragicum. Exemplum reipublicae recte institutae: unde discitur, quomodo arma contra Turcam sint capienda,* by Xystus Betulius. Augsburg. Reprinted at Cologne 1544, and at Bâle 1547[5]

[1] *Epitome Bibliothecae Conradi Gesneri,* I, 60 vo.; *Mistére du Viel Testament,* V, p. LIII. Soleinne in his *Dictionnaire,* I, page 83, follows the *Epitome* in referring this play to Carbonirosa. Now, Betulius is known to have presented a play on this subject at Bâle in 1535, while there is *Ein herrliche Tragedi wider die Abgötterey,* which was acted at Bâle, May 9, 1535, and is a condensed form of Betulius's *Beel Ain Herrliche Tragedi wider die Abgötterey,* Augsburg, 1539. Betulius, then, seems to have written a German play at Bâle in 1535 that has practically the same title as the Latin play assigned to Carbonirosa and published at Bâle in the same year. Hence it is probable that Betulius, rather than Carbonirosa, was the author of the play. Goedeke, *Grundrisz,* II, 345; Creizenach, *Geschichte,* III, 325.

[2] Soleinne, *Dictionnaire,* I, Nos. 502 and 503; Brunet, *Manuel,* I, 834 and II, 835; Goedeke, *Grundrisz,* II, 134; Creizenach, *Geschichte,* II, 120 and III, 320; Baechtold, *Geschichte,* 301; Pilger in *Zeischrift f. D. Philologie,* 1880, 129-217.

[3] Moratin, *Tesoro,* I, 78; Brunet, *Manuel,* V, 912. Paz y Mélia, *Catálogo de las Piezas de Teatro,* 388. The latter refers to MS 2501 of the Biblioteca Nacional at Madrid, which contains this piece. Barrera, *Catalogo,* 475 and 587; Gallardo, *Ensayo* I, 980 *seq.*

[4] The *Anábion, sive Lazarus Redivivus. Comoedia nova et sacre* by Joannes Sapidus, Cologne, 1539, might be cited here, as its author declares that it can be called *tragicomoedia.* Goedeke, *Grundrisz,* II, 135; Creizenach, *Geschichte des N. Dramas,* II, 104; Brunet, *Manuel,* V, 137.

[5] Soleinne, *Dictionnaire,* I, nos. 291 and 502; Brunet, *Manuel,* I, 834 and II, 835; Goedeke, *Grundrisz,* II, 134; Creizenach, *Geschichte,* III, 322. Bolte, in *Lateinische Litteraturdenkmäler,* VIII, *Einleitung,* page V, dates this play 1536, but he cites no authority for the date.

1542.—*Tragicomedia de Lysandro y Roselia llamada Elicia y por otro nombre quarta obra y tercera Celestina.* Madrid.[1]

1543.—*Christus redivivus, comoedia tragica sacra et nova* by Nicholas Grimald. Cologne. Acted in Merton College, Oxford, probably in 1540.[2]

1544.—*Comoedia Tragica, quae inscribitur Magdalena Evangelica* by Petrus Philicinus of Arras. Antwerp. Reprinted there 1546.[3]

1544.—*Hypocrisis. Tragicocomoedia* by Guilielmus Gnaphaeus (Willem van de Voldersgroft) of Gravenhage. Bâle.[4]

1546.—*Voluptatis ac Virtutis Pugna. Comoedia tragica et nova et pia,* by Jacobus Schoepper of Dortmund. Cologne. Reprinted there 1563.[5]

1546.—*Tragicomoedia Sant Pauls bekerung. Gespilt von einer Burgerschafft der wytberümpten frystatt Basel, im jor M. D. XLVI,* by Valentin Boltz of Rufach. Bâle, 1551.[6]

1547.—*Sapientia Solomonis, Drama comicotragicum* by Xystus Betulius. Published in *Dramata sacra ex Veteri Testamento desumpta,* Bâle 1547.[7]

1547.—*Protoplastus. Drama comicotragicum* by Hieronymus Ziegler of Rotenburg. Published in *Dramata sacra* just noted.[8]

1547.—*Nomothesia. Drama tragicomicum* by Hieronymus Ziegler. Published in *Dramata sacra* just noted.

[1] Brunet, *Manuel,* III, 1257; Barrera, *Catálogo,* 560.

[2] J. M. Hart in *Publications of Mod. Language Ass.,* XIV, 3; Creizenach, *Geschichte,* II, 138; Chambers, *Mediaeval Stage,* II, 450.

[3] Goedeke, *Grundrisz,* II, 137; Brunet, *Manuel,* IV, 607; Soleinne, *Dictionnaire,* I, no. 409; Creizenach, *Geschichte,* II, 138.

[4] Goedeke, *Grundrisz,* II, 133; Brunet, *Manuel,* II, 1630; Soleinne, *Dictionnaire,* I, no. 389.

[5] Goedeke, *Grundrisz,* II, 138; Brunet, *Manuel,* V, 215; Soleinne, *Dictionnaire,* I, no. 311.

[6] Goedeke, *Grundrisz,* II, 348.

[7] Soleinne, *Dictionnaire,* I, no. 502; Brunet, *Manuel,* I, 834 and II, 835. Goedeke, *Grundrisz,* II, 134.

[8] Gesner, *Epitome,* I, 52 Vo. Soleinne, *Dictionnaire,* I, no. 502; Brunet, *Manuel,* II, 835; Goedeke, *Grundrisz,* II, 137. For Protoplastus, cf. also Creizenach, *Geschichte,* II, 109.

1549.—*Ophiletes. Drama Comicotragicum argumento ex D. Matthaei Euangelio sumpto* by H. Ziegler. Ingolstadt (?).[1]

First half of the sixteenth century (?).—*Apollo e Leucotoe. Tragicommedia* by Francesco Sallustio Buonguglielmi of Florence. Florence.[2]

1551.—*Gollias.* Latin Tragicomedy given by students at the University of Coimbra (Portugal).[3]

1551.—*Monomachia Davidis et Goliae Tragicicomoedia nova simul et sacra* by Jacobus Schoepper. Antwerp.[4]

1552.—*Tragicomedia Chiammata Potentia d'amore* by Gerotheo di Magri di Mantoa. Ferrara.[5]

1553.—*Regales nuptiae drama comicotragicum ex Matth. 22. capite argumento sumpto* by Hieronymus Ziegler. Augsburg.[6]

1555.—*Parabola Christi de decem Virginibus in drama comicotragicum redacta* by Hieronymus Ziegler. Ingolstadt. Reprinted at Antwerp in 1556.[7]

1556.—*Adelphopolae. Drama comicotragicum historiam Josephi, Jacobi filii, complectens* by Martinus Balticus of Munich. Augsburg.[8]

1558.—*Drama Comico-tragicum, Danielis prophetae leonibus objecti et ab angelis Dei rursus liberati historiam complectens* by Martinus Balticus. Augsburg.[9]

[1] Gesner, *Epitome*, I, 52 vo. Soleinne, *Dictionnaire*, I, No. 305; Goedeke, *Grundrisz*, II, 137.

[2] Salvioli, *Bibliografia*, 326; Allacci, *Drammaturgia*, 97; Crescimbeni, *Comentarj della Poesia italiana*, II, 165.

[3] Braga, *Historia da Universidade de Coimbra*, I, 559 (Lisbon, 1892) and *Curso de historia*, 239; Creizenach, *Geschichte*, II, 80.

[4] Soleinne, *Dictionnaire*, I, no. 313; Brunet, *Manuel*, V, 215; Goedeke, *Grundrisz*, II, 138. Spengler in *Zeitschrift für die österreichischen Gymnasien*, XL, 442 *seq.*

[5] There is a copy in the Biblioteca Nazionale at Venice. Allacci in his *Drammaturgia*, 640, writes *Venice* for *Ferrara.*

[6] Gesner, *Appendix*, I, 52 vo.; Goedeke, *Grundrisz*, II, 137, does not give the *genre.*

[7] Soleinne, *Dictionnaire*, I, no. 308; Goedeke, *Grundrisz*, II, 137.

[8] Goedeke, *Grundrisz*, II, 141; Soleinne, *Dictionnaire*, I, no 320; Creizenach, *Geschichte*, II, 115.

[9] Goedeke, *Grundrisz*, II, 141.

1561.—*La Cangenia. Tragicomedia* by Beltramo Poggi of Florence. Florence.[1] [2]

1562.—*Finis Saulis et Coronatio Davidis, tragi-comoedia.* Represented at Prague.[3]

1563.—*Exodus sive transitus maris rubri comoedia tragica* by Cornelius Laurimanus of Utrecht. Louvain.

1566.—*Il Giudizio di Paride. Tragicommedia* by Gio. Maria Scotto. Naples.[5]

1566.—*Il Ratto d'Helena, tragicommedia* by Anello Paulilli.[6]

1567.—*Tragococomoedia. Von dem frommen Könige Dauid, und seinem auffrürischen Sohn Absolon* by Bernhard Hederich. Represented at Schwerin, Sept. 1. Represented there again in 1569. Published at Lübeck in 1569.[7]

1567.—Damon and Pithias by Richard Edwardes, who calls it in his prologue a "tragical comedy." It was "entered on the registers of the Stationers' Company in 1567 as 'a boke intituled the tragicall comodye of Damonde and Pethyas.' " It was printed in 1571 and in 1582.[8]

1567.—*Quintilia. Tragicomedia* by Diomisso Guazzoni of Cremona. Mantua. Reprinted there in 1579.[9]

[1] Allacci, *Drammaturgia,* 161; Salvioli, *Bibliografia,* 624; Soleinne, *Dictionnaire,* III, no. 4258; Riccoboni, *Histoire,* 144.

[2] *L'Invenzione della Croce di Gesu Cristo descritta in versi sciolti e in stile comico e tragico* (1561) by Beltramo Poggi may be cited here. Cf. Soleinne, *Dictionnaire,* III, no. 4291; Allacci, *Drammaturgia,* 466; Riccoboni, *Histoire,* 165.

[3] *Mistére du Viel Testament,* IV, p. xxv.

[4] Goedeke, *Grundrisz,* II, 139.

[5] Allacci, *Drammaturgia,* 414; Riccoboni, *Histoire,* 120 and 160.

[6] Soleinne, *Dictionnaire,* III, No. 4388; Riccoboni, *Histoire,* 120; Allacci, *Drammaturgia,* 629. The latter does not indicate the *genre.*

[7] Goedeke, *Grundrisz,* II, 402.

[8] Dodsley, Old Plays, IV, 1-104; Halliwell, *Dictionary of Old English Plays,* 70; Greg, *List of English Plays,* 36; Collier, *History of English Dramatic Poetry,* III, 3 *seq.*

[9] Allacci, *Drammaturgia,* 654; Soleinne, *Dictionnaire,* III, No. 4623; Brunet, *Manuel,* II, 1782. There are copies of the second edition at the Biblioteca Nazionale at Venice and the Biblioteca Ambrosiana at Milan.

1570.—*Sedecias* by Padre Luiz da Cruz. Represented by the Jesuits at Coimbra, Portugal.[1]

1570.—*Josephus*. *Tragicomedia* by Padre Luiz da Cruz.[2]

1558-1578.—*Prodigus*. *Tragicomedia* by Padre Luiz da Cruz.[2]

1571.—*Naboth*. *Tragicocomoedia sacra* by Cornelius Laurimanus of Utrecht. Utrecht.[3]

1571.—*Susannae Helchiae filiae tragica comoedia heroicis versibus expressa* by Carolus Godranius of Dijon. Dijon.[4]

1573.—*Ecclesia Militans. Tragicocomoedia bipartita, Christianae ejusdem Catholicae fidei incrimentum, persecutiones, haereses et alias ad supremum usque iudicii diem vicissitudines varias comprehendens* by Michael Hiltprand, a Jesuit. Dillingen, Bavaria.[5]

1575.—*Gedeon*. *Tragicocomoedia sacra* by Libertus ab Hauthem of Tongern. Liège.[6]

1575.—*A new Tragicall Comedie of Apius and Virginia* by *R. B.* London. Collier says this was probably acted in 1563.[7]

1575.—*The Glasse of Gouernement. A tragicall Comedie* by George Gascoigne.[8]

1576.—*Inclyta Aeneis: P. Virgilii Maronis, poetarum optimi, in regiam tragicocomoediam . . . redacta* by Joannes Lucienbergius. Frankfort-on-the-Main.[9]

[1] This is called a *tragicomedia* by Braga, *Curso de historia de litteratura*, 282.

[2] Braga, *Historia da Litteratura portugueza. Theatro no Secolo XVII*, 360.

[3] Soleinne, *Dictionnaire*, I, 83, suggests Philippus Morus of Utrecht as the author of this piece. Goedeke, *Grundrisz*, II, 139, assigns the play to Laurimannus, but he gives neither place nor date of its publication.

[4] Soleinne, *Dictionnaire*, I, page 83, Brunet, II, 1640; P. Papillon, *Bibliothèque des auteurs de Bourgogne*, I, 258, Dijon, 1745, two vols. in one.

[5] Goedeke, *Grundrisz*, II, 140; P. Bahlmann, *Jesuiten-Dramen der niederrheinischen Ordensprovinz*, 2, Leipzig, 1896.

[6] Goedeke, *Grundrisz*, II, 140

[7] Page 107 of introduction to reprint of this play in Dodsley, *Old Plays*, IV, 105-155. Cf. Greg, *English Plays*, 123; Halliwell, *Dictionary*, 20.

[8] Greg, *English Plays*, 40; Halliwell, *Dictionary*, 109; Collier, *English Dramatic Poetry*, III, 7.

[9] Soleinne, *Dictionnaire*, I, No. 329; Brunet, *Manuel*, III, 1216.

1578.—*Susanna. Comicotragoedia* by Peder Ienssön Hegelund. Copenhagen.[1] Translation of Betulius's play (see above under the year 1537).

1581.—*Susanna, comedia tragica.* Written in Portugal.[2] [3]

---

[1] Brunet, *Manuel*, VI, 920; *Mistére du Viel Testament*, V, p. *LXIX*.

[2] Braga, *Historia da Litteratura. Theatro no Secolo XVII*, 360.

[3] According to *Mistére du Viel Testament* (IV, p. xl) another tragicomedy is found in *La Coronazione del re Saul* by Giovanmaria Cecchi of Florence, represented "vers le milieu du XVI siècle." D'Ancona, *Sac. Rap.* III, 1, mentions the piece, but does not give its *genre*.

APPENDIX B.

FRENCH TRAGI-COMEDIES FROM 1552 TO 1636.

I.—The Sixteenth Century.[1]

1552.—*Tragique Comedie Françoise de l'homme iustifié par Foy. Galat III. Avez-vous receu l'Esprit par les oeuvres de la Loy, ou par la predication de la Foy?* (verses of 10 and 8 syllables; 5 acts) by Henry de Barran. Geneva (?). Published 1554, two years after it was written, as the author states in his prologue. Reprinted 1561, according to La Croix du Maine.[2]

1561.—*Tragi-comedie. L'Argument pris du troisieme chapitre de Daniel: avec le cantique des trois enfans, chanté en la fornaise. Matth. 10. Ne craignez point ceux qui tuent les corps, etc.* (verses of 12, 10 and 8 syllables without division into acts and scenes; chorus) by A. D. L. C. [Antoine de La Croix.] Paris. Dedicated to the Queen of Navarre. Called for brevity *Les Enfants dans la Fournaise.*[3]

[1] See above, page 36 *seq.*

[2] La Croix du Maine, *Bibliothèque*, 363; Beauchamps, *Recherches*, II, 26; Léris, *Dictionnaire portatif*, 177; La Vallière, *Bibliothèque*, I, 142; Mouhy, *Journal*, 135 and 137; Clément, *Anecdotes dramatiques*, I, 433; Soleinne, *Dictionnaire*, I, Nos. 736-37; Brunet, *Manuel*, I, 666; Ebert, *Franz: Tragödie*, 131; Petit de Julleville, *Répertoire du Théâtre comique*, 69; E. Picot, *Bulletin du protestant français*, 1892, 626 *seq.;* Lanson *Revue d'hist. litt.*, X, 414.

[3] Du Verdier, *Bibliothèque*, III, 111; Maupoint, *Bibliothèque*, 308; Beauchamps, II, 30-1; Léris, 127; La Vallière, I, 159; Mouhy, 160; Clément, I, 306; Soleinne, I, 156; Brunet, IV, 1; Faguet, *Tragédie française*, 102 *seq.;* Creizenach, *Geschichte*, II, 459; Lanson, *Revue d'hist. litt.*, X, 415.

December, 1560 — November, 1567. — *Tragicomédie La Gaule* (Alexandrines; 4 acts; chorus.) Dedicated to the King of France.[1]

1564.—*Genièvre* (?). Played at Fontainebleau, February 13, by members of the court.[2]

1572.—*Tragicomedie de Iob* (a prologue in Alexandrines and a *cantique de Iob* in seven-syllable verse are the only extant portions of the play) by Charles Tiraqueau and Scévole de Sainte-Marthe. Represented July 28 and 29, *au moustierneuf,* at Poitiers. Printed at Paris 1579 and at Poitiers 1600.[3]

1576.—*Lucelle. Tragi-comédie en prose françoise* (prose; 5 acts) by Louis Le Jars. Paris. Represented at Rouen in 1600 and 1606. Dedicated to M. Anibal de Saint Mesmyn Seigneur du Brueil.[4]

[1] It was written between Dec. 5, 1560, the date of the accession of Charles IX and Nov. 10, 1567, the date of the death of Anne, duc de Montmorency, *conestable.* See above, page 43. MS in Bibliothèque Nationale, *fonds fr.* 838; P. Paris, *Les MSS fr. de la Bibliothèque du Roy,* VI, 416-418; Abbé Migne, *Dictionnaire des Mystères,* 1394. Other writers on the French stage have overlooked this play.

[2] The play is lost. Jacques Madeleine in *Quelques Poëtes Français des XVIe et XVIIe siècles,* 5, 14-19, 359 *seq.* (Fontainebleau, 1900) cites Castelnau, Ronsard, Père Dan, Marcassus, Abel Jouan, Brantôme, and Vauquelin to establish the fact of its representation. Lanson in *Revue d'hist. litt.,* X, 200 and 423, after quoting Madeleine at length, writes "cette représentation éclatante était demeurée inconnue des historiens du théâtre, jusqu'à ce que M. Jacques Madeleine en réveillât le souvenir." He appears to have forgot Ebert, *Franz: Tragödie,* 140, where Castelnau's reference to the play is mentioned, as recently noted by H. Schlensog, *Lucelle,* 2. Strange to say, all these authors have failed to observe that Beauchamps, *Recherches,* III, 5, refers to the same play as a *comédie,* after the representation of which Castelnau recited verses before the King.

[3] *Les Oeuvres de Scevole de Sainte Marthe, ff.* I, 41b-43a and 144a-145b, Paris, 1579, 2 vols; reprinted at Poitiers, 1600. Cf. H. Clouzot, *L'Ancien Théâtre en Poitou,* 81-2; Lanson, *Revue d'hist. litt.,* 202; Morf, *ZFSL,* XIX, 46; *Journal historique de Denis Generoux, notaire à Parthenay* (1566-1576), published by M. B. Ledain, Niort, 1865; *Le Mistére du Viel Testament,* V, page VIII; Petit de *Julleville, Les Mystères,* I, 447;

[4] La Croix du Maine, II, 49; Du Verdier, II, 600; Maupoint, 90; Beauchamps, II, 45; Frères Parfaict, III, 377; Léris, 204; La Vallière, I, 213; Mouhy, 207; Pont-de-Vesle, *Catalogue,* 21; Clément, I, 498; Soleinne, I, No. 795; Brunet, III, 952; Morf, *ZFSL,* XIX, 50; Faguet, *Tragédie française,*

1578.—*La Celestine fidellement repurgée . . . par Jacq. de Lavardin, sieur du Plessis Bourrot, tragi-comédie jadis espagnole, composée in répréhension des fols amoureux, etc.* Paris. Reprinted there without date, and at Rouen, 1598. This was probably not considered a dramatic work.[1]

1579.—*Un Acte de la Tragicomédie de Tobie, ou sont représentées les Amours et les Noces du Ieune Tobie et de Sarra Fille du Raguel* (Alexandrines; one act and fragments; chorus) by Catherine Fradonet, Mlle des Roches. Paris. Reprinted at Poitiers 1583 and Rouen 1604. Incorporated into the tragicomedy on the same subject by Iacques Ouyn (1597). Dedicated " à ma mère."[2]

1580.—*Iokebed miroir des meres. Tragi-Comedie de Moyse, en son enfance exposé par sa mere au fleuve du Nil* (prose except the *cantique de Iokebed* in 6-syllable verse; 5 acts) by Pierre Heyns. Represented at Antwerp by the *disciples* of Heyns's school. Printed in 1597 at Harlem. Dedicated to Mlle Malapart, femme de M. André van der Meulen, jadis Deputé de Messeigneurs les Estats de Brabant.[3]

373-81; Pierre Toldo, *Revue d'hist. litt.*, V, 579-84; Hugo Schlensog, *Lucelle.* The latter compares the first and third editions with the reworking in verse by Duhamel (1607.) Though he knows that Toldo (p. 579) refers to the second edition (Rouen, 1600; catalogued Y Fh, 10360, in Bibliothèque Nationale), "der aber wohl mit dem von 1606 identisch sein dürfte" (Schlensog, *Lucelle,* 6), he does not seem to have examined it.

[1] Brunet, I, 1721 and Supp. I, 230. Magnin, *Journal des Savants*, April, 1843, p. 200.

[2] *Les oeuvres de Mes-dames des Roches de Poictiers mere et fille seconde édition corrigée et augmentée de la Tragi-comédie de Tobie et autres oeuvres poëtiques.* The dedication indicates that the play is the work of the daughter, a fact that has been overlooked by La Vallière. Beauchamps, II, 42; Léris, 325; Mouhy, 224 and 34; Soleinne, I, Nos. 787 and 789; Brunet, IV, 1342; Faguet, *Tragédie française,* 323-25; *Le Mistére du Viel Testament,* V, page xviii.

[3] *Comédies et Tragédies du Laurier*, Harlem, 1597; Beauchamps, II, 66; Léris, 226; La Vallière, I, 243 seq.; Mouhy, 316, 320; Pont-de-Vesle, 24; Clément, II, 410; Soleinne, 1, No. 817; Brunet, III, 151-52; Lanson, *Revue d'hist. litt.*, X, 206. Brunet shows, as cited, that La Vallière and those who have followed him are mistaken in stating that the work was published at Amsterdam.

1582.—*Bradamante. Tragecomedie* (Alexandrines; 5 acts) by Robert Garnier. Paris. Reprinted there 1585 and three times in 1599; in 1588 and 1589 at Toulouse; 1592, 1595, 1597 and 1600 at Lyons; 1592 at Antwerp; 1596 and 1599 at Rouen; 1598 at Niort. Thirty-two editions in the seventeenth century. Reprinted by W. Foerster, Heilbronn, 1883.[1]

1584.—*L'Ombre de Garnier Stoffacher, Suisse. Tragicomedie. Sur l'alliance perpetuelle de la Cité de Geneue auec les deux premiers et puissans Cantons Zurich et Berne* (Alexandrines; 3 acts; chorus) by Jos. Du Ch. S. de la Viol. (Josephe Du Chesne, Sieur de la Violette.) Geneva. Dedicated to Charles Baron de Zerotin, Seigneur de Namescht, etc. Represented at Geneva, Oct. 18, 1584.[2]

1858.—*Tragi-comédie en laquelle figure l'histoire des deux griëves tentations desquelles le patriarche Abraham a éte exercé* by Jean Georges *maitre d'école de Saint Julien.* Represented by school children at Montbéliard *sur la place des Halles.* Given again in 1609.[3]

1592.[4]—*Les Avengles. Trigicomoedie d'Epicure Napolitain d'Italienne faicte françoise . . . avec une trés-belle plaincte du*

[1] Maupoint, 59; Beauchamps, II, 40; Frères Parfaict, III, 454 *seq.;* Léris, 65; La Vallière, I, 189 and 199; Mouhy, 255; Soleinne, I, No. 772 *seq.;* Brunet, II, 1490; Ebert, *Franz: Tragödie,* 169-78; Faguet, *Tragédie française,* 212-36; Rigal in P. de Julleville's *Histoire de la langue et de la litt. fr.,* III, 312-15. F. Pasini, *La Bradamante di Roberto Garnier e la sua fonte ariostesca, Annuario degli studenti trentini,* 1901, 122 *seq.;* Th. Roth, *Der Einfluss von Ariost's Orlando Furioso,* 104-131. For the representation in 1611 and at other times, cf. Rigal, *Alexandre Hardy,* 93. Foerster's edition appeared in *Sammlung Französischer Neudrucke,* VI, *Heilbronn,* 1882-83, published by Karl Vollmöller; cf. also *ibidem,* III, pp. xiv-xviii.

[2] La Vallière, I, 255; Pont-de-Vesle, 22; Soleinne, I, No. 823; Brunet, II, 855; Lanson, *Revue d'hist. litt.,* X, 209.

[3] Lanson, *Revue d'hist. litt.,* X, 211 and 222.

[4] This year at Bordeaux: "Valleran joue des tragédies, tragicomédies et farces. Il y a une femme dans la troupe; elle ne joue pas la farce." Chronde J. de Gaufreteau, I, 306, cited by Lanson, *Revue d'hist. litt.,* X, 211. Thist note indicates that even in the sixteenth century the tragi-comedy was more closely allied to the tragedy than to the farce.

jaloux et de plus le recouvrement de leur veüe (prose, without division into acts or scenes) by R. D. J. (Roland du Jardin.) Tours.[1 2]

1595.—*Le Desesperé, tragicomedie pour exemplaire d'obeissance, poeme tres remarquable aux peres et enfans de famille* (Alexandrines, divided into acts) by Benoet Du Lac (anagram for Claude Bonet). Represented at Aix-en-Provence. Printed there, 1615.[3]

1595.—*Caresme prenant, tragicomedie facetieuse en laquelle il y a un coq a l'asne a quatre langues touchant plusieurs abus de ce temps* (eight-syllable verses; 5 acts) by Benoet Du Lac. Represented at Aix-en-Provence. Printed there, 1615.[3]

1597.—*Thobie. Tragi-Comedie nouuelle. Tiree de la S. Bible* (Alexandrines; 5 acts) by Iacques Ouyn Louerien except the fourth act and four pages of the fifth, which were composed by Mlle des Roches. Dedicated to Mme du Roulet. Privilege, Feb. 4, 1597. Printed at Rouen, 1606.[4]

1597.—*La Polyxene. Tragicomoedie nouvellement representee au College des Bons Enfans, le Dimanche 7 de septembre,* 1597. (Alexandrines; five acts; chorus) by Iean Behourt. Printed at Rouen, 1598. Dedicated to Madame de Montpensier.[5]

[1] Beauchamps, II, 62; Léris, II, 319; Clément, II, 319; Soleinne, III, No. 4132.

[2] The first example of an allied *genre* occurs (1594) in *Tragecomedie pastoralle ou Mylas* by Claude de Bassecourt, an imitation of Tasso's *Aminta*. See Claude de Bassecourt, *Trage-comedie pastorale et autres pieces*, Antwerp, 1594.

[3] A. Joly, *Note sur Benoet Du Lac*, Lyon, 1862; Petit de Julleville, *Répertoire*, 43, 53, and 400-01.

[4] *Diverses tragédies sainctes de plusieurs auteurs de ce temps. Recueillies par Raphael du Petit Val*, Rouen, 1606; Maupoint, 303; Beauchamps, II, 75; Frères Parfaict, III, 533; Léris, 325; La Vallière, I, 315-16; Mouhy, 320; Pont-de-Vesle, 26; Soleinne, I, Nos. 863 and 879; Brunet, IV, 302; Faguet, *Tragédie fr.*, 323-25; *Mistére du Viel Testament*, V, page xx.

[5] Beauchamps, II, 69; Frères Parfaict, III, 530; Léris, 269; La Vallière, I, 317-18; Mouhy, 321; Pont-de-Vesle, 24; Clément, II, 87; Soleinne, I, 864; Brunet, I, 736.

1597.—*La Nouvelle tragicomique* (Alexandrines, without divisions into acts or scenes) by Captain Lasphrise, [Marc de Papillon.] Paris. Reprinted there in 1599 and in 1855.[1]

1599.—*Amour Vaincu, tragecomedie. Représentée deuant tres-illustre Prince Henry de Bourbon, duc de Montpensier, etc. Et tres-excellente Princesse Catherine de Joyeuse, le* 10, *Septembre,* 1599, *en leur chasteau de Myrebeau et dédiée à leurs Grandeurs par Jacques de la fons natif dudit Myrebeau Aduocat en Parlement,* (verse; 5 acts.). Poitiers.[2]

II. The Seventeenth Century to Rotrou (1628).

1593-1601.—*Les Chastes et Loyales Amours de Theagene et Cariclée. Réduites du Grec de l'Histoire d'Heliodore, en huit Poëmes Dramatiques, où* [sicl] *de Theatre consecutifs* (Alexandrines; eight *journées* of 5 acts each) by Alexandre Hardy. Published at Paris in 1623 and 1628. Dedicated to *monsieur Payen, Sieur de Landes.* Called *tragi-comedie* in the title of the individual *journées.*[3]

1593-1624.—*Procris, ou La Ialousie Infortunèe. Tragi-comedie* (Alexandrines; 5 acts) by Alexandre Hardy. Published at Paris in 1624 and 1626; at Frankfort in 1625; at Paris and Marburg in 1884. Dedicated with other plays to the duc de Montmorancy [sic].[4]

1593-1624.—*Alceste ou La Fidelité, Tragi-comedie* (Alexan-

[1] *Les premieres oeuvres poetiques du Capitaine Lasphrise,* Paris, 1597 and 1599; Beauchamps, II, 70; Léris, 241; La Vallière, I, 322; Mouhy, 319; Pont-de-Vesle, 24; Clément, II, 438; Soleinne, I, No. 870; Brunet, III, 863 and Supp., I, 790 *seq.;* Sainte-Beuve; *Tableau,* 234; Viollet Le Duc in *Bibliothèque Elzévirienne, Ancien Théâtre françois,* VII, 463-91. Paris, 1855.

[2] Mouhy, 331; Soleinne, I, No. 869; Brunet, III, 746; Clouzot, *Ancien théâtre en Poitou,* 90.

[3] For a full account of Hardy, his works and their dates, see Rigal, *Alexandre Hardy,* a treatise that has superseded all previous works on the subject. for this play *ibidem,* 435-42; Lombard. *ZFSL* I, 395-97; La Vallière, I, 334-37.

[4] La Vallière, I, 338-39; Stengel, *Théâtre d'Alexandre Hardy,* I, 172-203; Lombard, I, 348; Rigal, *Alexandre Hardy,* 401-04.

drines; 5 acts) by Alexandre Hardy. Published and dedicated with the preceding.[1]

1593-1624.—*Ariadne Rauie, Tragi-comedie* (Alexandrines; 5 acts) by Alexandre Hardy. Published and dedicated with the preceding.[2]

1593-1625.—*Arsacome, Tragi-comedie* (Alexandrines; 5 acts) by Alexandre Hardy. Published at Paris in 1625 and 1632; at Paris and Marburg in 1884.[3]

1601.—*L'Aymée, jeu tragecomique* (verses of 6, 8, 10 and 12 syllables; 5 acts) by André Mage, Sieur de Fiefmelin. Represented after a banquet. Published at Poitiers. Republished without place or date. Dedicated to Anne de Pons, comtesse de Marennes et baronne d'Oléron.[4]

1601.—*L'Amour Divin tragecomedie. Contenant un bref discours des Saincts et sacrés mysteres de la Redemption de l'humaine nature* (Alexandrines; 5 acts) by Iean Gaulché. Troyes. Dedicated to Jean Angenoust, seigneur d' Auan.[5]

1604.—*Le Miror de L'union Belgique . . . en forme de Tragi-comedie* (Alexandrines; 5 acts) by Anthoine Lancel. Place not given. Dedicated to the *Estats generaux des Provinces Unies du Pays Bas.*[6]

1604.—*Iacob. Histoire Sacrée en forme de Tragi-comédie retirée des sacrés feuillets de la Bible, du commandement de la*

[1]La Vallière, I, 339-40; Stengel, I, 204-238; Lombard, I, 349; Rigal, *Alexandre Hardy*, 404-07.

[2]La Vallière, I, 340; Stengel, I, 239-70; Lombard, I, 350; Rigal, 408-11.

[3]La Vallière, I, 342; Stengel, II, 141-84; Lombard, I, 353; Rigal, 445-51.

[4]*Les oeuvres du sieur de Fiefmelin*, Poitiers, 1601; *La Polymnie ov diverse poesie d' A. M. S. de F.* Poitiers; Pont-de-Vesle 25; Soleinne, I, nos. 886 and 887; Brunet, II, 1247; Clouzot, *Ancien théâtre en Poitou*, 94; Lanson, *Revue d' hist. litt.*, X, 215-16. For a careful analysis of this play, I am indebted to the kindness and erudition of M. E. Ginot, librarian of Poitiers.

[5]Also in Bibliothèque Nationale, *MS. fr.* 9306. Beauchamps, II, 72; Léris, 224; La Vallière, I, 358; Mouhy, 354; Clément, II, 298; Soleinne, I, p. 227; Sainte-Beuve, *Tableaux*, 245-46; Brunet, II, 1503.

[6]Also in Bibliothèque Nationale, *ms. fr.* 9305. Beauchamps, II, 73; Léris, 225; La Vallière, I, 364; Clément, II, 432; Soleinne, I, p, 227; Brunet, III, 805.

Royne Marguerite Duchesse de Valois (Alexandrines and prose; 5 acts; chorus) by Anthoine de la Puiade. Bordeaux. Dedicated to M. Dusault, conseiller du Roy.[1]

1605.—*Tragi-comédie de S. Etienne, premier roy chrestien de Hongrie, estoc paternal de la très-noble et ancienne maison de Croy.* Represented by students of the Jesuit *collège à Mons en Henault,* Dec. 20. Published at Mons, 1605.[2]

1607.—*Lucelle, tragicomédie, mise en vers françois* (Alexandrines; 5 acts) by Jacques Duhamel. Rouen. This is a reworking of *Lucelle* by Louis Le Jars.[3]

1609.—*L'Ethiopique. Tragi-comédie des Chastes Amours de Theagene et Chariclée* (Alexandrines; 5 acts; chorus) by Octave-César Genetay, sieur de la Gilleberdiere. Rouen.[4]

1609.—*L'Innocence Descouverte, Tragi-comédie* (Alexandrines; 5 acts) by Iean Auvray. Rouen. Reprinted there in 1628. First published as Marfilie or Marfille.[5]

[1] *La Mariade, d'Anthoine de la Puiade,* 85-221, Bordeaux, 1605. Soleinne, I, No. 896; Brunet, III, 838; *Mistére du Viel Testament,* II p. xxxiii; Lanson, *Revue d'hist. litt.,* X, 220.

[2] Faber, *Théâtre français en Belgique,* I, 40 and IV, 340.

[3] Frères Parfaict, IV, 63; Léris, 204; La Vallière, I, 280; Mouhy, 358; Pont-de-Vesle, 21; Clément, I, 498; Soleinne I, No. 844; Brunet, III, 952; Schlensog, *Lucelle.*

[4] Beauchamps, II, 77; Frères Parfaict, IV, 124; Léris, 133; Mouhy, 385; Pont-de-Vesle, 28; Clément, I, 326; Soleinne, I, No. 925; Brunet, II, 1532.

[5] *Le Banquet des Muses . . . du Sieur Auvray,* Rouen, 1628; Maupoint, 176; Beauchamps, II 82; Frères Parfaict, IV, 414; Léris, 190; La Vallière, I, 425; Mouhy, 391; Clément, I, 450; Soleinne, I, No. 941; Brunet, I, 575-76; Beauchamps and La Vallière state that this play was first published in 1609, without place. Brunet posits the edition of 1609 as brought out at Rouen, *Chez J. Petit in*-12. Now, Soleinne mentions a play by the same author, published at Paris, 1609, 12mo, and called *Marfille.* It seems strange that Auvray, at the age of nineteen, would publish two plays in the same year. Moreover the heroine of *L'Innocence Descouverte* is named Marfilie, and it is a very common practice to name a tragi-comedy after the heroine. It seems, therefore, that the two plays are the same and that Marfille should be written Marfilie. This explains why *Marfilie* is known to no other Bibliographer than Soleinne. The early date of the play also explains its vulgarity, which is absent from the author's later tragi-comedies. As the author was a native of Rouen, it is probable that Brunet is correct in stating that the play was published there.

1609.—*Tragicomédie intittulée Jacob ou Antidolatrie. Tiree de la Saincte Escripture et des escriptz de Sainctz Pères.* Represented at Brussels, Sept. 14, by *la Jeunesse du College* of the Jesuits. Published at Brussels in 1609.[1]

1610.—*Genevre tragecomedie* (Alexandrines; 5 acts; chorus) by Claude Billard, Seigneur de Courgenay, Bourbonnois. Paris. Republished there in 1612.[2]

1610-1628.—*Elmire ou L'Heureuse Bigamie, Tragi- comedie* (Alexandrines; 5 acts) by Alexandre Hardy. Published at Paris in 1628; at Paris and Marburg in 1884. Dedicated to Monseigneur de Liancourt, marquis de Montford, etc.[3]

1610 (?)-1622 (?).—*Tragi-Comedie de la rebellion ou mescontentment des Grenouilles contre Jupiter* (Alexandrines; 4 acts). Rouen.[4]

1610 (?)-1622 (?).—*Tragi-comedie plaisante et facécieuse intitulée La Subtilité de Fanfreluche et Gaudichon et comme il fut emporté par le Diable* (verse; 5 acts.) Rouen. Republished at Paris, 1829-30.[4]

1610 (?)-1622 (?).—*Tragi-comédie des Enfans de Turlupin malheureux de nature, où l'on void les fortunes dudit Turlupin, le mariage d'entre luy et la Boulonnoise, et autres mille plaisantes ioyeusetez qui trompent la morne Oisiveté* (verses of ten syllables; 4 acts.) Rouen. Republished at Paris, 1829-30.[4]

[1] Faber, IV, 337.

[2] *Tragédies françoises de Claude Billard,* 163, *seq.,* Paris, 1610; *ibidem,* 1612; Maupoint, 151; Beauchamps, II, 84; Frères Parfaict, IV, 129; Léris, 164; Mouhy, 396; Clément, II, 405; Soleinne, I, Nos. 917 and 918; Brunet, I, 945; Th. Roth, *Einfluss von Ariost's Orlando Furioso,* 206-11, giving a detailed analysis. Brunet dates this play 1609, which is incorrect, as the published copy gives Feb. 27, 1610 and March 9, 1610 as the respective dates of the privilege and the completion of the printing.

[3] La Vallière, I, 348; Stengel, V, 66-109; Lombard, I, 362; Rigal, *Alexandre Hardy,* 488-94.

[4] The three plays were published, without date or name of author, at Rouen, *chez* Abraham Cousturier, from whose press works were printed as early as *Discours facétieux,* 1558 (cf. Soleinne, I, p. 88) and as late as *Tragédie de Suzanne,* 1614 (Cf. Soleinne, I, p. 227.) Beauchamps, II, 92-3,

1613.—*Tragicomoedie en trois actes dans laquelle on traitait de la Purification du temple de Jérusalem après la profanation faite par Antiochus.* Represented Sept. 22, at Valenciennes by *les Ecoliers des Jésuites.*[1]

1613.—*Clotilde trage-comedie* (Alexandrines; 5 acts; a non-lyric chorus) by Iean Preuost. Poitiers. Probably acted at Saint-Léonard de Limousin. Dedicated to Leonard de Chastenel, baron de Murat.[2]

1614.—*Zóanthropie, ou Vie de l'Homme, Tragico-medie* [sic] *morale* (Alexandrines; 5 acts) by François Auffray, Gentilhomme Breton. Paris. Reprinted at Paris and Rouen, 1615. Dedicated to France.[3]

dates the three plays about 1622; Léris, 328, dates the first about 1622, the third about 1620, assigning the authorship of the latter to Ville-Toustin; La Vallière, I, 453, mentions the first play without date, treating it with plays of the year 1613; Mouhy, 497-98, dates the first two 1622; Clément, II, 458, dates the first 1622, and the others 1620, following Léris in assigning the last to Ville-Toustin; Soleinne, I, Nos. 960, 996, and 519, and Brunet, V, 912, do not date; Migne, *Dictionnaire des Mystères,* 1347, 1387, 1453, 1555, assigns the last two to the sixteenth century. The last two were republished by Montaran, *Recueil de livrets singuliers et rares,* Paris, 1829-30. The *Enfans de Turlupin,* at least, could scarcely have been written earlier than 1610, and probably has a later date, for Turlupin was the sobriquet of Henri Legrand (1587-1636, cf. A. Jal. *Dictionnaire,* article on Legrand), who was too young before about 1610 to have a play named for him. His name is found in the title of Hardy's *Folies de Turlupin,* a lost play of unknown date, and in the *dramatis personae* of *Farce plaisante et recreative,* a piece attached to a tragedy of 1617 (La Vallière, I, 473.) From these considerations the dates 1610-1622 have been assigned to all three plays, as they are associated by their common publisher and by their bibliographers.

[1] The play is lost. Hécart, *Recherches sur les Théâtres de Valenciennes,* 5, Paris, 1816.

[2] *Les Tragedies et autres oeuvres poëtiques de Iean Preuost,* Poitiers, 1614; Beauchamps, II, 88; Léris, 83; Pont-de-Vesle, 29; Clément I, 211; Soleinne, I, No. 963; Brunet, IV, 867 and Supp, II, 296; Lanson *Revue d'hist. litt.,* X, 224.

[3] Beauchamps, II, 88; Léris, 348; La Vallière, I, 458; Mouhy, 435; Pont-de-Vesle, 29; Clément, II, 486; Soleinne, I, No. 966 and I Supp., 173; Brunet, I, 553-4; Lanson, *Revue d'hist. litt.,* X, 225.

1614.—*L'Ephesienne, Tragi-Comédie* (Alexandrines; 5 acts; chorus) by Pierre Brinon. Rouen.[1]

1614-1625.—*Cornelie, Tragi-comedie* (Alexandrines; 5 acts) by Alexandre Hardy. Published at Paris in 1625 and 1632; Paris and Marburg in 1884.[2]

1615-1625.—*La Force du Sang, Tragi-comedie* (Alexandrines; 5 acts) by Alexandre Hardy. Published at Paris in 1625; Paris and Marburg in 1884. Dedicated with other plays to *Monseigneur le Premier.*[3]

1615 (?)-1625.—*Felismene, Tragi-comedie* (Alexandrines; 5 acts) by Alexandre Hardy. Published and dedicated with the preceding.[4]

1615-1628.—*La Belle Egyptienne, Tragi-comedie* (Alexandrines; 5 acts) by Alexandre Hardy. Published and dedicated with *Elmire.*[5]

1616.—*Tragicomedie de l'Empereur Henry et Kunegonde, representée par les estudians de la Compagnie de Jesus à Malines,* July 15. Published at Antwerp, 1616.[6]

1617.—*Les Heureuses Infortunes, Trage-comedie* (Alexandrines; two parts of 5 acts each) by Bernier de la Brousse. Poitiers. Privilege, Oct. 16. Printed 1618.[7]

[1] Beauchamps, II, 86; Frères Parfaict, IV, 188; Léris, 128; Mouhy, 436; Pont-de-Vesle, 29; Clément, I, 308; Soleinne, I, No. 962; Brunet, I, 1261. The privilege of July 1, 1614, speaks of "deux Tragedies, l'une intitulée Baptiste, ou la Calomnie traduite de Buchanan et l'autre l'Ephesienne." From a careless reading of this passage, *L'Ephesienne* has been listed in the new catalogue of the *Bibliothèque Nationale* as a translation from the Latin of Buchanan, although Buchanan never wrote a work on this subject and although Brinon gives Petronius as his source.

[2] La Vallière, I, 342; Stengel, II, 92-140; Lombard, I, 352; Rigal, *Alexandre Hardy,* 474-77.

[3] La Vallière, I, 344; Stengel, III, 63-106; Lombard, I, 359-61; Rigal, *Alexandre Hardy,* 474-77.

[4] La Vallière, I, 345-46; Sainte-Beuve, *Tableau,* 240-42; Stengel, II, 143-87; Lombard, I, 361-62; Rigal, *Alexandre Hardy,* 477-81.

[5] See above, under the year 1610. La Vallière, I, 348; Stengel, V, 110-59; Lombard, I, 363; Rigal, *Alexandre Hardy,* 494-98.

[6] Faber, I, 40 and IV, 340.

[7] *Les Oeuvres Poëtiques du Sieur Bernier de la Brousse,* Poitiers, 1618; Maupoint, 161; Beauchamps, II, 89; Frères Parfaict, IV, 171; Léris, 174;

1618.—*Daphnis, célébrant l'Ascension du Christ, tragicomédie du professeur de rhétorique D. Candide Postrolumna.* Played, with musical accompaniment, before Saint François de Sales, May 27.[1]

1618.—*Aretaphile, Tragi-comédie* (Alexandrines; 5 acts) by Pierre Du Ryer. Acted at the Hotel de Bourgogne, but not printed.[2]

1619.—*Tragi-Comédie très célèbre des inimitables amours du Seigneur Alexandre et d'Annette* (verses of 8 syllables; 5 acts.) Troyes, 1619 and 1628. Soleinne states that there was an earlier edition of unknown date.[3]

1619.—*Tragecomedie sur Les Amours de Philandre et de Marisee* Alexandrines; 5 acts; chorus) by Gilbert Giboin. Lyon. Dedicated to Honoré d'Urfe.[4]

1619-1625.—*Dorise. Tragi-comedie* (Alexandrines; 5 acts) by Alexandre Hardy. Published and dedicated with *La Force du Sang.*[5]

1621-1626.—*Fregonde ou Le Chaste Amour, Tragi-comedie* (Alexandrines; 5 acts) by Alexandre Hardy. Published at Rouen, 1626. Dedicated to *Monseigneur le Prince.*[6]

1621 (?)-1626.—*Gesippe ou Les Deux Amis, Tragi-comedie*

La Vallière, I, 477; Mouhy, 471; Pont-de-Vesle, 29; Clément, I, 427; Soleinne, I, No. 1001 and I, Supp., No. 184; Brunet, I 802; Clouzot, *Ancien Théâtre,* 130.

[1] Fr. Mugnier, *Théâtre en Savoie,* 85.

[2] Bibliothèque Nationale, *ms. fr.,* 25496; Mahelot, *Mémoire,* fols. 35 vo and 36; Maupoint, 32; Beauchamps, II, 109; Léris, 36; La Vallière, I, 495 and 497; Mouhy, 473; Clément, I, 87; Soleinne, I, 1003; Philipp, *Pierre Du Ryers Leben,* 18. The last writer merely translates La Vallière's analysis of the play.

[3] Beauchamps, II, 91; La Vallière, I, 525-26; Clément, V, 303; Soleinne, I, No. 1009; Brunet, V, 913.

[4] Beauchamps, II, 91; Léris, 28; La Vallière, I, 524; Mouhy, 475; Clément, I, 68; Soleinne, I, No. 1008; Brunet, II, 1587.

[5] See above, year 1615; La Vallière, I, 346; Stengel, III, 188-226; Lombard, I, 362; Rigal, *Alexandre Hardy,* 481-83.

[6] La Vallière, I, 351; Stengel, IV, 126-64; Lombard, I, 363-64; Rigal, *Alexandre Hardy,* 483-88.

(Alexandrines; 5 acts) by Alexandre Hardy. Published and dedicated with the preceding.[1]

1621 (?)-1626.—*Phraarte ou Le Triomphe des Vrays Amans, Tragi-comedie* (Alexandrines; 5 acts) by Alexandre Hardy. Published and dedicated with the preceding.[2]

1622.—*La tres-saincte et admirable vie de Madame Saincte Aldegonde, patronne de Maubenge, tragicomédie,* by Denis Coppée. Liége.[3]

1622.—*Tragicomedie. Sainct Ignace de Loïola, premier Autheur et fondateur de la Compagnie de Jesus. Faicte à l'honneur de sa glorieuse canonization. Laquelle sera representée par les Escoliers du College de la Société de Jésus à Cassel le 27 de Mai.* Published at Ipre, 1622.[4]

1622.—*Clitophon, Tragi-comedie* (Alexandrines; 5 acts) by Pierre Du Ryer. Acted at the Hotel de Bourgogne, but not printed.[5]

[1] La Vallière, I, 351-52; Stengel, IV, 165-207; Lombard, I, 364; Rigal, *Alexandre Hardy,* 458-66.

[2] La Vallière, I, 352-53; Stengel. IV, 208-58; Lombard, I, 364-66; Rigal, *Alexandre Hardy,* 467-72.

[3] Faber, IV, 267.

[4] Faber, IV, 338.

[5] Bibliothèque Nationale, *ms. fr.* 25, 496; Mahelot, *Mémoire,* fols. 47 Vo and 48; *Ouverture des jours gras,* published by Ed. Fournier, *Variétés historiques,* II, 345-55; Maupoint, 75; Beauchamps, II, 109; Léris, 82; La Vallière, I, 498-501; Mouhy, 494; Pont-de-Vesle, 36; Clément, I, 210; Soleinne, I, No. 1003; Philipp, *Pierre Du Ryers Leben,* 18; Stiefel, *Nachahmung italienischer Dramen,* I, 259-60. All of these authors but Soleinne call the play *Clitophon et Leucippe,* the title of the Greek source of the play, but not of the play itself, which is called *Clitophon* in the manuscript and in seventeenth-century documents that refer to it. Du Ryer, furthermore, wrote the heroine's name *Lucippe,* indicating the letter *u* both by the ordinary symbol and by an unusual symbol, which he certainly means for *u,* for he employs it in words where there can be no doubt of its meaning, but which has been read *eu* by dramatic bibliographers under the influence of the Greek name, ordinarily transliterated, *Leucippe.* The date of the play is uncertain, as the manuscript gives 1632 and, at the same time, calls it the "seconde pièce de M. Du Ryer," who published *Argenis et Poliarque* in 1630 and *Argenis* in 1631. One of the statements in the manuscript is, therefore, incorrect. The facts, that Du Ryer published another play in 1632; that no play of his, unless it be *Clitophon,* appeared between 1618 and 1630; and that *Cli-*

1624.—*Pasithée. Tragicomedie* (Alexandrines; 5 acts) by P. Troterel sieur d'Aves. Rouen. Dedicated to Marie Catherine de Mouchy, Dame de Medany.[1]

1625.—*Chriseide et Arimand, tragi-comedie* (Alexandrines; 5 acts) by Jean Mairet. Published at Paris, 1630. Acted at the Hotel de Bourgogne.[2]

1625.—*Les Folies de Cardenio. Tragi-comedie* (Alexandrines; 5 acts) by Pichou. Privilege Aug. 20, 1625. Published at Paris, 1629, 1633 and 1871. Dedicated to Monsieur de Sainct Simon. Acted at the Hotel de Bourgogne.[3]

1626.—Sephœ, tragédie-comique du P. D. Amédée, *chancelier du collège à Annecy.* Represented Sept. 9.[4]

1628.—*Lambertiade, tragicomédie en laquelle seront mis sur le théâtre les plus beaux traits de la vie et mort du glorieux S. Lambert, évêque de Mastricht et de Liége.* Represented by the *escolliers du collége de la compagnie de Jesus à Lux* [*embourg,*] *en la salle dudit collége,* Sept 12. Published at Luxembourg, 1628.[5]

1628.—*Richecourt, Trage-comedie* (Alexandrines; 5 acts; chorus; partly in Latin) by Dom Simplicien Gody (?). Played

tophon and his first play, *Aretaphile,* are his only unpublished plays, make it probable that *Clitophon* was his second play and was, therefore, published before 1630, perhaps in 1622, which is the date assigned to the piece by all the bibliographers except Soleinne and Pont-de-Vesle, who follow the date given in the manuscript.

[1] Maupoint, 238; Beauchamps, II, 85; Frères Parfaict, IV, 375; Léris, 253; La Vallière, I, 373; Mouhy, 502; Pont-de-Vesle, 29; Clément, I, 40; Soleinne, I, No. 909; Brunet, V, 969.

[2] Mahelot, *Mémoire,* fols. 54 vo and 55; Maupoint, 71; Beauchamps, II, 112; Frères Parfaict, IV, 337; Léris, 79; La Vallière, II, 88; Mouhy, 484; Pont-de-Vesle, 37; Soleinne, I, No. 1056; Brunet, III. 1323; Rigal in Petit de Julleville's *Histoire de la Langue, etc.,* IV, 233; Bizos, *Etude,* 103 *seq.;* Dannheisser in *Rom. Forschungen,* V, 39-40.

[3] Mahelot, fols. 55 vo and 56; Maupoint, 144; Beauchamps, II, 103; Frères Parfaict, IV, 419; Léris, 157; La Vallière, II, 37; Mouhy, 545; Pont-de-Vesle, 34; Clément, I, 387; Soleinne, I, Nos. 1036-37; Brunet, IV, 633; Fournier, *Théâtre;* Rigal in Petit de Julleville's *Histoire de la Langue, etc.,* 224 and 226.

[4] The play is lost. Mugnier, *Théâtre en Savoie,* 86.

[5] Faber, IV, 340.

by the *Pensionnaires des Rr. Peres Benedictins de S. Nicolas.* Published at Saint-Nicolas-de-Port in Lorraine, 1628 and 1860. Dedicated to Anthoine de Lenoncourt, primate of Lorraine.[1]

1628.—*Tyr et Sidon, Tragi-comedie* (Alexandrines; two *journées* of five acts each) by Jean de Schelandre. Paris. Reprinted there, 1856. Preceded by a *preface au lecteur* in which François Ogier defends the *drame libre.*[2]

To this list may be added the following lost plays by Hardy, the plots of which, skilfully worked out by Rigal from references to them in Mahelot's Memoire, show that they were tragicomedies.

1593-1632.—*L'Inceste supposé.*

1600-1632.—*Ozmin.*

1615-1632.—*Pandoste* (two *journées*).

1612-1632.—*Le Frère indiscret*[3]

From the list have been omitted Hardy's *Aristoclée,* which is called both tragedy and tragi-comedy, but is undoubtedly a tragedy; his *Ravissement de Proserpine par Pluton* and *Gigantomachie,* which are not called tragi-comedies, and differ from them by their mythological plots, in which practically all the personages are divine, a usage unknown to French tragi-comedies; the *Ravissement de Céphale* (1608), a translation of an Italian musical melodrama and not a tragi-comedy, as it is called by Beauchamps, II, 78, and Clément, II, 119; and the unpublised *Isolite, ou l'Amante courageuse, Poëme tragi-comique,* the date of which is unknown.[4]

[1]Beaupré, *Recherches sur l'imprimerie en Lorraine,* 390-97, Saint-Nicolas-de-Port, 1845; Beaupré, *Richecourt, Tragi-Comédie, ibidem,* 1860; Soleinne, I, No. 1031; Brunet, II, 1641.

[2]Maupoint, 310; Beauchamps II, 78 and 100; Léris, 335; La Vallière, I, 408 and II, 1; Mouhy, 524; Pont-de-Vesle, 33; Clément, II, 481; Soleinne, I, No. 1030; Brunet, V, 195; *Bibliothèque Elzévirienne, Ancien Théâtre,* VIII, 5-225; Robiou, *Essai,* I, 406 *seq.;* F. A. Aulard, *Schelandre. Un romantique en* 1608, Poitiers, 1883; Rigal in Petit de Julleville's *Histoire de la Langue, etc.,* IV, 226 *seq.*

[3]Rigal, *Alexandre Hardy,* 542-56; Mahelot, Fols. 20 vo, 21 vo, 22 vo, 36 vo, 58 vo.

[4]Cf. La Vallière, I, 528.

Tragi-comédies pastorales are pastoral, rather than tragi-comedies. As, however, they show the effects of influence from the latter *genre,* those which appeared between 1600 and 1628 are here listed.

1613.—*L'Heureux desesperé. Tragi-comedie Pastorelle* by C. A. Seigneur de C. Paris.

1623.—*Le Pasteur fidelle, tragi-comedie pastoralle de Jean Baptiste Guarini,* translated by Anthoine de Liraud, Lyonnois.

1626.—*La Sylvie, Tragi-comedie pastorale* by Jean Mairet. Published at Paris, 1630.

1626.—*Carite, Tragi-comedie Pastorale.* Privilege, June 2. Published at Paris, 1627.

1627.—*Endymion ou le Ravissement, Tragicomedie pastoralle* by de La Morelle. Paris.

1627.—*Endymion ou le Ravissement, Tragicomedie Pastoralle* by de La Morelle. Paris.

1628.—*La Climène, Tragi-comedie Pastorale* by C. S. de la Croix. Privilege, Nov 24. Published at Paris, 1629.

1628.—*Agimee ou L'Amour Extrauagant, Tragi-comedie,* by S. B. [Sieur Bridard.] Privilege, Dec. 3. Published at Paris, 1629.[1]

III. From Rotrou's First Tragi-Comedy to the Cid (1628-1636).

1628.—*L'Hypocondriaque ou le Mort amoureux* by Jean Rotrou. Published at Paris 1631.[2]

1629.—*Ligdamon et Lidias ou La Ressemblance* by Georges de Scudéry. Published at Paris, 1631.[3]

1630.—*L'Inconstance Punie* by C. S. Sieur de la Croix. Paris.

1630.—*La Belinde* by N. de Rampale. Lyon.

[1] See above, page 132. For the author's name, see Soleinne, I, No. 1033.

[2] For the dates of Rotrou's plays, see Stiefel, *ZFSL,* XVI 1-49.

[3] For the dates of Scudéry's plays, see Batereau, *Georges de Scudéry.*

1630.—*La Genereuse Allemande ou Le Triomphe d'Amour* by Antoine Mareschal. Of its two *journées,* the first was published in 1631, the second in 1630, but the privilege for both is dated Sept. 1 of the latter year. Paris.

1630.—*Les Advantures Amoureuses d' Omphalle* by Grandchamp. Paris.

1630.—*Argenis et Poliarque ou Theocrine* by Pierre Du Ryer. Paris.

1631.—*Argenis,* the second *journée* of the preceding. Paris.

1631.—*La Madonte* by Jean Auvray. Paris.[1]

1631.—*La Dorinde* by Jean Auvray. Paris.

1631.—*Le Triomphe d'Octave César* by Père D. Charles-Jérôme Rosario, played at Annecy, Aug 16 and 17.[2]

1631.—*L'Infidelle Confidente* by Pichou. Paris.[3]

1631.—*Les Travaux d'Ulysse* by I. G. Durval. Paris.

1631.—*L'Indienne Amoureuse ou L'Heureux Naufrage* by Du Rocher. Privilege, June 14. Published at Paris, 1635.

1631.—*Le Trompeur puny ou l'Histoire septentrionale* by Georges de Scudéry. Published at Paris, 1633.

1632.—*Les Passions esgarees ou Le Roman du Temps* by de Richemont Banchereau. Paris.

1632.—*L'Esperance Glorieuse* by de Richemont Banchereau. Paris.

1632.—*L'Orizelle ou Les Extremes Monuuements d'Amour* by C. Chabrol. Paris.

1632.—*Lisandre et Caliste* by Pierre Du Ryer. Paris.

1632.—*Clitandre ov L'Innocence delivrée* by Pierre Corneille. Paris.

1632-1633.—*Le Vassal Genereux* by Georges de Scudéry. Published at Paris, 1635.

[1]The Frères Parfaict, IV, 494, date this play 1630 because Auvray alludes to it in the dedication of his *Dorinde.* As the privilege of the latter play, however, is dated May 30, 1631, this allusion is no proof that Madonte was not written in the early months of 1631. Its privilege is dated March 7, 1631.

[2]See Mugnier, *Théâtre en Savoie,* 87. The play is not extant.

[3]Privilege, March 8, before which date the author had been assassinated.

1632-1633.—*La Celiane* by Jean Rotrou. Published at Paris, 1637.

1633.—*Le Ravissement de Florisse ou l'Heureux Evenement des Oracles* by de Cormeille. Paris.

1633.—*Pyrandre et Lisimène ou L'Heureuse Tromperie* by François Le Metel de Boisrobert. Paris.

1633.—*La Virginie* by Jean Mairet. Published at Paris, 1635.[1]

1633.—*La Bourgeoise ou La Promenade de S. Cloud* by de Rayssiguier. Paris.

1633.—*La Comedie des Comediens* by Gougenot. Paris.

1633.—*La Fidelle Tromperie* by Gougenot. Paris.

1633.—*Les Heureuses avantures* by le Hayer du Perron. Paris.

1633.—*Les Occasions perdues* by Jean Rotrou. Published at Paris, 1635.

1633.—*L'Heureux Naufrage* by Jean Rotrou. Published at Paris, 1637.

1633-1634.—*La Pèlerine Amoureuse* by Jean Rotrou. Published at Paris, 1637.

1634.—*Cleagenor et Doristée* by Jean Rotrou. Paris.

1634.—*L'Innocente Infidelité* by Jean Rotrou. Published at Paris, 1637.

1634.—*La Soeur Valeureuse ou L'Aveugle Amante* by Antoine Mareschal. Paris.

1634.—*Alcimedon* by Pierre Du Ryer. Paris.

1634.—*Les Amours de Palinice, Circeine et Florice* by de Rayssiguier. Paris.

1635.—*La Celidee sous le nom de Calirie ou de la Generosité d'Amour* by de Rayssiguier. Paris.

1635.—*Les Thuilleries* by de Rayssiguier. Privilege, Dec. 31. Published at Paris, 1636.

1635.—*S. Sebastien Marytr* by Ivodevs de Croock. Represented at Audenarde, Sept. 21. Published at Ghent, 1635.[2]

1635.—*Orante* by Georges de Scudéry. Paris.

[1] Cf. Dannheisser, *Romanische Forschungen*, V, 47.

[2] Faber, IV, 337.

1635.—*Le Prince deguisé* by Georges de Scudéry. Paris.

1635.—*Agarite* by I. G. Durval. Privilege, March 13. Published at Paris, 1636.

1635.—*Le Jaloux sans Suiet* by Charles Beys. Paris.

1635.—*L'Ospital des Fous* by Charles Beys. Privilege, Nov. 21. Published at Paris, 1637.

1635.—*L'Heureuse Constance* by Jean Rotrou. Paris.

1636.—*Amélie* by Jean Rotrou. Published at Paris, 1637.

1636.—*Agésilan de Colchos* by Jean Rotrou. Published at Paris, 1637.

1636.—*La Belle Alphrède* by Jean Rotrou. Published at Paris, 1639.

1636.—*Les Deux Pucelles* by Jean Rotrou. Published at Paris, 1639.

1636.—*L'Amant libéral* by Georges de Scudéry. Published at Paris, 1638.

1636.—*Le Duelliste malheureux.* Rouen.

1636.—*Cleomedon* by Pierre Du Ryer. Published at Paris, 1637.[1]

1636.—*Le Cid* by Pierre Corneille. Published at Paris, 1637.[2]

[1] As the privilege is dated *le dernier Decembre*, 1636 the *achevé d' imprimer*, Feb. 21, 1636; and the title page, 1637, there is evidently an error somewhere. Beauchamps, II, 110, changes the privilege to Dec. 31, 1635, thus necessitating a second alteration, as the date of the title-page should be 1636 to coincide with that of the *achevé d'imprimer*. If, on the other hand, the error be located in the *achevé d'imprimer* and its date changed to 1637, the two other dates may be allowed to stand. An error, moreover, was more likely to occur in the *achevé d'imprimer* than in the privilege, a document in which the date was of particular importance. For these reasons it seems probable that the privilege was given Dec. 31, 1636, and that the publication was completed, Feb. 21, 1637.

[2] From this list have been omitted *L'Amphytrite* by Monleon, Paris, 1630, called a tragi-comedy by Léris, 31, but apparently not a dramatic composition; *Les amours infortunées de Léandre et d' Héron*, by de la Selve, Montpellier, 1633, on account of its unhappy *dénouement; L'Amour Sanguinaire*, 1633, the classification of which as a tragi-comedy is due to the unreliable testimony of Beauchamps, II, 131; and *Cloreste* cited by Beauchamps, II, 5, as a tragi-comedy by Baro, played in 1636, but evidently the same as that author's *Clorise*, a pastoral played before the queen in 1636.

BIBLIOGRAPHY [1]

Albert, Paul.—*La Littérature française au XVIIe Siècle,* Paris, 1895.

—— *La Littérature française des origines à la fin du XVIe siècle, Paris,* 1894.

Allacci, Leone.—*Drammaturgia di —, accresciuta e continuata fino all' anno MDCCLV,* Venice, 1755.

Ancien théâtre françois (*Bibliothèque elzévirienne*), Paris, 1854-57, 10 vols.

Ancona, Alessandro D'.—*Origini del Teatro in Italia,* Florence, 1877, 2 vols.

—— *Sacre rappresentazioni dei secoli XIV-XVI,* Florence, 1872, 3 vols.

Arnaud, Charles.—*Étude sur la vie et les oeuvres de l'abbé d'Aubignac et sur les Théories dramatiques au XVIIe siècle,* Paris, 1887.

Aubignac, François Hedelin Abbé d'.—*La Pratique du Théatre,* Paris, 1657.

Baechtoid, Jakob.—*Geschichte der deutschen Literatur in der Schweiz,* Frauenfeld, 1892.

Barrera y Leirado, Cayetano Alberto de la.—*Catálogo del Teatro Antiguo español,* Madrid 1860.

Batereau, Alfred.—*Georges de Scudéry als Dramatiker,* Leipzig Dissertation, Leipzig, 1902.

[1] This Bibliography contains works referred to more than once in the dissertation, and those from which general information has been derived regarding the tragi-comedies or the period in which they were written. The plays themselves are excluded, as they have been listed in the preceding appendices. The bibliography of works referred to on single subjects has been given in foot-notes at the places in the dissertation where reference to them is made.

BATINES, COLOMB DE.—*Bibliografia delle Antiche Rappresentazioni Italiane sacre e profane Stampate nei secoli XV e XVI,* Florence, 1852.

BEAUCHAMPS, DE.—*Recherches sur les Théatres de France,* Paris, 1735.

BIZOS, GASTON.—*Étude sur la vie et les oeuvres de Jean de Mairet,* Dissertation, Paris, 1877.

BRAGA, THEOPHILO.—*Curso de historia da litteratura portugueza,* Lisbon, 1885.

—— *Historia da litteratura portugueza,* Oporto, 1870, 14 vols.

BRUNET, J.-C.—*Manuel du Libraire et de l'Amateur de Livres,* Paris, 1860-64, 5 vols.

—— *Table méthodique,* 1865.—*Supplément* (by P. Deschamps and G. Brunet), 1878-80, 2vols.

BRUNETIÈRE, FERDINAND.—*Alexandre Hardy* (review of Rigal's work with this title), *Revue des Deux Mondes,* 1890, CI, 693-706.

—— *Conférences de l'Odéon*: *Les époques du théâtre français,* Paris, 1896.

—— *L'Évolution des Genres dans l'Histoire de la Littérature,* Paris, 1892.

—— *L' Évolution d'un Genre.—La Tragédie, Revue des Deux Mondes,* 1901, VI, 123 *seq.*

CARDUCCI, GIOSUÈ.—*L'Aminta del Tasso e la vecchia poesia pastorale, Nuova Antologia,* 1894, LII, 5-21.

—— *Precedenti all' Aminta del Tasso, ibidem.* 581-99 and LIII, 5-23.

CERVANTES SAAVEDRA, MIGUEL DE.—*Novelas exemplares,* edition of Perpignan, 1816, 4 vols.

CHAMBERS, E. K.—*The Mediaeval Stage, Oxford,* 1903, 2 vols.

CHAPPUZEAU, SAMUEL.—*Le Théatre françois où il est traité de l'usage de la comédie,* Lyon, 1674.

CHASLES, ÉMILE.—*La Comédie en France au seizième siècle.* Paris, 1862.

CHASSANG, A.—*Des essais dramatiques imités de l'antiquité au XVe et au XVIe siècles,* Paris, 1852.

CLEMENT ET L'ABBE DE LA PORTE.—*Anecdotes dramatiques,* Paris, 1775, 3 vols.

CLOETTA, WILHELM.—*Beiträge zur Litteraturgeschichte des Mittelalters und der Renaissance,* Halle, 1890-92, 2 vols.

CLOUZOT, HENRI.—*L'Ancien Théâtre en Poitou,* Poitiers, 1901.

COLLIER, J. P.—*The History of English Dramatic Poetry,* London, 1831, 3 vols.

CREIZENACH, WILHELM.—*Geschichte des neueren Dramas,* Halle, 1893-1903, 3 vols.

CRESCIMBENI, GIO. MÁRIO.—*Comentarj intorno all' istoria della Poesia italiana,* republished by T. J. Mathias, London, 1803, 3 vols.

DACIER, ÉMILE.—*La Mise en scène à Paris au XVIIe siècle. Mémoire de Laurent Mahelot et Michel Laurent,* Paris, 1901.

DANNHEISSER, ERNST.—*Zur Chronologie der Dramen Jean de Mairet's, Romanische Forschungen,* 1890, V, 37-64.

DODSLEY, ROBERT.—*Old English Plays,* fourth edition by W. C. Hazlitt, London, 1874-76, 15 vols.

DUVAL, HENRI.—*Dictionnaire des ouvrages dramatiques, depuis Jodelle jusqu'à nos jours,* Manuscripts 15048-61 in the Bibliothèque Nationale, nineteenth century.

DU VERDIER, see below, under JUVIGNY.

EBERT, ADOLF.—*Entwicklungs-Geschichte der Französischen Tragödie,* Gotha, 1856.

FABER, F.—*Histoire du théâtre français en Belgique,* Brussels, 1878-80, 5 vols.

FAGUET, ÉMILE.—*La Tragédie française au XVIe Siècle* Paris, 1883.

—— *Les Manifestes dramatiques avant Corneille, Revue des cours et conférences,* 1900, IX, No. 6, 241-50.

FEUERLEIN, EMIL.—*Die italienische Komödie des 16 Jahrhunderts in ihren Anfängen, Preuszische Jahrbücher,* 1881. XLVII, 1-24.

FOERSTER, WENDELIN.—*Les Tragédies de Robert Garnier,* vols. III, IV, V and VI of *Sammlung Französischer Neudrucke,* edited by Karl Vollmöller, Heilbronn, 1881-88.

FOLLIOLEY, L. H.—*Histoire de la littérature française au XVIIe siècle,* Tours, 1885, 3 vols.

FONTENELLE, BERNARD LE BOVIER, SIEUR DE.—*Oeuvres,* Paris, edition of 1825, 5 vols.

FOURNEL, VICTOR.—*La Littérature indépendante et les écrivains oubliés,* Paris, 1862.

FOURNIER, ÉDOUARD.—*Le Théâtre français au XVIe et au XVIIe siècle,* Paris, 1871, 2 vols.

—— *Variétés historiques et littéraires* (Bibliothéque elzévirienne), Paris, 1855-63, 10 vols.

GALLARDO, BARTOLOMÉ JOSÉ.—*Ensayo de una Biblioteca española,* Madrid, 1863-89, 4 vols.

GESNER, KONRAD.—*Appendix Bibliothecae,* Zurich, 1555.

GINGUENÉ, P. L.—*Histoire littéraire d'Italie,* Paris, 1824, 9 vols.

GODEFROY, FRÉDÉRIC.—*Histoire de la littérature française depuis le XVIe siècle jusqu'à nos jours,* Paris, 1878-81.

GOEDEKE, KARL.—*Grundrisz zur Geschichte der Deutschen Dichtung,* Dresden, 1884-1905, 8 vols.

GREG, WALTER WILSON.—*A list of English Plays written before* 1643 *and printed before* 1700, London, 1900 (printed for the Bibliographical Society).

GUARINI, GIOVANNI BATTISTA.—*Opere,* Verona, 1737-38, 4 vols.

GUIZOT, F. P. G.—*Corneille et son temps,* Paris, 1865.

HALLIWELL, JAMES O.—*A Dictionary of Old English Plays,* London, 1870.

HARTMANN, MAX.—*Lateinische Litteraturdenkmäler des XV und XVI Jahrhunderts,* Berlin, 1891-99, 14 vols.

HÉCART, G. A. J.—*Recherches sur le théâtre de Valenciennes,* Paris, 1816.

Hispaniae Illustratae, Frankfort, 1603, 4 vols.

JAL, AUGUSTE.—*Dictionnaire critique de biographie et d'histoire,* Paris, 1872.

JUVIGNY, RIGOLEY DE.—*Les bibliothèques françoises de la Croix du Maine et de du Verdier,* Paris, 1772-73, 6 vols.

LACROIX, PAUL (BIBLIOPHILE JACOB).—*XVIIe siècle. Lettres, sciences, et arts,* Paris, 1882. See, also, under SOLEINNE.

LA CROIX DU MAINE, see above, under JUVIGNY.

LA MESNADIERE, H.-J. P. DE.—*La Poëtique,* Paris, 1640.

LANSON, GUSTAVE.—Corneille, Paris, 1898.

—— *Études sur les origines de la tragédie classique en France, Revue d'histoire littéraire de la France,* 1903, X, 177-231 and 413-36.

——*Études sur les rapports de la littérature française et de la littérature espagnole au XVIIe siècle, ibidem,* 1896 and 1897, III, 45-70 and 321-31 and IV, 61-73 and 180-194.

—— *L'Idée de la tragédie en France avant Jodelle, ibidem,* 1904, XI, 541-85.

LA VALLIÈRE, LE DUC DE. — *Bibliothèque du théatre françois depuis son origine,* Dresden, 1768, 3 vols.

LÉRIS, DE.—*Dictionnaire portatif des théàtres,* Paris, 1754.

LESSING, GOTTHOLD EPHRAIM.—*Hamburgische Dramaturgie,* Vol. VII of his *Sämmtliche Schriften, Leipzig,* 1853-1905, 20 vols.

LIVET, CH.—*Précieux et Précieuses,* Paris, 1860.

LOMBARD, E.—*Étude sur Alexandre Hardy, Zeitschrift für neufranzösische Sprache und Literatur,* 1879, I, 161-85 and 348-97.

LOTHEISSEN, FERDINAND.—*Geschichte der Französischen Literatur im XVII Jahrhundert,* Vienna, 1877-84, 4 vols, in 2.

MAHELOT, LAURENT.—*Mémoire,* MS. *fr.* 24330 in the Bibliothèque Nationale.

MARSAN, JULES.—*La Pastorale Dramatique en France à la fin du XVIe et au commencement du XVIIe siècle,* Dissertation, Paris, 1905.

MARTINENCHE, ERNEST.—*La comedia espagnole en France de Hardy à Racine,* Paris, 1900.

MAUPOINT.—*Bibliothèque des théatres,* Paris, 1733.

MIGNE, J. P. ABBÉ.—*Dictionnaire des mystères in Nouvelle Encyclopédie théologique,* Paris, 1853, 44 vols.

MORATIN, L. F. DE.—*Obras,* Madrid, 1830-31, 4 vols.

MOREL-FATIO, ALFRED.—*La Comedia espagnole du XVIIe siècle,* Paris, 1885.

MORF, HEINRICH.—*Die französische Litteratur in der zweiten Hälfte des sechzehnten Jahrhunderts, II, Zeitschrift für französische Sprache und Litteratur,* 1897, XIX, 1-61.

MOUHY, C. DE F. CHEVALIER DE.—*Journal chronologique du Théâtre français* (1220-1773,) MSS. *fr.* (9229-35) in Bibliothèque Nationale, eighteenth century.

MUGNIER, FRANCOIS.—*Le Théâtre en Savoie, Chambéry,* 1887.

MYSING, OSCAR.—*Robert Garnier und die antike Tragödie,* Leipzig Dissertation, Leipzig-Reudnitz, 1891.

NICERON, J. P.—*Mémoires pour servir à l'histoire des hommes illustres dans la république des lettres,* Paris, 1729-45, 43 vols in 44.

NISARD, DÉSIRÉ.—*Histoire de la littérature française,* eighth edition, Paris, 1881, 4 vols.

OCHOA, EUGENIO DE.—*Tesoro del Teatro español,* Paris, 1838, 6 vols.

PAPILLON, PHILIBERT.—*Bibliothèque des Auteurs de Bourgogne,* 1745, 2 vols in 1.

PARFAICT, FRÉRES.—*Histoire du Théatre françois,* Paris, 1745-49, 15 vols.

PARIS, GASTON and ULYSSE ROBERT.—*Miracles de Nostre Dame* (*Société des anciens textes français*), Paris, 1876-93, 8 vols.

PARIS, A. PAULIN.—*Les Manuscrits François de la Bibliothèque du Roi,* Paris, 1836-48, 7 vols.

PAZ Y MÉLIA, ANTONIO.—*Catálogo de las Piezas de Teatro que se conservan en el departamento de manuscritos de la Biblioteca Nacional,* Madrid, 1899.

PELLISSON FONTANIER, PAUL and P. J. T. ABBÈ D'OLIVET.—*Histoire de l'Académie française,* edition of Paris, 1858, 2 vols.

PETIT DE JULLEVILLE, LOUIS.—*Histoire de la langue et de la littérature française,* Paris, 1896-99, 8 vols.

—— *Histoire du théâtre en France. La Comédie et les moeurs en France au moyen-âge,* Paris, 1886.

—— *Histoire . . . Les Comédiens en France au moyen-âge,* Paris, 1885.

—— *Histoire . . . Les Mystères,* Paris, 1880, 2 vols.

—— *Histoire . . . Répertoire du théâtre comique en France au moyen-âge,* Paris, 1886.

PHILIPP, KURT.—*Pierre Du Ryers Leben u. dramatische Werke* Leipzig Dissertation, Zwickau, 1905.

PONT-DE-VESLE, DE.—*Catalogue des livres imprimés et manuscrits,* Paris, 1774.

PUIBUSQUE, A. L. DE.—*Histoire comparée des littératures espagnole et française,* Paris, 1843, 2 vols.

REINHARDSTOETTNER, KARL VON.—*Plautus. Spätere Bearbeitungen plautinischer Lustspiele,* Leipzig, 1886.

RICCOBONI, LUIGI.—*Histoire du Théâtre italien depuis la décadence de la Comédie Latine,* Paris, 1728.

RIGAL, EUGÈNE.—*Alexandre Hardy et le Théâtre français à la fin du XVIe et au commencement du XVIIe siècle,* Dissertation, Paris, 1889.

——*De l' établissement de la tragédie en France, Revue d' art dramatique,* Jan. 15, 1892.

—— *Le Théâtre au XVIIe siècle avant Corneille,* in Petit de Julleville's *Histoire de la langue, etc.* (cf. above, *s. v.*) IV, 186-259.

——*Le Théâtre de la Renaissance, ibidem,* III, 261-318.

——*Le Théâtre français avant la période classique,* Paris, 1901.

ROBIOU, FÉLIX.—*Essai sur l' histoire de la littérature et des moeurs pendant la première moitié du XVIIe siècle,* Paris, 1858.

ROTH, TH.—*Der Einfluss von Ariost's Orlando Furioso auf das Französische Theater* (*Münchner Beiträge zur Romanischen und Englischen Philologie*), Leipzig, 1905.

ROTHSCHILD, JAMES DE.—*Le Mistére du Viel Testament,* Paris, 1878-91, 6 vols.

ROYER, ALPHONSE.—*Histoire universelle du théâtre, Paris,* 1869-78, 6 vols.

SAINTE-BEUVE, C. A.—*Tableau historique et critique de la Poésie française et du Théâtre français au XVIe siècle,* Paris, edition of 1893.

SALVIOLI, GIOVANNI and CARLO.—*Bibliografia Universale del Teatro Drammatico italiano,* Venice, 1894-1904.

SAUVAL, HENRI.—*Histoire et Recherches des Antiquités de la Ville de Paris,* Paris, 1724, 3 vols.

SCALIGER, J. C.—*Poetices,* edition of Geneva, 1594.

SCHACK, A. F. VON.—*Geschichte der dramatischen Literatur und Kunst in Spanien,* Frankfort, 1854, 3 vols.

SCHLENSOG, HUGO.—*Lucelle, tragicomédie en prose française von Louis le Jars* (1576) *und Lucelle, tragicomédie mise en vers français von Jacques Duhamel* (1607), Greifswald Dissertation, Freiburg, 1906.

SOLEINNE, MARTINEAU DE.—*Bibliothèque dramatique,* edited by P. L. Jacob (Paul Lacroix), Paris, 1843-4, 5 vols.

STEFFENS, GEORG.—*Rotrou Studien I. Jean de Rotrou als Nachahmer Lope de Vega's,* Göttingen Dissertation, Oppeln, 1891.

STENGEL, E.—*Le Théâtre d' Alexandre Hardy,* Marburg and Paris, 1884, 5 vols.

STIEFEL, A. L.—*Die Nachahmung italienischer Dramen bei einigen Vorläufern Molières. I. D'Ouville,* Berlin, 1904.

—— *Über die Chronologie von Jean Rotrou's dramatischen Werken, Zeitchrift für französische Sprache und Litteratur,* 1894, XVI, 1-49.

——*Über Jean Rotrous Spanische Quellen, ibidem,* 1906, 195-234.

Storia letteraria d'Italia da una Società di Professori, Milan, without date.

TILLEY, ARTHUR.—*The Literature of the French Renaissance,* Cambridge, 1904, 2 vols.

TITON DU TILLET.—*Le Parnasse françois,* Paris, 1732.

VAUQUELIN, SIEUR DE LA FRESNAYE, JEAN.—*Diverses poésies,* edited by Julien Travers, Caen, 1869-72, 3 vols.

VIEL-CASTEL, LOUIS DE.—*Essai sur le théâtre espagnol,* Paris, 1882.

LIFE.

Born at Richmond, Virginia, November 10, 1882, I was educated at private schools, including that conducted by Captain W. Gordon McCabe, and at the University of Virginia, where I was a student from September, 1900, to June, 1903, graduating with the degrees of A. B. and A. M. After spending a year as instructor at the University School of Montgomery, Alabama, I entered the Johns Hopkins University in the fall of 1904, taking French as a principal subject, Spanish and Italian as first and second subordinate subjects, and following courses offered by Professors Elliott, Ogden, Armstrong, Marden, Shaw, Keidel, Warren, Vos, and Bloomfield. Since coming to the University, it has been my good fortune to hold two Virginia Scholarships and the Fellowship in the Romance Department for the current year. The summers of 1905 and 1906 were passed in Europe, principally at Paris, where I was occupied, during the second summer, with the collection of material for my dissertation.

It gives me much pleasure to thank Professor R. W. Wilson of the University of Virginia for early instruction in Romance languages, and the professors whose lectures I have attended at the Johns Hopkins for the information and inspiration that they have afforded me. I would express to Professor Armstrong my appreciation of his careful and comprehensive courses on the French language; I would acknowledge the benefit received from Professor Ogden's expression of enlightened literary views, his suggestion of the subject of my dissertation, and the assistance that he has rendered me during its progress. To Professor Elliott I am particularly indebted for a most careful criticism of my dissertation and for wise and sympathetic guidance in various fields of literary and philological research.

HENRY CARRINGTON LANCASTER.

BALTIMORE, April 21, 1907.

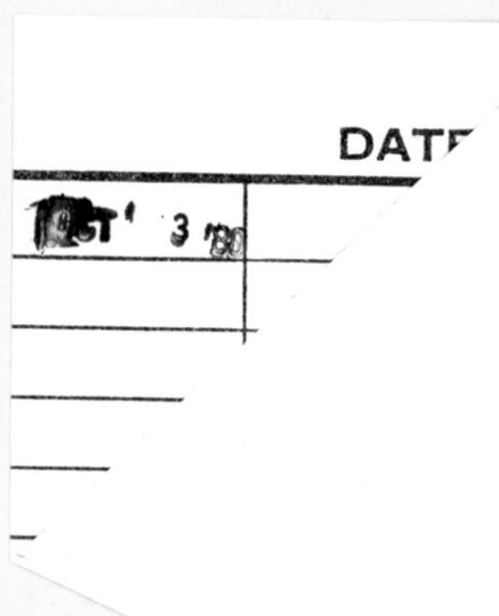
DAT
OCT 3 '80